The Complete Guide to
Offshore Residency,
Dual Citizenship
and
Second Passports

Robert E. Bauman, JD

THE
SOVEREIGN
SOCIETY

The Complete Guide to Offshore Residency, Dual Citizenship and
Second Passports

Robert E. Bauman and The Sovereign Society, Ltd. 2004

The Sovereign Society
5 Catherine Street, Waterford, Ireland

Fourth Edition, August 2004

ISBN 1-90590-11-6

Printed by Victor Graphics, 1211 Bernard Drive, Baltimore, Maryland 21223

The Sovereign Society advocates full compliance with all applicable tax
and financial reporting laws. The U.S. government taxes all worldwide
income wherever it is earned and wherever the U.S. person may live or
have residence(s). U.S. citizens and resident aliens (known in tax law as
„U.S. persons‰) must, by law, report all of their income annually and pay
U.S. taxes accordingly. If a U.S. person has direct or indirect control
over an offshore bank account or other financial account, this fact must
be reported. If the aggregate amount of financial activity in such accounts
amounts to $10,000 or more in a year, additional reporting is required.
You should consult with a qualified attorney or accountant to insure
that you know, understand and meet these and other reporting requirements.

The Complete Guide to
Offshore Residency,
Dual Citizenship
and
Second Passports

ROBERT E. BAUMAN, JD

THE SOVEREIGN SOCIETY, LTD.
5 Catherine Street
Waterford, Ireland
TEL: 1 888 358 8125
Internet: http://www.sovereignsociety.com
E-mail: info@sovereignsociety.com

Table of Contents

PART I — PASSPORT HISTORY

PART II — ECONOMIC CITIZENSHIP PROGRAMS

PART III — COUNTRIES BY REGION

Section 1. North America

Section 5. Middle East and Africa

Section 6. Asia and Oceania

Foreword

Thoughts on Second Citizenship for U.S. Citizens

MARSHALL J. LANGER, JD

Mr. Langer, a member of the State of Florida (U.S.) bar, practiced law in Miami for 35 years prior to moving to London in 1985. He now divides his time between London and Barbados, where he lives. Formerly a partner in the Miami law firm of Shutts & Bowen, he remains of counsel to that firm. He was also adjunct professor of law at the University of Miami Law School. In 1990, he received the Florida Bar Association's award as "Outstanding Tax Attorney of the Year."

Mr. Langer is a graduate of the Wharton School of Finance of the University of Pennsylvania, where he received a BD in economics, and the University of Miami Law School, where he received his juris doctor degree, summa cum laude. He has lectured worldwide at seminars and tax institutes and is the author of many articles and books on taxation and related topics. Perhaps his best known book is *The Tax Exile Report*, but he also authored a leading book on tax haven countries, *Practical International Tax Planning*. He is also co-author (with Rufus Rhodes JD) of a six-volume treatise entitled, Rhoades & Langer, *U.S. International Taxation & Tax Treaties*, which is updated quarterly and stands as the "bible" on international tax matters.

Benjamin Franklin, one of the most astute and beloved of all the founders of the American nation, once observed: "Where liberty dwells, there is my country."

Well-known for his broad minded views and liberality, with that utterance Franklin may have been expanding on another famous statement he made shortly after signing the U.S. Constitution on September 17, 1787. Leaving Independence Hall in Philadelphia, he was asked by a citizen: "What have you given us?" Franklin replied: "A republic, if you can keep it."

Whether we have remained true to the intent of America's Founding Fathers is certainly open to question in our day and time.

That question certainly applies to the size, scope, and power of the federal government, especially as manifested in its oppressive and complex taxation laws and policies. So acute has the tax issue become for people of wealth that many are seeking a home in other nations; more hospitable places where taxes are low or non-existent and where America's original ideals are still alive.

The United States is certainly not alone in imposing oppressive and exorbitant taxes. The United Kingdom, Germany, France, and many other countries take well over half of a citizen's income to finance the insatiable demands of the ever-growing welfare state.

For such reasons, citizens of many countries should, and indeed have a right to consider, the possibility of acquiring a second citizenship, particularly in a country where taxes are more reasonable. Beyond that, there exists the possibility of making a home in your new country, and eventually leaving your native citizenship behind.

It may seem a radical idea to those born and bred in one country, but almost anyone with the financial means and a determined will can become an international citizen. This is accomplished by acquiring a legal second citizenship, and with that enhanced status comes an official second passport. This new passport can expand your legal rights, allowing world travel unmolested by curious border guards and nosey customs and tax officials. It can open doors that otherwise would forever remain closed to you. Best of all, a second citizenship/passport can serve as the key to reducing your taxes and protecting your assets — or even your life.

In this edition of *The Complete Guide to Offshore Residency, Dual Citizenship & Second Passport*, you will discover how this second passport "magic" can work for you.

The Tax Exile

As I explained in my book, *The Tax Exile Report*, only a few countries impose taxes based on nationality. To escape taxes in these countries, you may have to change your nationality. Unless you already have a second nationality, you must first acquire a second one before you can abandon your original nationality.

Unless you are a citizen of the United States, the Philippines, Eritrea, Finland, Greece, the Netherlands, or Sweden, retaining your present citizenship will not cause tax problems after you move your home to another country or acquire a second citizenship. These are the only countries that impose tax burdens based on mere citizenship, regardless of where their citizens live.

The U.S. rule holds that a U.S. citizen or resident alien is liable for taxes on all his or her worldwide income wherever it is earned and wherever they may live. Many countries exempt their citizens from taxes while they live abroad, although an increasing number are beginning to adopt the "no escape" U.S. tax view. Among the nations I have named, the U.S. is one of the few countries that make a serious effort to collect taxes from its citizens living in other nations. Not content with that, the U.S. also tries to collect taxes from some of its former citizens, claiming the right to do so for up to ten years after they relinquish citizenship.

As you can see, an American cannot become a "tax exile" so long as he or she remains a U.S. citizen. Moreover, if you decide to abandon U.S. citizenship, you first must acquire another nationality as well as a passport on which to travel. The U.S. State Department now concedes an American citizen's right to have dual nationality and to acquire that other nationality voluntarily without automatically losing American citizenship. But the first step is to acquire another nationality.

Why Second Citizenship?

Aside from taxation, there are many compelling reasons for becoming a dual national. For example, if you are fortunate enough to acquire citizenship in one of the countries presently a member of the European Union (EU), you gain the right to live and work in any of these 25 countries. In addition, you may be entitled to second citizenship if your parents or any of your grandparents were born in an EU country, although the rules vary among countries. It is certainly worth your consideration, at least in the context of your financial and retirement planning.

Now that you know expatriation may be required to lower your tax burden, you must determine whether it makes sense for you to become a tax exile. Only you can decide whether it is worthwhile for you to develop your own ultimate estate plan.

Examine your present will and estate plan. How much will you and your spouse pay in taxes when you pass your estate to your heirs? How much would these taxes be reduced if you became a tax exile? How much of your present income now goes to pay income taxes? How much would that income tax be reduced if you became a tax exile?

The Decision Is Yours

After you carefully analyze these questions and the answers, you are likely to reach one of three conclusions:

1.   You enjoyed learning about the possibilities, but becoming a tax exile would be too disruptive to your present and future lifestyle. You will stay and pay. Your children and grandchildren will have to make do with whatever is left after taxes.

2.   You feel that the savings during your lifetime and to your heirs would be great, but you can't afford to move now. You will begin to take steps that will make it possible for you to move when you can.

3.   You are ready, willing and able to become a tax exile now. The after-tax savings will improve your lifestyle for the rest of your life, and the eventual savings to your family will be substantial.

If you have reached option two or three, you have further work to do. Sit down with your legal and tax advisors and work out your plan. This is an area where no two plans can ever be the same. You already have a general idea of the steps you must take to leave your present home country.

Residency Questions

At a minimum, you must terminate your existing residency. You will want to determine whether you must sell or lease your home, or whether you can keep it for visits.

Must you establish one specific home base or can you be a perpetual tourist with homes in several different places? Which country or countries will be best for you to move to? Have you already visited or lived in them or in similar foreign countries? Have you gathered all the information you possibly can concerning living conditions there? Are you satisfied that your new base has adequate facilities for health care and your other needs?

Should you terminate your present residence at or near the end of a tax year, or can you do it when it is most convenient for you? Are you subject to a departure tax if you leave? How many days a year can you spend visiting your friends and family in your present home country after you leave? Must you stay at a hotel or can you rent an apartment or home for your visits? Can you keep a car or should you rent one during your visits? Will it be safe for you to keep any bank accounts or investments in your present home country after you leave?

Must you also change your domicile? If so, how will you and your heirs be able to prove that you have made the change? What is your domicile of origin? What is your present domicile? What happens if you leave your present domicile without establishing a new one? Do you retain your present domicile? Do you revert to your domicile of origin? Must you change both your residency and your domicile at the same time, or can you change your residency now and your domicile later?

Can you retain your present citizenship? Even if you can, would you feel safer or more comfortable if you had a second nationality and another passport? Does your present passport make it difficult for you to travel to certain parts of the world that you would like to visit? Trace your family history and that of your spouse. Does your ancestry entitle you to obtain citizenship somewhere? Does your present country permit dual nationality? Does it make sense for you to obtain another nationality now, so that you can terminate your present nationality when, and if, you consider it necessary to do so? Do you know where and how you can obtain another suitable nationality? If you keep your present nationality and passport, must you use that passport to enter and leave your present country? Do you know how to terminate your present nationality when, and if, you decide to do so? Are you subject to a departure tax or ongoing taxation if you give up your citizenship?

Are you married and, if so, are your assets subject to community property rules? Are those rules consistent with your own wishes? Will your spouse take the same steps you do to become a tax exile? If you are not married, do you have an ongoing relationship with someone to whom you plan to leave part of your estate? Will that person be treated as unrelated for gift or inheritance tax purposes in your present or proposed future home country?

How much of your present income comes from sources in your present home country? Will you still be taxed on that income if you leave? If so, can you change the source of that income to reduce or eliminate such taxes? Can you use your new home country's tax treaties to reduce the tax at source on any of your income?

How much of your assets are located in your present home country? Will you still be taxed on gifts or other transfers of those assets after you leave? If so, can you change the location of those assets to reduce or eliminate gift and death taxes?

Do you know when to take each of the steps required to achieve the most beneficial results? Will most of your beneficiaries move with you or will some, or all, of them remain in your present home country? If they remain behind, are there special steps you need to take to ensure that they are not pounced on for taxes on your estate after you are gone?

Your own personal circumstances may require you to take steps that are different from those that might be suitable for someone else. Check each step carefully. Develop your own ultimate estate plan. If you want to become a tax exile, do it right or don't do it at all.

Which Country — Which Passport?

A most important consideration when seeking another citizenship is how easily you can travel using that country's passport. The goal is to enjoy as much visa-free travel as possible, especially to those countries you wish to visit regularly. The next best choice is a passport with which you can reasonably expect to obtain multiple-entry visas to those same countries. You don't want a passport that severely restricts your ability to travel, and some do.

How do you compare the usefulness of some of the "instant" passports available under the several "economic citizenship" programs explained in this book? If you have a clean personal and business record and are prepared to make the required financial investment, you can obtain citizenship and a passport from Dominica, or St. Kitts and Nevis within a few months. Since each of these countries are members of the British Commonwealth, their passports allow you relatively visa-free entry to the U.K., Switzerland, Canada, and about 90 other countries. You still will need a visa to visit most EU countries or the United States. But with a passport from any of those two British Commonwealth countries, you will have no trouble obtaining visas to visit other countries not on the Commonwealth visa-free list.

In summary, I am certain that in these pages you will find your potential second home nation, and with it a passport to greater economic and personal freedom. If I can assist you in that quest, please contact me. Good luck!

London, May 2004
Marshall J. Langer

Prologue

Thoughts on Second Citizenship: A Global Perspective

CHRISTIAN H. KALIN

Christian H. Kälin is a director and partner of Henley & Partner, Inc. in Zurich, Switzerland. Mr. Kälin is a specialist in international residence and citizenship matters and related tax planning. He can be contacted at Henley & Partners AG, Kirchgasse 22, 8001 Zurich, Switzerland; Tel: +(41) 44-266 22 22; Fax +(41) 44-266-22 23; E-mail: christian.kalin@henleyglobal.com.

Every day, people from around the world, with diverse backgrounds, come to Henley & Partners seeking advice on alternative residence and citizenship. We realize that there is no substitute for professional, personal assistance from an experienced advisor. But now, for the first time in my experience, this well-researched volume provides an authoritative overview of what is available in the field of second passports and foreign residence. In these pages are proof of the many opportunities and possibilities afforded by acquiring an alternative citizenship.

There are many valid reasons to consider acquiring an alternative citizenship and second passport.

As a citizen and passport holder of two or more countries, one can travel or move one's residence more easily, particularly in an emergency. The right to travel, to enter or leave a country, at some point, may become crucial. This flexibility may even save your life. Perhaps, you are a citizen of a well regarded, major country, and you think you will never need an alternative citizenship and passport. You may not foresee any problems now. Your current passport may permit travel almost anywhere without the need for a visa.

But an alternative passport is similar to an insurance policy. It's something you should have well before an emergency arises. Depending on your country's international reputation, your present passport may restrict your movements. Or it may expose you to difficulties when you travel or attempt to conduct business internationally. Using a different, alternative passport can restore your personal security, ease of travel, and allow hassle-free border crossings.

Those who disagree with government policies in their home country face a special dilemma. Perhaps, you don't want your children and grandchildren exposed to physical danger or forced into mandatory military service. You and your family may face persecution on ethnic, political, religious, or other grounds. Whatever your situation, now or in the future, you should have the ready option to seek a safe haven without first having to apply for an official entry visa or residence permit.

While some countries still officially discourage dual or multiple nationality for their citizens, most governments now accept this as a fact of international life. Dual nationality is the inevitable result of the increased mobility of large numbers of people and of the growth of a more and more integrated world economy. In recent years, many countries have amended citizenship laws to recognize these new realities. Until the distant day when the concept of global citizenship achieves universal acceptance, acquiring and using more than just one citizenship can enhance your personal liberty in many ways.

Today, a person of talent and means need not limit his or her personal life and professional business to only one country. Residence in a foreign country can enrich your life. It can offer new and expanded opportunities. Moreover, a new life abroad is far easier when one acquires second citizenship in the country you choose to make your home. As you will learn in these pages, many countries willingly offer serious investors and wealthy individuals special, expedited status leading to official residence and, usually later on, citizenship, often in a matter of weeks or months.

In today's world of guarded international borders, strict entry controls, and complex immigration laws, it has become more difficult to acquire alternative citizenship — unless you know and understand how it can be done.

Nevertheless, there are still many possibilities to explore.

Foreign persons willing to create employment through business investment in other countries, usually, are welcomed officially with open arms. Established nations such as Ireland, Austria or Switzerland, as well as many developing countries, have incentive programs aimed at attracting foreign investors. These governments offer grants, subsidies, and substantial tax breaks. Resident foreigners can benefit from special tax exemptions and regimes, freedom from currency exchange controls, and other financial advantages. Depending on the country, a financially independent foreigner may be very privileged indeed.

Many countries allow a foreign national to establish residence simply upon showing sufficient financial support from abroad without the need for local employment. There are few restrictions on operating your own tax-free business offshore. In some countries, wealthy foreigners are better treated than local citizens. In scores of attractive places worldwide, visitors are welcome, tourism is a national priority, and paying guests are very well treated.

Based on our extensive experience at Henley & Partners, we know that some countries, such as The Bahamas, Hong Kong, Monaco, Malta, Croatia or Switzerland, are especially attractive places for establishing an alternative residence. Others are of special interest for acquiring full citizenship in a relatively short period of time, such as Australia, Austria, Canada, or the United Kingdom. If your goal is visa-free access throughout Europe, a residence permit in a EU/Schengen member country is ideal.

Currently only Austria, the Commonwealth of Dominica and St. Kitts & Nevis offer citizenship in return for investment under what are also called "Economic Citizenship Programs." These countries offer the opportunity to legally acquire a second nationality quickly and simply, without any residence requirements or disruptions of present life. A passport issued by internationally neutral Austria is one of the best travel documents in the world, and even a St. Kitts & Nevis passport allows visa-free access to over 100 countries and territories worldwide.

There is another important, economic reason to consider second citizenship — the continuing drain of high taxes imposed by the major industrial nations. Following the unfortunate lead of the United States, some other nations now impose taxes on their non-resident citizens in one way or another. Thus, alternative residence and citizenship are becoming increasingly important in international tax and estate planning.

Many of the world's most affluent people have chosen legally to avoid excessive taxation by a change of residence. For them, that means more freedom, flexibility, and security, all achieved simply by moving their residence abroad. Moreover, these tax-planning moves do not normally require surrender of their home country citizenship, with the important exception of US citizens. Accordingly a growing number of people do choose to acquire new citizenship.

Foreign residence and alternative citizenship can return countless benefits in life. Your personal situation may make it worth considering these options. Whatever your personal status, at Henley & Partners we are ready to advise and assist you.

Zurich, August 2004

Christian H. Kälin

PART I
Passport History

PART I
Passport History

ROBERT E. BAUMAN, JD

Robert E. Bauman, is a member of the District of Columbia bar and a former state senator and member of the U.S. House of Representatives from Maryland. He is a graduate of George-town University's Edmund A. Walsh School of Foreign Service and the GU Law Center. He is the author of *The Gentleman from Maryland* (Hearst Book Pub., NYC, 1985), *How to Lawyer-Proof Your Life* (Shot Tower Press, Boca Raton, Florida, 1995), co-author of The *Offshore Money Manual 2000*, (The Sovereign Society, 1999), and editor of *Forbidden Knowledge* (The Sovereign Society, 2004). His writings have appeared in *The Wall Street Journal*, *The New York Times*, *National Review*, and other publications. He is also legal counsel to the Sovereign Society and Editor of its *Sovereign Society Offshore A-Letter*, a free, 5-day-a-week e-mail newsletter.

The United Press International news dispatch on June 17, 1985, datelined Algiers, was terse: "A body identified by a freed TWA flight attendant as Robert Stethem was hurled off the Boeing 727 onto the airport tarmac on Friday night. The body was later taken to a U.S. airbase for identification."

The dead American was U.S. Navy Petty Officer Stethem, a victim of the terrorist hijacking over Greece of Trans World Airlines Flight 847, carrying 153 people as it flew from Athens to Rome. The young sailor was returning from an assignment in Nea Makri, Greece. Over several days, the terrorists, later identified as Iranian Shiite Muslims based in Syria, forced the Boeing 727 to Beirut, then to Algiers, back to Beirut and again to Algiers. Groups of passengers were released during the initial stops. The dozen terrorists threatened to blow up the airplane if anyone approached it on the tarmac.

The terrorists systematically forced all passengers to show their passports, targeting U.S. and Israeli citizens for special, unwanted attention. During a violent rampage, they beat Robert Stethem to death. Although in civilian clothes, Petty Officer Stethem was singled out from the passengers as a U.S. Navy sailor and American citizen, and killed when terrorist demands were not met.

On June 30, 1985, the hijackers were allowed to go free and, nearly 15 years later, some of those believed to be responsible are thought to be in Lebanon, Libya, or Iran. One is in prison in Germany. At the time, a U.S. State Department spokesman claimed the Iranian Embassy in Syria was "the mastermind" behind this and other Lebanese Shiite airline highjackings.

No doubt you have lost count, as have I, of the many similar, brutal terrorist attacks that have occurred since that June day in 1985. Not all involved airplane highjackings, but many have resulted in random death and injury to foreign nationals unlucky enough to be in the wrong place at the wrong time. In the 1980s alone, 17 American citizens were kidnapped and held by Arab terrorists. The entire U.S. Embassy staff in Tehran, Iran was held hostage for more than a year in 1979-80, and, in the mid-1980s, the U.S. Embassy in Beirut was destroyed, along with the lives of many U.S. Marines.

Would Robert Stethem's young life have been spared had he been able to produce a different passport, say that from a more neutral, less targeted nation such as Canada? Of course, we will never know.

The point is that second passports should not be viewed as sinister evidence of international criminal intent or illegal tax evasion, but as an intelligent means of defending oneself in the highly dangerous and volatile age in which we are forced to live.

A second passport could save your life and the lives of those you love.

Passports — a Modern Invention

Foreign travel in the modern world means having to deal with all the inconveniences imposed by national sovereignty — international borders, customs officials, passports, visas, and identity documents. It means having to put up with officious customs officers, bribe-seeking border guards and unreasonable, unexplained delays.

It may seem difficult to believe, but until shortly before the First World War (1914-19), official passports were almost never required by most countries. In those much slower moving times, document-free international travel was the general rule. Before the last century, passports were usually special travel documents used to protect official emissaries of nation states at war with each other, allowing safe conduct for surrender or peace negotiations.

The first modern travel document known as the "Nansen Passport" was issued to White Russian faction refugees in the prolonged civil war that followed the 1918 anti-Tsarist Russian Revolution led by the Bolsheviks.

That document took its name from Fridtjof Nansen, a Norwegian explorer (later a delegate to the ill-fated League of Nations in Geneva), who first proposed the passport concept. This passport, administered by the League, successfully served hundreds of thousands of refugees as a travel and identity document until the outbreak of World War II in September 1939. The International Refugee Organization (IRO) replaced the defunct League's Nansen Passport Office from 1930 to 1945, but had no authority to issue refugee documents.

In a 1951 treaty, the "Convention on the Status of Refugees" (CSR), the United Nations (U.N.) attempted to define the rights of international refugees. Effective in 1960, after the required 35 countries ratified it, the U.N. CSR authorized signatory countries to issue travel documents for those they determined eligible for refugee status, applying the Convention's criteria. Since each nation interpreted the CSR in its own fashion, the world soon became cluttered with thousands of refugees fleeing from wars, ethnic conflicts, famine, and pestilence. These unfortunates were admitted by some countries, rejected by others, and the result was misery on a grand scale in places as diverse as the Balkans, Israel and Palestine, Hong Kong, Vietnam, Cambodia, Rwanda, and numerous other countries.

On the subject of the right of persons to travel freely, the United Nations Universal Declaration of Human Rights states:

Article 13 – Everyone has the right to freedom of movement and residence within the borders of each state. Everyone has the right to leave any country, including his own, and to return to his country.

Article 15 – Everyone has the right to a nationality. No one shall be arbitrarily deprived of his nationality nor denied the right to change his nationality.

It goes without saying that these so-called "rights" of free movement, travel and residence have been, and are, systematically violated by almost every nation, including dictatorships and democracies. The United States and the United Kingdom are among the worst violators when it suits the political convenience of the government in power at the moment.

Politics dominates the recent history of world refugee problems.

In 1956, the U.S. Government under President Dwight Eisenhower welcomed thousands of refugees from the failed Hungarian revolt against the Russian-backed Communists who at the time dominated Hungary. During four decades of the Castro regime in Cuba, the U.S. has repeatedly admitted tens of thousands of Cuban refugees, who, with their offspring, now constitute a majority of U.S. citizens in south Florida.

In contrast, in what has been called a racist policy, during the early 1990s, the U.S. turned away thousands of Haitian "boat people" trying to escape dictatorship and poverty. In a shameful act, the British refused to give citizens of Hong Kong full U.K. citizenship rights when Communist China took over the colonial government in 1997, mainly because of a feared U.K. voter backlash against admitting more immigrants "of color."

More recently, the Balkan wars involving Serbia, Bosnia, Albania, and Kosovo have produced hundreds of thousands of refugees whose fate seemed the least concern of many national leaders, including their own.

Who Needs a Second Passport?

The English political philosopher, Edmund Burke (1729-97), observed in another time: "Early and provident fear is the mother of safety."

That is still good advice for any potential world traveler. Having to be "politically correct," or "PC" as they say, often means travel using a national passport that keeps the bearer as far away as possible from international controversy. It may be a fact of your political life that your home nation's passport may provide you little or no safety margin, but another nation's passport will.

Some countries are more popular and accepted in the world than others. Some countries are respected in some parts of the world, despised in others. Some countries are universally condemned and ostracized. Whichever categories your nation happens to fall into at the moment is likely to reflect on your fate when you present your passport bearing the official stamp of your government.

As I noted, travel in the Middle East or the Balkans, parts of Russia or Asia using a U.S. passport can make you an instant target for terrorist groups. If your government is out of world favor at the moment, your passport could be confiscated, revoked, or suspended at will, as happened to citizens of the Republic of South Africa during the apartheid years.

It's a fact of international political life that citizens of certain countries, the U.S. among them, find travel abroad difficult. For many reasons, some countries impose strict visa requirements each time a foreign national wants to enter their country. It's their way of keeping out troublemakers and other supposed "undesirables."

When I served as a member of the United States Congress, I was asked by a personal friend, a Catholic priest, to intercede with the South African Embassy in Washington, D.C. so that he could obtain a visa to visit that nation. He wished to spend several months there working with members of his religious order, but the apartheid regime diplomats apparently suspected he might engage in anti-apartheid political activities. It required a personal telephone call and my assurances in writing to the South African ambassador, a personal friend of mine, to obtain the visa.

Americans who want to visit Cuba can expect similar troubles. At this writing, for decades it has been illegal for U.S. citizens to visit Cuba because of the official U.S. embargo aimed at toppling Fidel Castro's Communist dictatorship. However, this situation is now easing.

Even a national whose passport usually allows easy international access can find a visa denied due to temporary travel restrictions during trade sanctions or political disturbances. And even if you finally do obtain a desired visa, it can take weeks of procedural delays.

As the unfortunate case of TWA passenger Robert Stethem demonstrates, holding second citizenship and a passport issued by a small, peaceful, non-controversial country can save your life when traveling in times of political unrest, civil war, and in other delicate situations abroad. For good reasons, countless thousands of international businessmen, and others, active worldwide consider an alternative passport as their best life insurance.

In an unsettled, ever-changing world, acquiring a second citizenship can be a wise decision, an investment in your future. Your second citizenship is a choice for life, which can act as a protective shield extended to your spouse and children as well. Moreover, there is usually no need to surrender or change your present nationality while you enjoy the benefits of your second passport.

Home Government Coercion

There is another disturbing trend that makes a second passport a great value. In various ways, governments increasingly use issuance of a passport to their own citizens as a means of coercion. In the United States, for example, a citizen can be denied a passport simply for being in debt to the Internal Revenue Service or because of other problems with federal government agencies.

Since 1986, the U.S. State Department has been informing the IRS of all persons who renew their U.S. passports using a foreign address. Since passport renewals require an applicant's Social Security number, this is also used by the IRS to see if applicants have filed income tax returns. In 1998, an IRS official speaking in Zurich said a special effort was being made by the agency to track all U.S. citizens who renewed U.S. passports while living in Switzerland, for reasons we can surely guess.

There is a growing tendency in important countries to follow the lead of the United States in taxing non-resident citizens. Alternative citizenship is, therefore, increasingly important as a powerful tool for truly international tax planning. As a national of two different countries, you also can enjoy extra privacy in your banking and investment activities.

An even more immediate threat can arise from your own government. Depending on your nation's policies, your government may use your passport to restrict your basic human right to travel, rather than to guarantee it. Use of your passport can be made contingent on payment of your taxes, however unreasonable, and on reporting of worldwide income and assets. Issuance of your passport allows your government to control, restrict, monitor, and record your travels.

Now you can begin to see why a second passport may be highly useful. Your qualification for a second nation's passport, one that comes with no restrictive strings attached, can serve as your passport to freedom. It can be your key to a whole New World of free movement, expanded international investment, greater flexibility, and adventure. In addition, it can mean safe passage as compared to delay or even worse.

Dual Nationality

There is little doubt that government bureaucrats and tax collectors see dual nationality as a serious threat to their control over the citizenry that they pretend to serve. As more U.S. citizens acquire dual nationality, the debate is intensifying. Eager to work abroad free of red tape and restrictions, or to strengthen ties with their ancestral lands, record numbers of people are obtaining a second, foreign passport.

Dual nationality simply means that a person legally is a citizen of two countries at the same time, qualified as such under each nation's law. This status may result automatically, as when a child born in a foreign country to a U.S. citizen becomes both a U.S. citizen and a citizen of the country where he or she is born. Or it may result from operation of law, as when a U.S. citizen acquires foreign citizenship by marriage to a spouse from another nation, or a foreign person naturalized as a U.S. citizen retains the citizenship of their country of birth.

Under U.S. law, a second passport does not jeopardize American citizenship. U.S. citizens, including dual nationals, must use a U.S. passport to enter and leave the United States. Dual nationals may also be required by the foreign country to use their passport to enter and leave. Use of the foreign passport does not endanger U.S. citizenship.

Many countries won't permit their citizens to hold a passport from another nation. This was the case in the U.S. until 1967, when the U.S. Supreme Court upheld the right of U.S. citizens to hold a second, foreign passport. Before that time, the official rule was that a person acquiring second nationality automatically lost U.S. citizenship. Since 1967, the government generally presumes a U.S. citizen does not wish to surrender citizenship. Proof of that intention is required before expatriation is officially recognized. The burden of proof is on the government to show intentional abandonment of U.S. citizenship. This presumption is set forth in a U.S. Department of State publication, Advice About Possible Loss of U.S. Citizenship and Dual Nationality, (1990). As a matter of policy, the U.S. Government recognizes dual nationality but does not encourage it because of what it views as problems and conflicts that may result.

No doubt, legal tax avoidance is at the top of the U.S. Government's list of major "problems" it sees resulting from Americans enjoying dual nationality.

The law of most countries holds that the exercise and acquisition of dual citizenship need not affect a person's original national legal status. Many people are automatically entitled to dual citizenship under various nation's laws, such as American grandchildren of Irish grandparents. In addition, a growing number of countries now issue "economic citizenship" based on investment by a foreign national in the issuing country. This may confer a limited or full citizenship status on the recipient, but it does not usually affect that person's original citizenship.

In the final analysis, it is the law of the nation that is seeking to impose its control over a dual national that determines whether expatriation, or loss of citizenship, occurs. Dual nationals owe allegiance and obedience to the laws of both countries of which they are citizens. Either country has the right to enforce its laws, especially when the person is physically within that country.

Some countries demand that a foreign national seeking citizenship formally renounce his or her original national allegiance. That, in theory, is the rule of the U.S. Although all naturalized U.S. citizens must take an oath which requires them to "renounce allegiance" to any other nation, in fact, new U.S. citizens do not have to surrender their previous nationality or passports. But, in varying degrees, the renunciation rule is followed in Italy, France, Spain, and Portugal. Other countries, notably Japan and the People's Republic of China, automatically exclude from citizenship any child born from the matrimonial union of one of their citizens and a parent from a foreign nation.

The trend toward multiple nationalities has the potential to turn upside down traditional notions of how people think of themselves, their careers, and their communities. It's drawn a flurry of attention from scholars, many of whom believe nationalities are artificial and, thus, interchangeable. "Most academics are happy to declare the end of the nation-state," says T. Alexander Aleinikoff, who studied international migration trends for the Carnegie Endowment for International Peace. Aleinikoff continues, "Dual citizenship is seen as a part of that."

Some critics worry that the trend has dangerous implications for a unified society. "If people can become dual citizens, why not have allegiances to three, four or even eight countries?" asks Mark Krikorian, director of the Center for Immigration Studies. A conservative think tank in Washington, D.C., Mr. Krikorian worries that native-born Americans will be harmed by a loosening of the traditional notion of "us" and "them."

Fueling the soul searching over identity and nationality is the fast spread of capital and culture around the world. Rapid transportation and instant communication links make it possible for many people to literally call home anywhere they can plug in a modem or get a dial tone.

"Whether you're a migrant or a hi-tech worker, you can move around the globe and you're not boxed in to any one single notion of belonging or identity," said Noah Pickus. He is a professor of public policy at Duke University, who edited a book forecasting migration and citizenship in the 21st Century. Pickus predicts that, "This is an emotional issue that has far-reaching implications we can only begin to imagine at this point."

In recent years, Americans with dual nationality have served as officials in the governments of Yugoslavia, Armenia, and Estonia. A retired U.S. Government employee, Valdas Adanikus, was elected president of his native Lithuania, while a former New York City attorney, Lionel Fernandez, is just beginning a second, non-consecutive term as president of the Dominican Republic.

France and the United Kingdom are among the major powers allowing dual nationality. In recent years, Colombia, Ecuador, Brazil, and the Dominican Republic have allowed their citizens to hold a second passport. South Korea and the Philippines are considering it. And, in a move that substantially boosted the number of the world's dual citizens, Mexico in 1998, began allowing its nationals to hold a U.S. passport. Naturalized Mexican Americans are allowed to reclaim their Mexican passport, though they can only vote in Mexico in person.

Scholars say that increasing numbers of U.S. immigrants are maintaining ties to their homelands, just as native-born Americans are reconnecting to roots overseas. "The old model of nationality is outmoded in this globalizing world," says Aiwa Ong, an anthropologist at the University of California at Berkeley. Ms. Ong, who wrote a book on the trend, calls the new way of living "flexible citizenship." Other scholars prefer the term "transnationals."

In the U.S., one of the questions most hotly debated by scholars is whether the oath of allegiance, required for all naturalized citizens, should be altered. The oath requires new citizens to swear off fidelity to other countries, but has little practical effect since the Immigration and Naturalization Service doesn't even ask new citizens whether they retain the passport of their country of origin. In fact, no one knows just how many citizens claim a second nationality.

Millions of Americans are eligible to become dual citizens based on their family ties to foreign lands that allow dual citizenship. (See the chapters on Ireland, Italy, and Germany). The requirement for gaining citizenship in many countries is the being born there, or the birth there, of a parent or grandparent. Relying on U.S. Census data, some estimates say that the pool of eligible American dual nationals grows by at least 500,000 each year, based on the number of U.S. children born to foreign-born parents.

In supporting dual citizenship, some governments have an economic incentive to maintain, or even strengthen, ties with emigrants who settled in the U.S. or other wealthy countries. An estimated 30% of all Latino immigrants to the U.S. send money back to native countries, and governments fear these remittances may decline over time.

Do Americans Need a Second Passport?

People of means living in places where it seems civil war never ends — like the Balkans, home to the shattered pieces of the former Yugoslavia, or people facing continued political uncertainty, such as Hong Kong since the 1997 handover to Communist Beijing — obviously can use a safe refuge for escape. If besieged people enjoy the legal status afforded by a second nationality, their chance of safety is far more certain. In a time when threats turn into physical menace, they simply head to their "other" country.

But what about American citizens? The "good old U.S.A." has been the favorite destination of millions of refugees throughout its history, and remains so. The Statue of Liberty in New York harbor still welcomes those "huddled masses" and "wretched refuse" from other shores who want to become Americans.

So why would any U.S. citizen need to acquire a second nationality, and the additional passport that goes with that expanded political status?

One very good reason: increasingly, the U.S. Government imposes highly burdensome restrictions on the freedoms that the nation's Founders set down in the U.S. Constitution. For people of wealth, in particular, there is now an extensive web cast to catch persons "the government" decides may be doing something wrong. And the current definition of "wrong" is so expansive as to be all-inclusive in the bureaucratic mind.

For example, the very fact that one has an offshore bank account, creates an offshore trust, or owns shares in an international business corporation — any and all of these innocent financial choices can suggest potential tax evasion in the jaundiced eyes of the IRS.

What About the British?

The same holds true of the official attitude of the United Kingdom and its bureaucrats.

It is estimated that in recent years 600,000 or more U.K. citizens have been driven into exile because of high taxes. Once domiciled abroad, in Italy, Portugal, Singapore, or Bermuda, many Britons used to return home like migratory birds to spend six months annually "vacationing" in England. Stay one day more and under the law, they would be liable to pay U.K. income taxes.

Realizing this, the tax collector, Her Majesty's Inland Revenue Service, adopted rules making long stays by former Britons more difficult. Today, if a British person maintains a home or apartment within the U.K., even a single day's visit results in full income taxes on all worldwide income. Without a U.K. home, the allowable non-taxable visit is 90 days per year, but only after an initial three-year continuous absence.

However, consider the alternative using a second passport.

If former residents enter and leave the U.K. using a legitimate, non-British passport, entry and departure records produced no tax demands. The person comes and goes free from Inland Revenue's counting of days. That's because U.K. law allows unrestricted dual citizenship and does not dictate which passport you must use if you are lucky enough to have dual citizen status.

A similar "days-in, days-out" rule applies in the U.S.

A foreigner who establishes residence in the U.S. for over 122 days annually, and engages in what could be called "business activity," can be held liable for U.S. income taxes on all worldwide income. The IRS may decide he/she is a "U.S. person," as this legal status is called, for tax purposes. He/she may have to submit to an unpleasant grilling to get tax clearance before being permitted to leave. The IRS also counts any legal resident alien in the U.S. as a "U.S. person" for tax purposes.

Multinational Corporations Do It

There is an apt analogy between multinational corporations doing business around the world, and individuals that legally hold dual or multiple citizenship, using their passports for world travel and business.

By registering and qualifying under local laws in more than one political jurisdiction, a corporation has the right to do business in each country where they qualify. Or a corporation in one nation may choose to set up a subsidiary company in a foreign nation where they do business. The subsidiary company may be owned by a parent company in a foreign land, but the local government treats it as one of their own domestic corporations (i.e., as a local citizen).

In fact, to induce a foreign company to set up shop, many governments offer special concessions, tax holidays, discounts on energy and raw materials, free land, subsidized local labor, cash grants, and other attractions. Why? Because ruling powers want to stay in office and that's easier to do when the local populace is employed and prosperous.

The major impetus to form multinational businesses, however, did not arise because of extravagant foreign inducements. This international movement didn't grow primarily to exploit profitable local opportunities in foreign lands. Instead, explosive growth of the multinationals came about, in part, to evade undue business restrictions and confiscatory high taxes in the company's home nation.

Now, the same pressures are forcing individual citizens to look elsewhere for protection from high taxes and excessive government control.

Until relatively recently, many countries did not permit their citizens to have foreign bank accounts, own foreign currencies, or hold foreign investments. Those that did allow these financial activities abroad still imposed strict reporting requirements, currency controls, costly exit permits, and special transactions taxes. But, "dual nationals," as dual citizens are also known, like multinational corporations, can move about the world in such a way as to minimize or avoid currency and other controls.

Dual nationality is not without its inherent contradictions.

Members of Mick Jagger's famous Rolling Stones rock music group moved to France in order to escape high British income taxes. Yet, many wealthy (and not so wealthy) Frenchmen have moved to the U.K. in order to avoid high French taxes. This anomaly exists because most high tax countries often exempt foreigners who reside within their borders less than six months a year.

A foreign citizen who winters in California for four months, travels or lives outside the U.S. for three months, then spends the remaining five months in his own country, may be able to avoid paying taxes anywhere! More importantly, this roaming individual can escape currency controls, investment restrictions, and the burdensome paperwork that comes with permanent attachment to one place on the map.

In order to enter a foreign country and live there for six months as a tourist, one generally needs a passport. Some countries also require foreign tourists to obtain a "visa," a prior written permission to enter that country, which is attached to your passport. And in order to remain longer, to work or to purchase a home, a "residence permit" is needed. "Non-work residence permits" are typically granted to entrepreneurs and others who do not compete in the local job market.

Citizenship and Passports

Before going further, let's examine the elements of citizenship and the meaning of passports.

Citizenship can be loosely defined as the legal relationship between a person and the sovereign nation in which he/she lives, a status defined by the law of that nation, conferring or limiting the person's duties and rights. Only through the formal process of citizenship acquisition, called *naturalization*, can one legally acquire the right to a second passport.

A *passport* is a personal identification and travel document for international use issued by a sovereign nation, usually to its own citizens, but to others as well.

Most familiar are government issued passports based on a person's national citizenship. However "official" they may appear to be, passports sold or "issued" by some commercial sellers may be illegal and, therefore, useless. Many governments designate attorneys and others to act as their official agents on second citizenship matters. Also, there are special travel documents such as diplomatic passports and other temporary travel documents issued by international organizations or individual countries. Diplomatic passports are only legal if issued by the proper authorities of the nation or international organization and only if the passport holder is properly accredited in the receiving nation.

Dual or Alternative Citizenship

Under the laws of most countries, it is legal and proper for some qualified persons to enjoy what is called "dual citizenship," sometimes also called "alternative citizenship." This dual status also may confer the right to have and use a second passport.

Legal grounds that can allow a person to have or acquire dual citizenship status are:

1) *being born within the borders of a nation's territory*; the 14th Amendment to the U.S. Constitution grants citizenship to any child born within American territory, regardless of the citizenship of the parents. Other countries conferring automatic citizenship on those born within their jurisdiction include Argentina, Australia, Barbados, Belize, Bolivia, Brazil, Canada, Chile, Cost Rica, the

Dominican Republic, Ecuador, Greece, Honduras, Israel, Italy, Jamaica, Lebanon, Malta, Mauritius, Mexico, New Zealand, Panama, Paraguay, Portugal, St. Kitts and Nevis, Spain, Thailand, Trinidad, Turkey, Uruguay, and Venezuela;

2) *descent from a foreign citizen parent or grandparent*; making ancestry a basis, as in Ireland, Germany, Spain, or Greece;

3) *marriage* to a foreign citizen;

4) *religion*; as in Israel; and

5) *formal naturalization*; meaning applying and qualifying for citizenship status. The process for receiving the privilege of naturalization varies among countries. Usually, a certain period of residence is required (e.g., five years in the U.S.), plus good character and an absence of any criminal record may be among other requirements.

Some countries demand that a foreign national seeking naturalized citizenship formally renounce his or her original national allegiance. That is the U.S. law, but as we explained, it simply is not being enforced, even though the citizenship oath includes such a statement. The same rule is followed in varying degrees in Italy, France, Spain, and Portugal. Other countries, notably Japan and the People's Republic of China, automatically exclude from citizenship any child born from the matrimonial union of one of their citizens and a parent from a foreign nation.

Second Passports: Important Considerations

Legality

The single most important consideration when evaluating the usefulness of an alternative citizenship is that it be legal in every respect. That fact may seem obvious, but the proliferation of fly-by-night passport fraud operations requires not only this reminder, but strict adherence to it when making second passport plans and decisions.

If you are going to spend a considerable sum of money to acquire a second citizenship and then use a second passport as your basis of personal international movement, you should demand that these documents and your status be in strict accord with the constitution and laws of the issuing nation.

A few countries actually do have provisions in law that give the head of government, or other government ministers, discretion regarding the granting of citizenship to foreign nationals in exceptional cases. Even then, if criminal bribery is involved, the person acquiring the passport may face revocation of this previously granted citizenship after a subsequent political change in government. Persons with such documents frequently are subject to blackmail by being forced to pay further "fees" later on. That is why it is imperative that second citizenship must be firmly based upon clear provisions in the existing law of the issuing nation.

The prospective second passport client most at risk is one lured into an "instant" or "immediate" passport deal that promises to waive residency requirements and grant quick citizenship. Immediate passports are a favorite lure for attracting unsuspecting and ill informed would-be buyers who need and want a quick passport, but haven't done sufficient investigative groundwork.

And even legal passport programs can come and go swiftly, so a candidate must always determine what actually is current. Ireland had an immediate citizenship program for wealthy investors, but ended it in 1996. A similar Cape Verde economic citizenship program ended in 1997. The same year, the Seychelles canceled their program in the face of European Union complaints about its questionable operation.

A recent Internet search using the terms "second passport" and "economic citizenship program" produced scores of Internet sites offering allegedly "instant" passports from Argentina, Brazil, Chile, the Dominican Republic, Greece, Guatemala, Honduras, Panama, Paraguay, Peru, Tonga, Vanuatu, Venezuela, and Western Samoa. None of these countries has such an official program. The reasonable implication is that what these sites offer is either fraudulent and/ or illegal.

All of this may also reflect a little known fact; that there is an expansive, lucrative underground black market in forged and faked passports. In October 1997, forged Canadian passports were carried by two Israeli hit men who took part in an unsuccessful assassination attempt in Jordan. Even legal passports can go astray. In 1998, the Western Samoan Government announced 150 of its official passports simply had been "lost." Since then thousands of official passports have been stolen or lost in France, Australia, Finland and Belgium.

Passport Fraud

A few years ago, had you read the classified advertisements in such respectable journals as the *The International Herald Tribune* and *The Economist,* you would have seen an ad that promised to provide a "European Union passport, fully registered and renewable" for only

US$19,500. A contact telephone number in Ireland was listed.

When we made inquiries of this advertiser, the person who answered the telephone said that, for a price, his company could arrange "official citizenship" in the Netherlands and/or Switzerland. When we asked for citations to specific Dutch and Swiss laws authorizing the sale of such passports, the spokesperson gave several answers: a) the company had a special deal with senior Dutch and Swiss officials; b) they had arranged an accelerated naturalization process; and c) their legal counsel, who could explain more fully how all this worked, was away at the moment.

Consular officers at both the Swiss and Dutch Embassies were astonished when told about the company and their claims. The officials confirmed what we already knew. Neither nation has ever had an economic citizenship/passport program at any price. They assured us that their national police authorities would be immediately alerted about this passport fraud and actions taken to end it.

We cite this example only because it is typical of the passport frauds that abound in offshore publication ads, even in well-respected publications like these. As we said, the Internet is loaded with hundreds of passport fraud Web sites masquerading as legitimate passport services, many claiming to have official sanction from the countries whose "passports" they hawk.

Throughout this report, you will find numerous references to true passport frauds involving counterfeit documents. We also tell you about passport frauds resulting from corrupt and dishonest officials in some countries, now and in the past, such as Belize and the Dominican Republic, where there may also be legitimate second passport programs.

Unlike the fraudulent passport huckster and their false claims, what you read here you can believe and rely upon. We're not selling passports. We're speaking the truth.

International Recognition

Before you acquire a second passport, be certain that it is one that commands widespread acceptance and prestige in the international community. If it's not likely to be recognized by all other countries, it is worthless from the start.

In this age of instant communications, it takes only hours, certainly no more than a few days, before customs and immigration officials worldwide know when a passport is called into question. In 1992, this happened with official, but illegally issued Dominican Republic passports, mentioned above, and, in 1999, with passports issued by Panama. In the latter case, a high passport official resigned alleging she had been pressured into issuing passports to various foreign business associates of the outgoing president. At this writing, an investigation continues, but you can be certain that when, and if, the facts are revealed, anyone holding such a passport will soon find it worthless.

Of course, if you intend to become a citizen of another nation, and possibly spend time there, your consideration should include geographic location, language, stability of the political and legal system, the banking and business environment, visa-free travel possibilities, and, of course, total initial and future costs.

Do You Need a Lawyer?

There is something to be said for dealing directly with the officials of the nation from which you seek a second citizenship. This can be done at the appropriate embassy in your nation's capital city or at a local consulate. Information and applications can be obtained by telephone or facsimile.

But that assumes you have the time, expertise, and patience to navigate the often tedious bureaucratic route that can take months or even years. Working directly with diplomatic and consular officials eliminates the middleman and probably lessens the chance of fraud or mistakes. Nevertheless, it is better to employ an experienced attorney based in your own nation or intended country, who is an established, reputable professional specializing in immigration and passport matters. These experts usually know the legitimate shortcuts and have personal acquaintances with the involved foreign nation officials. That can speed up your application and approval process considerably.

Caution may dictate using an escrow agent; a trustworthy third party that holds your citizenship and passport fees until the transaction is complete. A bank, law firm, solicitor, or other escrow agent can serve this purpose. The agent will hold your money, usually in the form of a certified check payable to the agent, will receive your passport or other documents, permitting you to inspect them before a final payment is made. If you are satisfied after a genuine passport or other documents have been delivered, the escrow agent makes payment and delivers the passport to you. An agent's fee for services will range from 1-10% of the transaction value. In most second passport cases, "advanced fees" should be avoided. If you are willing to place cash in escrow, expense advances should seldom be required.

The Sovereign Society Worldwide Immigration Assistance Program

By special arrangement with one of the world's leading international immigration service firms, **Henley & Partner, Inc.** and with selected attorneys, The Sovereign Society is able to offer its members considerably reduced fees on acquisitions of permanent residency and second citizenship in almost every nation. These special fee reductions apply to economic citizenship programs, residency pending naturalization, naturalization, and other programs offered by various countries to foreign nationals.

Recommended Service Providers

Henley & Partner, Inc. is recognized as one of the world's leading service firms for international immigration and citizenship law. The firm also offers services in corporate location, international tax, and estate planning.

They can advise you on all aspects of current residency and citizenship programs available in the nation of your choice. They offer expert information on second passports, the advantages and disadvantages of various options, special situations and current events affecting citizenship. They maintain offices and associates in all countries offering economic citizenship programs as well as other major countries.

Henley & Partner, Inc. maintains an international network of immigration specialist attorneys, tax consultants, investment advisors, and other professionals who are experts in their fields. They emphasize practical and speedy solutions consistent with the best current advice available. Topics for which assistance is available include not only second passports and immigration, but also taxation, private law, insurance, real estate, corporate and personal relocation, and government procedures in all countries.

All services and contacts are completely confidential and strict privacy is assured. Inquiries should be directed to: Henley & Partner, Inc., Mr. Christian H. Kälin, Haus zum Engel, Kirchgasse 22, 8001 Zurich, Switzerland; Tel: +(41) 44-266-22 22; Fax: +(41) 44-266-22 23; E-mail: Zurich-office@henleyglobal.com; E-mail: christian.kalin@henleyglobal.com; Web site: http://www.henleyglobal.com.

Recommended Visa Publication

Since 1963, the "Travel Information Manual" (TIM) has supplied the air travel industry with reliable and comprehensive up-to-date country information on entry and health requirements as well as visa, customs, and currency regulations. The TIM booklet, issued monthly, offers a complete package to help travelers save time, and avoid fines and delays. Contact: Tel: +(31)(0) 20-316-3714; Fax: +(31)(0) 20-316-3801; E-mail: mwesterwaal@iata.nl.

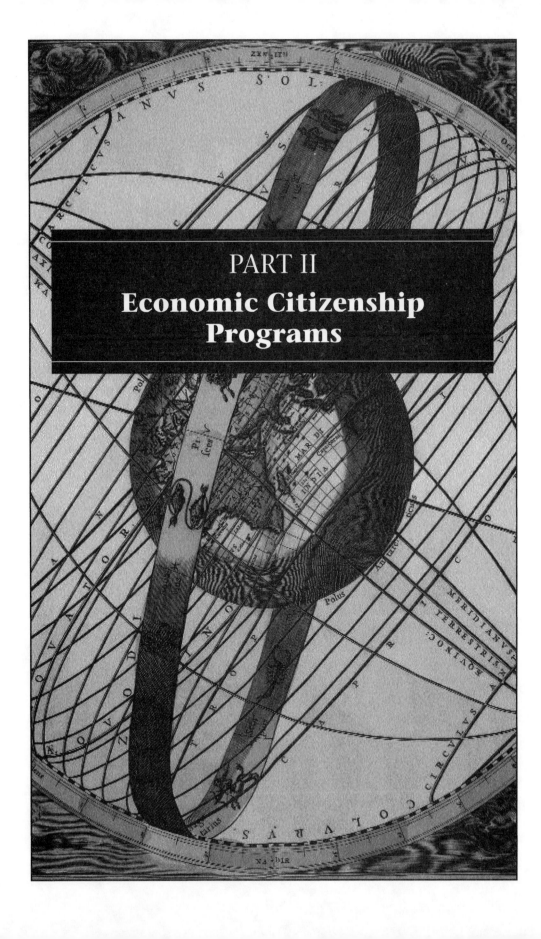

PART II
Economic Citizenship Programs

Economic Citizenship Programs

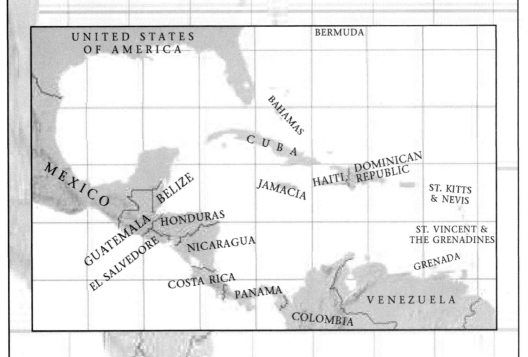

Part II

Economic Citizenship Programs

Residence, rather than full citizenship, is granted by most countries to wealthy foreign investors and other individuals. Only very few countries grant official citizenship based on economic considerations without residency requirements. These so-called "economic citizenship programs" offer an opportunity to acquire a new nationality quickly and simply, without major disruptions to your life.

Because "citizenship" is a legal relationship between a person and his/her national government, that government has the power to define by law the criteria for its citizenship. Very few countries (two at this writing) have enacted explicit laws that grant citizenship to foreign nationals based purely on economic considerations, and without imposing actual residence requirements. Included in this group are **Dominica** and **St. Kitts-Nevis**.

Before considering the two national programs that do exist, here's a reality check. You may have seen advertisements in the pages of the *International Herald Tribune* Tribune or other offshore publications offering "official passports" from a long list of countries. You're told that all you need to do is pay the price asked. The implication in such ads is always that the passports offered are somehow "official," yet buying from this seller allows you to avoid going through official channels to obtain the prized passport.

We have to accept the fact that, in almost every country, it may be possible to make direct payments, bribes, to dishonest government officials in return for passports and citizenship documents. If these documents are not issued under a currently authorized, legitimate government program, then these actions are illegal and buying them may constitute a crime. Those so foolish as to acquire passports in this backdoor way run the serious risks of exposure, arrest, and deportation.

However, there are indeed legal, valid "economic citizenship programs" available to those willing to pay the price. **Australia**, **Canada**, **Portugal**, **Switzerland**, **United Kingdom**, and the **United States** are all examples of countries that offer varying degrees of residency and/or citizenship to wealthy individuals and investors. But only a few offer fast, immediate *quid pro quo* citizenship in return for investments, including the **Commonwealth of Dominica** and **St. Christopher** and **Nevis**, both in the Caribbean area. Many other nations offer what amounts to economic residency, but not citizenship.

Austria also allows citizenship if a foreign national person invests substantially in the country, but the process for obtaining this is difficult and limited to special circumstances. The **Dominican Republic** also offers quick citizenship after a minimum residence period of only six months if you invest in a local business or real estate. However, the Dominican Republic has suffered passport issuance scandals in recent years and this weighs against the nation as a choice for obtaining a second passport.

Each of these programs grants citizenship, evidenced by an official naturalization certificate, or certificate of registration, identifying the named person as entitled to citizenship rights with some qualifications. The official passport is granted after the naturalization process. In each of these countries, the entire process usually takes less than 90 days.

Commonwealth of Dominica

CAPITAL:	ROSEAU
POPULATION:	69,655
LANGUAGE:	ENGLISH (OFFICIAL), FRENCH PATOIS
CURRENCY:	EAST CARIBBEAN DOLLAR (EC$)
AREA:	751 SQUARE KM
ETHNIC GROUPS:	EUROPEAN, SYRIAN, CARIB AMERINDIAN, BLACK
RELIGION:	ROMAN CATHOLIC 77%, PROTESTANT 15%, OTHER 6%, UNAFFILIATED 2%

PASSPORT HIGHLIGHTS: Dominica's economic citizenship program is considered one of the world's best. Since its inception in 1991, it has operated successfully, but not always smoothly. For the foreseeable future, a single investor may acquire Dominican citizenship via a direct cash contribution of US$100,000 to government and private projects; the sum is raised to US$150,000 for a family of up to four persons. A citizen of Dominica has the right to live and work there at any time. Holders of a Dominica passport can travel on it without a visa to more than 100 countries and territories, including the U.K., Canada, Switzerland, Sweden, and Hong Kong.

Dominica is located at the northern end of the Windward Chain of the Lesser Antilles in the Caribbean Sea, between the French islands of Guadeloupe and Marie Galanty to the north, and Martinique to the south. A volcanic island plunging steeply into the sea on all sides, Dominica lacks substantial beaches. Thus, it was overlooked in the Caribbean tourism boom of the past quarter-century, which saw massive hotel and resort development elsewhere throughout the region. It has nonetheless undergone a steady increase in the affections of eco-tourists and nature lovers who flock to Dominica for its largely unspoiled landscapes, romantic in their grandeur: "Too much blue, too much purple, too much green. The flowers too red, the mountains too high, the hills too near," as Jean Rhys, a native Dominican, has a character say in her novel, Wide Sargasso Sea. Nature treks and reef diving are common topics in travel writing about Dominica, but – apart from reggae festivals – night life is not.

Known as the "Nature Island" of the Caribbean, Dominica boasts a wide range of unique nature attractions, including unspoiled rain forests, an abundance of spectacular waterfalls in its 365 rivers, the second largest volcanic boiling lake (92° C) in the world, and world-class hiking in many nature reserves. The island is also a bird watcher's paradise and offers fabulous scuba diving in the coral reefs with 30-meter underwater visibility.

While not exactly cut off from the world – the island is readily accessible by air from Antigua, Barbados, and Puerto Rico. People settling in Dominica may find themselves a little bit away from the beaten track, as air connections to mainland destinations are not as frequent as elsewhere in the Caribbean. There are plans for a new international airport.

With a perfect Caribbean climate, the island covers an area of almost 800 square kilometers and supports a population of about 65,000 citizens, including some 3,000 descendants of the original Carib native peoples. Dominicans are some of the friendliest of all Caribbeans. English is the official language, but early French rule is evident in a local Creole dialect.

Independent since 1978 and a full member of the British Commonwealth, Dominica enjoys a Westminster-style parliamentary government, free elections, and has had several peaceful transfers of political power. There is a strong local currency and little crime. Unlike some other nations offering economic citizenship, Dominica's program has had a reasonably good reputation despite its admitted problems.

The economy depends on agriculture and is highly vulnerable to climatic conditions, notably tropical storms. Agriculture, primarily bananas, accounts for 20% of GDP and employs 40% of the labor force. Tourism has become a major growth sector offering good investment opportunities, but it is not yet well developed because of the rugged coastline, lack of beaches, and the lack of an international airport. Hurricane Luis devastated the country's banana crop in September 1995; tropical storms wiped out one-fourth of the crop in 1994 as well. The economy began to recover in mid-1998, fueled by increases in construction, soap production, and tourist arrivals.

The nation is relatively poor and the Dominica Government is adopting a structured approach to economic development through a number of programs, including promotion of Dominica as an eventual offshore banking and company formation center, and an attractive economic citizenship program. Other possible investment benefits offered include business tax holidays of up to 15 years, unrestricted repatriation of profits, economical hydroelectricity, and the possibility of tax-free entry of produced goods into the U.S. market — a proposal suggested by the U.S. Government, but not yet adopted.

Economic Citizenship Program

Several nations have adopted statutory laws that allow foreign persons to acquire citizenship in exchange for a direct financial contribution to the country's economic development. The consensus among those who follow such matters closely is that Dominica has one of the best economic citizenship programs. Since its inception, the program has operated successfully, but has not been without problems. With its important banana export industry struggling, in 1991, Dominica began offering economic citizenships to foreign nationals who invested in local development projects, mainly in the tourism industry.

Dominica began its citizenship program by permitting the immigration minister to waive citizenship residency requirements in special circumstances. Initially, the waiver program sought to attract applicants from Hong Kong and Taiwan. The first attempt required qualified applicants to invest US$35,000 in a company that planned to build a small luxury hotel. This qualified the applicant, spouse, and two children under 18 years old for full citizenship. Later, the government asked for an additional US$25,000 to be paid to the hotel promoter.

This arrangement worked reasonably well until after the June 1995 election, when a new government took office. Despite criticism of the original program, the new government honored its past commitments until a dispute arose between the new prime minister and the hotel promoter. Construction of the hotel halted and individuals with pending citizenship applications had their applications delayed indefinitely, although they had already paid for shares in the hotel development. Eventually, the dispute was resolved and hotel construction resumed.

In spite of some problems, since 1991, more than 1,000 foreign persons have been granted economic citizenship in return for investments ranging from US$35,000 to US$75,000. More recently, the economic citizenship program has broadened; placing new emphasis on capital investments directed by the government itself.

In elections on February 1, 2000, the Labor Party narrowly defeated the incumbent government. The new government pledged to continue the economic citizenship program, while reviewing and making improvements based on comprehensive proposals received from Henley & Partner, Inc. In the opinion of experts, Dominica continues to offer unmatched expertise and experience in administering one of the world's most successful economic citizenship programs.

The Dominica program is specifically authorized by the nation's constitution (section 101). The government has set a limited quota of applications as authorized in section 8 of the Citizenship Act (Chapter 1) and associated policy guidelines.

The new Dominica citizen has the right to live and work there at any time. Equally important, as a citizen of a British Commonwealth nation, the new citizen enjoys special rights and privileges within the United Kingdom. In addition, they can travel on their Dominica passport without a visa to more than 100 countries and territories, including the U.K., Canada, Switzerland, Sweden, and Hong Kong. Dominica passports are valid for ten years and are readily renewable. Those who receive such passports are not liable for any taxes in Dominica on income earned outside the nation.

Payment/Investment Options

Over the years, there have been several sanctioned investment routes to acquire economic citizenship, including investment in long-term and low-yield government bonds, direct cash contribution to the government, or investments in particular projects. For example, a number of Taiwanese and Hong Kong residents received passports from Dominica after making investments of US$35,000 in shares of the country's first luxury hotel project, with an additional fee of US$25,000 paid to the hotel developer. The current Labor Government's position is that money contributed to acquire citizenship should go to specific projects only, which makes sense and distinguishes this program from others. The present guidelines for economic citizenship name school construction, renovation of the hospital, construction of a national sports stadium, and promoting the offshore sector as targets for these cash inputs. For now, and in the foreseeable future, there are two options to acquire citizenship:

The "family option," a direct cash contribution to the government of US$150,000 for a family of up to four persons (applicant, spouse, and two children under 18 years old), plus US$25,000 for each additional child. With registration and professional fees of approximately US$15,000 added to the basic figure, applicants can anticipate a total cost of US$165,000. One-third of the funds are earmarked for specific private-sector projects that benefit the development of the country, with the remaining two-thirds applied to public-sector budgets; or "single option," under which an individual applicant's $100,000 investment is to be divided equally between public and private-sector projects.

The government guarantees the return of all investment funds if an application is rejected for any reason or withdrawn, but some US$2,200 in processing fees is non-refundable. Since granting citizenship is at the sole discretion of the government, there is no guarantee that applications will be approved.

Application Procedure

An application for Dominica citizenship for one family (including the main applicant, spouse and two unmarried dependent children under the age of 18) must be accompanied by copies of passports, birth and marriage certificates, and police clearances (see below). The applicant must also contribute to the nation's economy using one of the options described above.

The Minister of Finance of Dominica appoints official foreign agents to administer the application process on behalf of the government. Approval normally requires no more than three to four weeks. Usually, there is a need for the main family applicant to visit the country for a few days to be interviewed by the Minister of Legal Affairs or his representative. However, the agent can arrange for an approved applicant to have the interview and the taking of the "Oath of Allegiance" before a consular officer at a Consulate of Dominica abroad, or in special circumstances, even in the applicant's home country or elsewhere. Citizens of Dominica are allowed to hold dual citizenship, and the acquisition of citizenship is not reported to other countries.

Required Documents

The following documents must accompany an application. If they are not in English, they must be translated and certified by a professional translation service on the firm's letterhead bearing its signature and stamp. Certified document copies in the original language must also be provided.

Document:	For:
Application form	each person, including children
Personal information form	each person, including children

Document:	For:
Business background information	each working adult
Birth certificate (certified copy)	each person, including children
Marriage certificate (certified copy)	Married couples
Divorce certificate (certified copy)	Divorced persons
Medical certificate, including HIV Test (original)	each person, including children
Certificate of no criminal record (original)	each person (16 years and over)
Two (2) personal references (originals)	Main applicant
Bank reference (original)	Main applicant
Copy of passport or ID document (certified copy)	each person, including children
Twelve (12) color passport photos	Each person, including children

Contacts

For citizenship information and assistance, **Henley & Partner, Inc.**, 10 Castle St., Roseau, Commonwealth of Dominica. Tel: 1 767 449 98 00 Fax: 1 767 449 97 77. E-mail: dominica-office@henley global.com Web site: http://www.henleyglobal.com/dominica0.htm Virtual Dominica Web site: http://www.delphis.dm/home.htm.

United States: U.S. citizens may enter Dominica without a passport for tourist stays up to three months, but must carry an original document proving U.S. citizenship, such as a U.S. passport, Certificate of Naturalization, Certificate of Citizenship, or certified copy of a U.S. birth certificate, photo identification, and a return/onward ticket. For further information concerning entry requirements, contact the Embassy of the Commonwealth of Dominica, 3216 New Mexico Avenue, NW, Washington, D.C. 20015; Tel: (202) 364-6781, or the Consulate of the Commonwealth of Dominica in New York.

Americans living in or visiting Dominica may wish to register at the Consular Section of the U.S. Embassy in Bridgetown, Barbados. http://bridgetown.usembassy.gov

Travelers may contact the Embassy to obtain updated information on travel and security on Dominica. The U.S. Embassy is located in

Bridgetown at the Canadian Imperial Bank of Commerce (CIBC) Building on Broad Street, telephone (246) 436-4950, web site http://bridgetown.usembassy.gov. The Consular Section is located in the American Life Insurance Company (ALICO) Building, Cheapside, telephone (246) 431-0225, fax (246) 431-0179, website http://bridgetown.usembassy.gov. The hours of operation are 8:30 a.m. to 11:30 a.m. and 1:00 p.m. to 2:00 p.m., Monday – Friday, except Barbadian and U.S. holidays.

St. Christopher & Nevis

CAPITAL:	BASSETERRE
POPULATION:	38,763
LANGUAGE:	ENGLISH
CURRENCY:	EAST CARIBBEAN DOLLAR (EC$)
AREA:	93.2 SQUARE KM
RELIGION:	ANGLICAN, OTHER PROTESTANT, ROMAN CATHOLIC

PASSPORT HIGHLIGHTS: Applicants for economic citizenship must invest US$250,000 in an "approved investment project." Government registration fees are now US$35,000 for a main applicant and US$15,000 for each spouse and dependent child under 18. Young adult family members over 18 must pay US$35,000 each. In addition, professional fees are US$15,000 for the main applicant and US$5,000 for each additional family member.

If there is one haven country that has all the things needed for smooth offshore financial operations, it's the two-island Federation of Saint Christopher (locally called "St. Kitts") and Nevis (pronounced KNEE-vis).

It's in the Leeward Islands in the eastern Caribbean, located 225 miles east of Puerto Rico and about 1,200 miles south of Miami. Each tropical island is a volcanic mountain rising about 1,000 meters from the sea, with about 75% of the total population living on St. Kitts. The islands' balmy, virtually unchanging weather and splendid beaches and accommodations have made them a popular vacation spot, offering a wide range of recreational amenities. Visitors to St. Kitts and Nevis tend find the islands' pace to be more leisurely even than that of other Caribbean holiday spots.

The British first settled the islands in 1623, however, control was disputed with the French, until 1783, when the British won. Independence was achieved on September 19, 1983 and the federation is now a member of the British Commonwealth. It is a parliamentary democracy based on the Westminster model, but the constitution of St. Kitts and Nevis allows either island to secede upon a referendum vote.

In August 1998, defying international pleas, residents of the seven-mile-long island of Nevis voted on whether to secede from St. Kitts and become the smallest nation in the Western Hemisphere. Approval of two-thirds of the island's voters was required for secession. The vote was 2,427 for secession and 1,418 against, falling just short of two-thirds.

The vote was the culmination of a struggle that began with Britain's colonization in 1628. In 1882, Britain stripped Nevis of its legislature and wed it to St. Kitts. When the islands became independent in 1983, Nevis reluctantly joined in a federation with neighboring St. Kitts, but Nevisians insisted on a constitutional clause allowing them to break away. After years of complaining that they are treated like second-class citizens by the federal government on St. Kitts, they invoked that right with the failed 1998 referendum. Nevis retains the right to secede, and proponents vow that they will try again.

International Financial Center

Nevis, which has its own Island Assembly, has a no nonsense banking and business privacy law that even the U.S. Government can't crack. Its pro-offshore laws have existed for two decades — so there is plenty of experience and precedent in the local courts — and the legislative assembly keeps the applicable laws current. There are well-established service companies that can do what you want, and many have convenient U.S. offices.

The Nevis independence movement owes much to its success as the business-friendly "Delaware of the Caribbean." Over the last two decades, its parliament has adopted and constantly updated excellent offshore corporation, trust and limited liability company laws, augmented by strict financial privacy. There are no exchange controls and no tax treaties with other countries. As a matter of official policy, the government does not exchange tax or other information with any other foreign revenue service or government. Unsuccessful moves by the St. Kitts-based Government to take over the offshore Nevis financial sector have spurred secession.

Asset Protection Trusts

Building on their reputation for statutory corporate cordiality, in 1994, the Island Assembly adopted the Nevis International Trust Ordinance, a comprehensive, clear and flexible asset protection trust

(APT) law. This law is comparable — and in many ways superior — to that of the Cook Islands in the South Pacific, already well known as an APT world center.

The new Nevis law incorporates the best features of the Cook Islands law, but is even more flexible. The basic aim of the law is to permit foreign citizens to obtain asset protection by transferring property titles to an APT established in Charlestown, Nevis.

Nevis simply is taking advantage of the worldwide growth in medical, legal, and professional malpractice law suits. Legislative and judicial imposition of no-fault personal liability on corporate officers and directors has become a nasty fact of business life. A Nevis trust places personal assets beyond the reach of foreign governments, litigious plaintiffs, creditors, and contingency-fee lawyers.

Under the 1994 law, the Nevis judiciary does not recognize any non-domestic court orders regarding its domestic APTs. This forces a foreign judgement creditor to start all over again, retrying in Nevisian court with Nevisian lawyers. A plaintiff sues an APT must first post a US$25,000 bond with the government to cover court and others costs before a suit will be accepted for filing. In addition, the statute of limitations for filing legal challenges to a Nevisian APT runs out two years from the date of the trust creation. In cases of alleged fraudulent intent, the law places the burden of proof on the foreign claimant.

This small, two-island country's greatest assets are its considerable natural beauty and Nevis as a financial center. To exploit potential tourism, the government has agreements with foreign-owned hotel and condominium developments. St. Kitts is a popular tourist destination, with white sand beaches, deep sea fishing, golf, tennis, and   casino gambling. Since 1994, the federation has been part of the Association of Caribbean States (ACS) trading bloc of over 60 million people.

Fast Tax Haven Citizenship

St. Kitts and Nevis's excellent citizenship program was established in 1984 and is governed by the Citizenship Act of 1984 (Section 3). It is the oldest of such national programs and offers the benefits of visa-free travel to over 90 countries. The Citizenship Act provides for persons to be registered as non-voting citizens if "the Cabinet is satisfied that such a person has invested substantially in the country."

Under current economic citizenship procedures, an applicant must invest US$150,000 in "approved investment project." Government registration fees are now US$35,000 for a main applicant and US$15,000 for each spouse and dependent child under 18. Young adult family members over 18 must pay US$35,000 each. In addition, professional fees are US$15,000 for the main applicant and US$5,000 for each additional family member.

These figures appear expensive compared to other programs described in this report, but St. Kitts and Nevis citizens enjoy one major difference. The country has no personal income tax, no capital gains tax, and no inheritance or gift taxes. There is also no corporate tax on offshore earnings or assets. There is a 2.5% tax on the purchase of condominiums and a 4% tax on the purchase of single-family homes. Legal fees on property transactions generally run at 1.5%.

Processing time for applications takes up to three months and dual nationality is permitted, with no residency requirement.

Documents that must be submitted include: 1) application for citizenship; 2) birth and marriage certificates; 3) a police certificate or affidavit showing no criminal record; 4) evidence of financial assets; and 5) a medical certificate showing a negative HIV test result.

Visiting Foreigners

A valid passport or birth certificate and photo ID that contains both name and date of birth are required of U.S. citizens entering St. Kitts and Nevis. Visitors should also have a valid return airplane ticket. Stays up to one month are granted and anyone requiring an extension must apply to the Ministry of National Security. There is an airport departure tax and an environmental levy. U.S. citizens entering with documents should take special care in securing those documents while traveling. For further information, contact the Embassy of St. Kitts and Nevis, 3216 New Mexico Avenue, NW, Washington, D.C. 20016; Tel: (202) 686-2636, fax (202) 686-5740 or the Permanent Mission to the U.N. in New York, or via the Internet at www.stkittsnevis.org.

Contacts

United States: The U.S. does not maintain an embassy on St. Kitts and Nevis. For assistance, contact the U.S. Embassy located in Bridgetown at the Canadian Imperial Bank of Commerce (CIBC) Building on Broad Street, telephone (246) 436-4950, web site http://bridgetown.usembassy.gov/. The Consular Section is located in the American Life Insurance Company (ALICO) Building, Cheapside; Tel. (246) 431-0225, fax (246) 431-0179. The hours of operation are 8:30 a.m. to 11:00 a.m. and 1:00 to 2:00 p.m., Monday to Friday, except Barbados and U.S. holidays.

Airport departure taxes are US$10. For further information, contact the Embassy of St. Kitts and Nevis, 3216 New Mexico Avenue, NW, Washington, D.C. 20016; Tel: (202) 686-2636, or the Permanent Mission to the U.N. in New York.

United Kingdom: High Commissioner resides at Bridgetown, Barbados. British High Commission, Price Waterhouse Center, Old Parham Road, St. John's, Antigua; Tel: +(268) 462-0008/9; Fax: +(268) 462-2806. British Consulate, Honorary British Council, P.O. Box 559, Basseterre, St. Kitts; Tel: +(869) 466-5620; Fax: +(869) 466-8889.

For St. Kitts & Nevis citizenship information and assistance, contact Henley & Partners, PO Box 481, 3 Church St., Basseterre, St. Kitts, West Indies, Tel: 1 869 465-1711, Fax: 1 869 465-1004. E-mail: caribbean-office@henleyglobal.com Web site: http://www.henleyglobal.com/stkittsnevis.htm

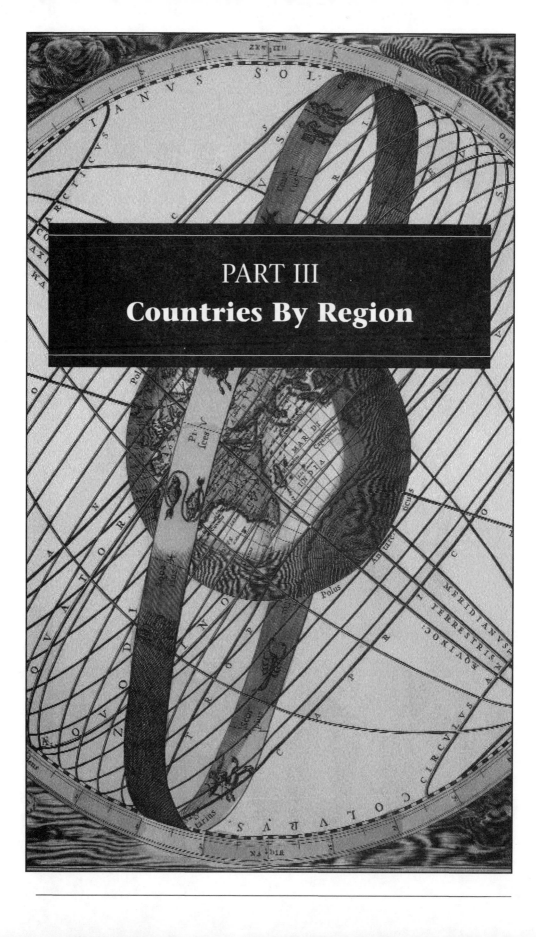

PART III
Countries By Region

Section 1.
North America

CANADA

UNITED STATES
OF AMERICA

MEXICO

CUBA

Canada

CAPITAL:	OTTAWA
POPULATION:	32,207,113
LANGUAGE:	ENGLISH 59.3% (OFFICIAL), FRENCH 23.2% (OFFICIAL), AND OTHER 17.5%
CURRENCY:	CANADIAN DOLLAR (C$)
AREA:	9,976,140 SQUARE KM
ETHNIC GROUPS:	BRITISH ISLES ORIGIN 28%, FRENCH ORIGIN 23%, OTHER EUROPEAN 15%, AMERINDIAN 2%, OTHER, MOSTLY ASIAN, AFRICAN, ARAB 6%, MIXED BACKGROUND 26%
RELIGION:	ROMAN CATHOLIC 46%, PROTESTANT 36%, OTHER 18%

PASSPORT HIGHLIGHTS: Canada welcomes immigrants with the financial means to invest in approved instruments or projects valued at a minimum of C$400,000, as well as those moving to the country to start their own business or participate in a going business concern.

Canada is the premier nation in the world for exercising, perhaps, the most effective wealth protection strategy — expatriation. However, for a U.S. citizen (and many others), expatriation means renouncing citizenship and becoming a foreign national — a Canadian.

Radical? You bet.

But wealthy Americans stand to lose millions of dollars to the IRS. Consider this; at death, the U.S. Government could take up to 55% of the assets you leave to your children — and that's after having paid up to 38% of your earnings in federal income taxes every year. Throw in state and local income and sales taxes, and you stand to lose well over half your earnings during your lifetime. For those with estates worth millions, the prospect of having their money enrich the bloated coffers of the IRS can be enough to force them to take drastic avoidance measures.

One of the options they are increasingly turning to is expatriation. Perhaps, more surprising, many of them are expatriating to Canada.

Why Canada?

Canada and the United States have long been staunch allies. These friendly neighbors share the largest undefended border in the world. A day-trip between the two countries requires only a short discussion with an unarmed customs official. International incidents occasionally arise, but for the most part are resolved before tempers flare. In all, the two countries do more than merely coexist; they share an amicable relationship unprecedented in world history.

More and more Americans are beginning to take advantage of these close ties. Every day, thousands choose Canada as an excellent place to visit, do business, even live — and with good reason. In 1992, leading economists at the United Nations headquarters in New York researched the best countries in which to live and work. They judged Canada number one. Japan came in second, the United States only sixth and the United Kingdom tenth. A 2003 survey of quality of life conducted by the U.S. human resources consulting firm Mercer found Vancouver, Calgary, Toronto, Ottawa, and Montreal (in that order) among the top 30 cities in the world. Montreal, lowest Canadian City in the grouping, has a score equal to that of the top-ranked U.S. City, Honolulu.

The factors the U.N. officials used in making their choice include Canada's high standard of living, minimal social class divisions, low crime rate, clean environment, beautiful scenery, economic opportunities, government support services, extensive infrastructure, comprehensive shopping and sports facilities, affordable housing, and the generous hospitality of the Canadian people.

Despite long harsh winters, a continuing bilingual English-French problem, and long-standing separatist sentiments in the province of Quebec, overall, the U.N. officials found Canada to be the most attractive nation in the world. Indeed, the French-Canadian poet Gilles Vigneault summed up the atmosphere and the allure of his land: "My country is no country, it is the Winter/.../My road is no road, it is the Snow/.../... I cry out/To all the people of the Earth/My home is your home/Between my four walls of ice/I make the time and the space/To set the fire and the place/For all humans, far and wide/For humanity is my race." Many observers believe Canada has the best prospects for sustained national growth since the end of World War II.

Canada is not without its problems. In 1998-99, the Canadian dollar hit an all-time low, with the "loonie" — so-called for the bird on the face of the dollar coin — at about C$1.50 to the US$1.00. While Canadian wages in the last 20 years have increased 17% more than in the U.S., productivity has grown only 36% compared to 70% in the U.S. Worse, government spending is over 35% of GDP, while it is only about 20% in the U.S.

Expatriation is a drastic measure, but it may be the only escape for the wealthiest of us. This is definitely not a strategy for everyone, but read on to see if it makes sense for you. There are certain trade-offs involved, and each must be researched and considered carefully. Most importantly, you must do it correctly to make it work. This chapter will explain the intricacies of expatriation, and why Canada might be the right place to go.

Immigration in Canada

The virtues of Canada as the place to live are known around the world. Recent immigration figures attest to the fact. In recent years, for example, Canada's population of 30 million has increased annually by about 200,000 immigrants. A modern nation built by European settlers, Canada has increased its flow of immigrants by three-fold since 1985. The top sources of immigrants have been the United States, India, Vietnam, Poland, the United Kingdom, the Philippines, Guyana, and El Salvador. The increasing numbers have also included many wealthy Asians, especially residents of Hong Kong, although some of these have returned home as dual nationals.

Canada now has the highest per capita immigration rate of any nation in the world, an influx that has caused widespread public demand for limitations. A May 1995 poll showed three out of five Canadians favor a five-year moratorium on all new immigration. Some immigrants are more welcome than others for a variety of reasons. As you will learn in a moment, you may be just the type of new citizen Canada welcomes with open arms.

About one in six Canadians is foreign-born, double the ratio in the United States. Canada admits aunts, uncles, nieces, nephews, and fiancees. Common law spouses and same-sex partners are recognized under Canadian law but not for immigration purposes. On arrival, so-called "landed immigrants" — those given residence status — immediately are entitled to the same menu of health, welfare, and university benefits as lifelong Canadian citizens.

An increasingly popular practice is to apply for refugee status, and then disappear during the one-year review period. That abuse has increased 20-fold during the 1990s, reaching 4,203 documented cases last year. Among nationalities, Chinese are the worst abusers of the system, with 53% of claimants vanishing after being released on refugee status during the first half of 1999. During that time, 95% of Chinese claimants in Montreal and 72% of Chinese claimants in Vancouver disappeared. Most are presumed to have sneaked or been smuggled across the border to the United States.

There is now pending in parliament revised Canadian immigration legislation to tighten residency requirements to ensure that all immigrants are physically present within Canada for at least 1,095 days (three full years) in a five-year period prior to becoming eligible to apply for citizenship. The period need not be continuous, so long as the total time accumulates. This restriction was proposed because of court rulings holding residence did not require physical presence. The courts had said that lengthy periods of time out of Canada did not impair an immigrant's right to apply for citizenship, if the person had sufficient ties to Canada through the presence of family members or the ownership of a home.

About Canadian Taxes

Before we get to the good news — the big tax break for new immigrants — you should know that the Canadian tax system is tough and comprehensive. Combined Canadian federal and provincial personal income taxes range from 48 to 54%, depending on the province. And the Canadian tax burden has been a direct cause of capital flight, which is relatively unrestricted, as you shall see below.

Does this seem like a good place to go for tax relief? Probably not at the moment. However, there is one very attractive feature of Canadian tax policies; unlike the United States, Canada does not tax the worldwide income or foreign assets of its non-resident citizens. Canada taxes only the worldwide income of its resident citizens and resident aliens who live in Canada at any time during the calendar year. "Residents," by law, include individuals, corporations, and trusts located in Canada.

Enjoying Life Tax-Free

However tough Canadian taxes may be for the average native-born citizen living within the Canadian border, there exists a huge loophole available only to wealthy, new immigrants. This major tax saving was deliberately written into law to encourage new arrivals with financial means. This preference for new citizens with substantial investment capital can translate into huge tax savings and far-reaching financial gains for you and your business. Here's why:

A qualified immigrant accepted for eventual Canadian citizenship is eligible for a complete personal income tax moratorium for the first five calendar years of residence in Canada — zero taxes if the source of your income is an offshore, non-Canadian trust or corporation. You can easily create such entities before you move to Canada and become a citizen. (As a general rule, Canada has a three-year residence requirement after immigrant admission before citizenship is granted, but a five-year residence is required in order to be eligible for this very special tax break).

Canadian citizens and resident aliens employed by certain "international financial centers" are forgiven 50% of all income taxes.

Canada has abolished its federal death taxes. The heirs of a wealthy American with an estate of US$3 million or more pay a marginal rate as high as 55%. In total, your heirs could lose as much as 60% of your estate in U.S. federal death taxes. Anything you leave over US$675,000 is subject to at least a 37% marginal rate, and as high as 55% (although there are increased estate tax exemptions for certain groups, including small business owners and family farmers). Worse still, state estate taxes and probate fees are added to these hefty federal sums. In sharp contrast, Canadians pay no federal estate taxes. The federal estate tax was abolished in 1971, but the provinces do impose death duties and these fees can be considerable.

After living five years tax-free in Canada as a new citizen, you can move your residence to another country and you then pay taxes only on income earned or paid from within Canada. You pay no taxes on your worldwide income. Most Americans living abroad do not enjoy this distinct tax advantage, although some qualify for the US$80,000 annual earned income exclusion under U.S. law.

A Scenario

Let's suppose you, as an American citizen, wish to sell an established business, or convert fixed assets into liquid cash for investment or other purposes. Depending on how long you have held the property and how the liquidation deal is structured, you may face U.S. capital gains taxes at the current maximum rate of 20%. Depending on your tax bracket, income taxes can be 40% or more. In either case, a major part of the cash proceeds from the sale or conversion will be devoured by the U.S. Internal Revenue Service and state tax authorities — before you ever see a thin dime.

How can you avoid this enormous tax burden?

What if you transfer the title of the U.S. business to a foreign trust (with the property owner — you — as the beneficiary) or to a corporation you control, conveniently located in a low or no-tax off-shore jurisdiction? Moreover, what if, after the trust or corporation receives title, you apply for and receive Canadian citizenship, later renounce U.S. citizenship, and become a legal resident of Canada for at least five years?

That offshore trust or corporation can pay you benefits and income for five years — tax-free — if you carefully follow the regulations that govern this incredible tax break. You can be a free spirit with absolutely no income or capital gains tax liability in either the U.S. or Canada.

Sounds too good to be true? Read on.

Testing the Waters

Maybe you would like to test the northern waters before making any major decision about a future in Canada. Fortunately, Americans thinking about emigrating can explore life north of the border for an extended period. The North American Free Trade Agreement (NAFTA) allows reciprocal extended stays of up to one year, and visas are routinely granted. Americans employed in certain occupations can enter, live, and work in Canada without a permit, and with no prior approval. The number of one-year extensions is unlimited.

Those welcome to work in Canada include those Americans who do research and designing, purchasing, sales and contract negotiation, customs brokering, financial services, public relations, advertising, tourism, and market research. It also includes professionals, so long as they are paid by a U.S. source.

Again, entry to either country requires no special visa or passport, only proper personal identification such as a state or provincial motor vehicle operator's license or voter card. Tourists are allowed to stay for at least 90 days without special permission.

Open Door for Immigrant Investors

Canada's immigration process, as in Australia and New Zealand, assesses prospective immigrants based on a points system weighted in favor of certain professional and occupational skills. Existing categories include: 1) Independent immigration, possibly with a job offer; 2) Employer sponsored immigration; 3) "Entrepreneur" immigration, for those with a substantial amount (e.g., C$150,000) to invest in their own business; 4) Immigration as a self-employed professional in a limited number of unique occupations, such as an artist or writer; 5) Immigration as a close relative of a Canadian or permanent resident; and 6) "Investor" immigration by investing at least C$400,000 in an approved investment.

If you are interested in obtaining Canadian citizenship, you should first fully explore any possible family ties you might have in the country. The Canadian Government will help you learn if you are eligible for citizenship based on ancestry. Any Canadian Consulate will provide a personal history information form to be completed and submitted with copies of relevant birth records to the Registrar of Canadian Citizenship in the capital city of Ottawa. A "Certificate of Canadian Citizenship" is automatically issued to anyone who qualifies for citizenship by family descent. If you are lucky enough to qualify, this is the least complicated basis on which to establish a new legal residence in Canada. Though there certainly is concern among Canadians about increased immigration, Canada keeps the official welcome mat out for skilled workers and professionals — especially, for wealthy investors who wish to become Canadian citizens.

Independent applicants for permanent residence are rated on a point system that takes into account age, education, fluency in English and French, financial standing, occupational or professional experience, local demand for certain types of workers, geographic destination, and a personal assessment of the applicant. These factors comprise a 100-point scale. Seventy points and above is passing.

Completely separate from the point system for admissions, Canadian law favors, as a special independent class, certain preferred immigrants including investors, entrepreneurs, the self-employed, and those who will add to the "cultural and artistic life" of the nation. With minor variation in each of the provinces, investor-immigrants generally must have a net worth in excess of C$800,000 and be willing to invest at least C$400,000 in Canada for a minimum three to five-year period. Another alternative is to pay a flat C$95,000 fee, in which case, no other investment need be guaranteed.

With proof of sufficient assets and an attractive business plan, especially one creating new jobs for Canadians, your permanent resident status and eventual citizenship is almost assured. Government loan guarantees and other assistance may be available for immigrants willing to invest larger sums of C$750,000 or more. Wealthy Hong Kong Chinese who have settled so successfully in Vancouver have used this strategy to their great advantage.

For potential investor visa applicants, the government rolls out the proverbial red carpet, officially known as the "Business Migration Programme." Business experience, marketing skills, contacts within Canada, an adequate credit rating, and available funds all greatly increase your chance of success. Applicants are usually required to submit detailed business proposals or general business plans. One must accompany the application for permanent residence. Such plans must detail the nature of the business, operating procedures, essential personnel (which may just be the applicant), a marketing plan, and a financial strategy.

Canadian Immigration Process

The immigration process begins with a visit to the Canadian Embassy. It is located at Fourth Street and Pennsylvania Avenue, NW, Washington, D.C. You can also try a Canadian Consulate, located in New York and other major U.S. cities.

There, you receive an "Immigration Questionnaire" requiring basic personal information about you, your spouse, and family. Within a few weeks, a more detailed questionnaire will be presented if the applicant is initially found acceptable. After this second document is reviewed, a personal interview and medical examinations are needed.

If all goes well, you will shortly receive a visa for entry into Canada as a landed immigrant: "Welcome, bienvenue à Canada."

A distinct advantage that comes with this new citizenship is the international official acceptance of the Canadian passport, one of the most respected in the world. Moreover, as citizens of a member nation of the British Commonwealth, Canadians are allowed to enter Britain without obtaining a prior visa.

It is worth noting that Canada recognizes the principle of dual nationality. They allow successful applicants for citizenship to retain their nationality of origin. For reasons that will become obvious in a moment, that choice is not a viable option for an ex-American expatriating to Canada.

The Big Change — U.S. Expatriation

The potential immigrant from America will eventually have to give up United States citizenship, formally renouncing his or her U.S. status in a way that carefully avoids identifying the purpose as avoidance of U.S. taxes. If they think you skipped just to avoid taxes, the

IRS can pursue you and any U.S. income or assets you may have left "south of the border."

Under current U.S. law, a citizen who is suspected of giving up U.S. citizenship for the principal purpose of avoiding taxes can still be taxed on U.S. source income for up to ten years after leaving the country. This is under section 877 of the Foreign Investors Tax Act of 1966, restated in 1996 amendments. Even if you die during that period, the IRS can go after any estate assets still located in the U.S., or any payments made to U.S. beneficiaries and heirs of the decedent's estate.

However, as we advise elsewhere in these pages, don't get too nervous. In reality, this law leaks like a sieve. Long before renouncing U.S. citizenship, you can systematically restructure your assets by sending wealth abroad. This will keep your assets outside the grasp of the IRS. The U.S. Treasury openly admits monitoring such subjective private transactions is all but impossible.

The difficulty for the IRS in proving an individual's intentions makes these recent anti-expatriation laws so much political hot air. By the time someone at the U.S. Department of Justice thinks they know what your intent might have been, you will have come and gone from the United States — along with your liquid assets and wealth.

Do It the Right Way

Here's how to expatriate from the U.S. and avoid pitfalls along the way:

It is crucial to obtain proper legal advice on expatriation in order to be effective in surrendering citizenship. The worst outcome is to wind up with ambiguous dual nationality status. In this case, you go through an extended period retaining not only U.S. citizenship, but citizenship in another country as well. You may then find yourself within the potential grasp of two government taxing authorities.

Generally, an ex-American who properly surrenders citizenship is treated by U.S. law as a non-resident alien and taxed at a flat 30% rate on certain types of passive income derived from U.S. sources, and on net profits from the sale of a U.S. trade or business at regular graduated rates. Expatriates can safely spend only about 122 days a year within the United States. After that, they expose themselves to IRS claims for full U.S. taxation based on alien residency.

Another strict caution: you must be certain to obtain valid foreign citizenship before you surrender your U.S. citizenship — if you fail to do so, you could become a "stateless" person, the proverbial "man without a country." A person without a passport and a nationality is legally lost in this world of national borders and bureaucratic customs officials, and is not entitled to the legal protection of any government.

Valid surrender must be an unequivocal act in which a person manifests an unqualified intention to relinquish U.S. citizenship. In order for the surrender to be effective, all of the conditions of the statute must be met; the person must appear in person and sign an oath before a U.S. consular or diplomatic officer, usually at an American Embassy or Consulate. Surrender of citizenship not in the form prescribed by the U.S. Secretary of State has no legal effect. Because of the way in which the law is written and interpreted, Americans cannot effectively renounce their citizenship by mail, through an agent, or while physically within the United States.

Once surrender is accomplished before an American diplomatic or consular officer abroad, all documents are referred to the U.S. Department of State. The Office of Overseas Citizens Services reviews them to ensure that all criteria under the law are met, but the State Department has no discretion to refuse a proper surrender of citizenship. This personal right is absolute.

Long before such a drastic final step is taken towards ending U.S. citizenship, the new Canadian immigrant should have his or her official Canadian citizenship in order, papers in hand, and an established residence in their new homeland. This will most likely be in the metropolitan areas of Montreal, Toronto, or Vancouver, where the vast majority of immigrants decide to live.

Offshore Trust Immigration

But enough about the "how" of expatriation for now. Let's discuss the "why." What exactly can you gain by becoming a Canadian citizen? One of the foremost benefits is the ability to take advantage of an immigrant offshore trust.

The key to eligibility for this unusual tax-free "window of opportunity" is found in section 94(1) of Canada's Income Tax Act of 1952 ("the Act"). In essence, section 94 ensures that an immigrant who has never been a Canadian resident can live in Canada and earn tax-free foreign source income from a non-resident trust or affiliated corporation for the first five calendar years of the immigrant's Canadian residency.

There is only one danger. It is important to note that this strategy has not been fully tested in court. Here's the problem: before you surrender U.S. citizenship, you must have already attained citizenship in

Canada. This requires fulfillment of at least the first three of your five-year exemption period. As a U.S. citizen, during that time you are subject to taxation on your worldwide income, including anything you earn from the trust. As of now, the IRS has not hauled anyone in on this issue, but they might. Even if they do, however, you still come out ahead. At least the last two of your five-year exemption would be completely tax-free.

The Beneficiary

To qualify for this big tax break, the arrangement must include an immigrant residing in Canada and either:

(a) A foreign corporation or a trust with which the immigrant is "closely tied;" or

(b) A foreign affiliate corporation controlled by a person resident in Canada, as defined by law (about which we will have more to say later).

The essential factor is that the non-resident trust must have one or more beneficiaries who are Canadian residents, or the offshore corporation must be "closely tied" in some manner to one or more Canadian residents.

The beneficiaries likely will be your family members, and can include yourself. The foreign trustee will follow your instructions on how the trust assets should be invested and income disbursed.

A "beneficial interest" in a non-resident trust is defined as belonging to a person or partnership that holds any right — immediate or future, absolute or contingent, conditional or otherwise — to receive any of the income or principal capital of the trust, either directly or indirectly (Subsection 248(25) of the Act). It would be difficult to find a broader definition of "beneficial entitlement" than this — and the implications for tax avoidance are obvious and potentially enormous.

What's more, Canadian tax officials and court cases have repeatedly stated that such immigration trusts and related businesses, when properly created and managed abroad, are not an abuse of the tax laws. That's because section 94 clearly is designed as a vehicle for exempting new immigrants from taxation for the stated period of five years. In the case of almost every other tax-avoidance scheme, Revenue Canada would pounce. Here, the law does more than permit tax avoidance, it approves and encourages it.

Only a change in Canadian law by Parliament could remove this generous tax break, and there is no current talk of removing a provision that has been so successful in attracting needed capital and business to the nation.

Business Immigration

Canada admits immigrants under a "Business Class," with these main categories:

1. **Entrepreneur**: A qualified applicant can receive Canadian permanent residence based on an investment, plus active participation in a business or commercial venture within Canada. The person must intend to, and have the ability to, establish, purchase, or make a substantial investment (at least one-third ownership) in a business or commercial venture that meets any two of the following criteria: Annual sales of C$500,000 or more; profit of C$50,000 or more; immigrant's share of net assets equal to C$125,000 at end of one year of operation; or creating employment opportunities for at least two Canadian citizens or permanent residents, other than the entrepreneur or his/her dependants.

   What may be a "substantial investment" is not defined, but is a matter of discretion on the part of the visa officer. Prospective business ability is based on an applicant's past business or managerial track record. To qualify under this category, an applicant must provide proof of a personal net worth of C$300,000 and have two to three years of business experience.

   There are a number of strings attached to this immigration category. In addition to creating a business and new jobs, the applicant must participate actively in the business management and furnish continuing proof of these facts to immigration officers when requested. So-called "landed immigrants" must report to immigration officers every six months. Failure to comply can lead to deportation.

2. **Investor**: Canadian permanent residence is granted to a qualified applicant who makes an irrevocable five-year passive investment of at least C$400,000 in an approved Canadian company. Under the more expensive option, the applicant receives a guarantee of a minimum return on capital, plus interest for investment in a number of approved Canadian investor programs.

   As with the "entrepreneur" immigrant category, applicants must provide proof of a successful business history and a personal net worth in excess of C$800,000 derived from business. The disadvantage of this immigration category is that an applicant is forced to tie up a significant portion of wealth for five years. This problem can be eased with available loan programs for the investor that can supplement the investor's personal contribution. This option does not require hands-on management, thus is more suitable to those who travel extensively abroad on business. Such travel does not jeopardize a person's permanent residence status once the investor status is granted.

Visiting Canada

When entering from the U.S., a U.S. passport or proof of U.S. citizenship and photo ID is required. U.S. citizens entering Canada from a third country must have a valid passport. A visa is not required for U.S. citizens entering from the U.S. for a stay up to 180 days. Anyone with a criminal record (including a DWI charge) should contact the Canadian Embassy or nearest Canadian Consulate before travel. A waiver of exclusion may be available but several weeks processing are required and a fee must be paid. Contact the Embassy of Canada at 501 Pennsylvania Avenue, NW, Washington, D.C. 20001; Tel: (202) 682-1740; web site http://www.canadianembassy.org; or the Canadian Consulates in Atlanta, Boston, Buffalo, Chicago, Dallas, Detroit, Los Angeles, Miami, Minneapolis, New York, San Juan, or Seattle.

Due to concern over child abduction, single parents, grandparents, or guardians traveling with children often need proof of custody or notarized letters from the other parent authorizing travel. Anyone under age 18 and traveling alone should carry a letter from his/her parent or guardian authorizing the trip.

Contacts

United States: U.S. citizens living in or visiting Canada may register at the Consular Section of the U.S. Embassy in Canada. The U.S. Embassy is in Ottawa, Ontario at 490 Sussex Drive; Tel: (613) 238-5335; Fax: (613) 238-5720; web site: http://www.usembassycanada.gov.

U.S. Consulates are located in: **Calgary, Alberta:** 615 Macleod Trail SE, Suite 1050, Tel: (403) 266-8962, emergency after-hours Tel: (403) 228-8962 then pres '0'; Fax: (403) 264-6630; **Halifax, Nova Scotia:** 1969 Upper Water Street, Suite 904, Purdy's Wharf Tower II, Tel. (902) 429-2480; emergency-after hours (902) 429-2485; Fax (902) 423-6861; **Montreal, Quebec:** 1155 St. Alexander Street, Tel: (514) 398-9695, emergency after-hours Tel: (514) 981-5059, Fax: (514) 398-0702; **Quebec City, Quebec:** 2 Place Terrasse Dufferin, Tel: (418) 692-2095, emergency after-hours Tel: (418) 692-2096, Fax: (418) 692-4640; **Toronto, Ontario:** 360 University Avenue, Tel: (416) 595-1700, emergency after-hours Tel: (416) 201-4100, Fax: (416) 595-5466; and

Vancouver, British Columbia: 11095 West Pender Street, Tel: (604) 685-4311, Fax: (604) 685-7175.

United Kingdom: The British High Commission is located at 80 Elgin Street, Ottawa K1P 5K7; Tel: +(613) 237-1530; Fax: +(613) 237-7980; Web site: http://www.britain-in-canada.org/.

British Consulates are located in: **Toronto:** 777 Bay Street, Suite 2800, College Park, Toronto, Ontario M5G 2G2, Tel: +(416) 593-1290, Fax: +(416) 593-1229, Web site: http://www.uk-canada-trade.org/; **Montreal:** Suite 4200, 1000 De La Gauchetière West, Montreal, Quebec H3B 4W5, Tel: +(514) 866-5863, Fax: +(514) 866-0202, Web site: http://www.uk-canada-trade.org/; **Vancouver:** 111 Melville Street, Suite 800, Vancouver, British Colombia V6E 4V6, Tel: +(604) 683-4421, Web site: http://www.softlink.org; **Halifax/Dartmouth:** 1 Canal Street, P.O. Box 605, Dartmouth, Nova Scotia B3Y 2Y9, Tel: +(902) 461-1381, Fax: +(902) 463 7678; **St John's:** 113 Topsail Road, St. John's, Newfoundland A1E 2A9, Tel: +(709) 579-2002, Fax: +(709) 579-0475; **Quebec City:** Suite 700, 1150 Claire Fontaine, Quebec City, Quebec G1R 5G4, Tel: +(418) 521-3013, Fax: +(418) 521-3098; **Winnipeg:** 229 Athlone Drive, Winnipeg, Manitoba R3J 3L6, Tel: +(204) 896-1380, Fax: +(204) 269-3025.

Recommended Attorney

David Melnik, JD, QC, of Toronto, Canada serves a member of the Sovereign Society Council of Experts. He headed his own law firm (1962-76), then became chief executive officer of Vanguard Trust Ltd. of Canada. He also served as policy advisor to the Premier of the Province of Ontario. He taught at the University of Toronto and York University in their Masters in Business programs. Mr. Melnik serves as a director of several U.S. and Canadian corporations and also lectures worldwide. He is co-author of *The Offshore Money Manual* (The Sovereign Society) and of *Your Money and Your Life*, (The Oxford Club, 1999). Contact: 350 Lonsdale Road Suite #311, Toronto ON M5P 1R6 Canada, Tel: +416.488.7918 Fax: +905.877.7751 E-mail: dm1976cp@netcom.ca Mr. Melnik's assistant is Carol Bruce, Tel: +905.877.3156

Republic of Mexico

CAPITAL:	MEXICO CITY (WORLD'S LARGEST CITY)
POPULATION:	104,907,991
LANGUAGE:	SPANISH
CURRENCY:	MEXICAN PESO (MEX$)
AREA:	1,972,550 SQUARE KM
ETHNIC GROUPS:	MESTIZO (AMERINDIAN-SPANISH) 60%, AMERINDIAN OR PREDOMINANTLY AMERINDIAN 30%, WHITE 9%, OTHER 1%
RELIGION:	ROMAN CATHOLIC 89%, PROTESTANT 6%, OTHER 5%

PASSPORT HIGHLIGHTS: In addition to generous programs allowing non-Mexican retirees and persons living on relatively modest fixed incomes to establish residency there, Mexico grants special residency permits to investors placing at least 1.8 million pesos in approved investment vehicles.

Mexico, the southern part of the North American continent, dominates Central America by its sheer size. The United States forms its northern border, while Guatemala and Belize lie to the south. Its eastern seaboard is the Gulf of Mexico and to the west is the Pacific Ocean. Some 50% of the country has a hot and dry climate with many arid desert regions, while 25% of the land in the south is a tropical rain forest. Mountainous, with several peaks of over 5,000 meters, climate varies considerably across the country and at various altitudes.

In the tenth century A.D., Mexico had one of the most highly developed civilizations in the world. Under dominance of the Aztecs, it built an empire of over 15 million people. Spanish Conquistadors arrived in 1519 and, within two years, the Aztecs were defeated and Spanish control consolidated. With silver deposits and other mineral wealth, New Spain, as it was then called, became an important part of the Spanish Empire. Remnants of Mexico's pre-Columbian and colonial past are abundant throughout the country, constituting a major asset in the world's cultural heritage.

As Spain's European influence waned, agitation for Mexican independence grew. In 1824, a federal republic was formed and, in 1836, Spain formally recognized Mexico's independence, the same year Texas, colonized by the U.S., separated from Mexico. An 1846 Mexican-American war over territorial issues was settled with Mexico ceding almost half its claimed territory to the U.S. For the next 70 years, Mexico suffered endless revolutions and internal power struggles. For most of the last century, one political party, the Institutional Revolutionary Party (or PRI) dominated the government, entrenching its power and corruption.

By the 1980s, socialist economics and deficit spending produced a deepening financial crisis, repeated peso devaluations, and continuing social unrest. In 1995, a severe economic crisis followed the announcement of a huge international trade deficit. An estimated US$11 billion fled the country as investors pulled out. Severe austerity measures and a multi-billion dollar bale out by the United States kept Mexico afloat. Another peso devaluation devastated middle class wage earners. By the end of the century, Mexico was in economic recovery and able to repay U.S. loans.

Mexico now has a semi-free market economy with a mixture of modern and outmoded industry and agriculture, increasingly dominated by the private sector. The number of state-owned enterprises has fallen from more than 1,000 in 1982 to fewer than 200 in 1998, but some of these are major industries such as oil and natural gas. The government is slowly privatizing and expanding competition in sea ports, railroads, telecommunications, electricity, natural gas distribution, and airports. A strong export sector helped to cushion the economy's decline in 1995 and led to the recovery in 1996 and 1997. In 1998, private consumption became the leading driver of growth, which was accompanied by increased employment and higher wages.

Diversity of possible lifestyles in Mexico has made the country a major magnet for expatriates and retirees from developed countries across the entire Northern Hemisphere. One can live either very inexpensively or, for those on less limited budgets, quite luxuriously there. Well known colonies of expatriates have been established throughout the country, particularly in highland areas with temperate climates. Popularity of these localities is somewhat subject to fashion: for example, Lake Chapala not far from Guadalajara is a "hot" destination at present. Other towns with large immigrant populations include Cuernavaca, Puebla, San Miguel de Allende, and Mexico City.

Mexico can be said to be a "high crime" nation, especially in Mexico City, but in rural areas as well. Robbery, carjackings, kidnapping for ransom, and street crime are rampant, often with the complicity of local police. Criminals posing as taxi drivers are a special threat. Extreme caution is advised at all times, especially when traveling anywhere by car.

Dual Nationality

A major change to the Mexican Constitution on March 20, 1998, allowed, for the first time, the principle of dual nationality to all former Mexican citizens who have obtained citizenship from another nation. All such persons now may apply for reinstatement of their original Mexican citizenship, the largest group being the hundreds of thousands of Mexican-Americans who have become U.S. citizens. Since the U.S. also recognizes dual nationality, this presents no problem for naturalized U.S. Mexican-Americans. Those who have their Mexican citizenship reinstated will have all privileges that status confers, except voting rights in Mexican elections. Dual nationals are not, however, subject to compulsory military service. If they formally re-establish residence in Mexico, they can vote as well.

Mexican law now recognizes dual nationality for Mexicans by birth, meaning those born in Mexico or born abroad to Mexican parents. U.S. citizens who are also Mexican nationals are considered Mexican by local authorities. Travelers possessing both U.S. and Mexican nationalities must carry with them proof of their citizenship of both countries. Under Mexican law, dual nationals entering or departing Mexico must identify themselves as Mexican.

Residence & Citizenship

Mexico has by statute created a variety of residence, visa and immigration plans in an effort to attract foreign nationals for varying reasons. Some are aimed at wealthy U.S. persons across the border. Others are geared to attract immigrants who possess needed skills or those who can demonstrate that they are of independent means.

Visitante Rentista

One residence category is known, in Spanish, as *Visitante Rentista*. It is directed toward nationals from western countries such as the U.S., Canada, Australia, and those in Europe. Mexican Consulates in those countries will issue a visa valid for one year, renewable in Mexico, to those who can demonstrate proof of a minimum monthly income of US$1,156 for the head of family, plus US$578 for each dependant.

Immigrante Rentista

The *Immigrante Rentista* visa program works in much the same way, except that it is granted directly by the Mexican Government and is valid for a period of five years. The basic requirement is proof of a monthly income of at least US$1,800 for a head of household and US$ 900 for each dependant. This is the path to eventual Mexican citizenship.

Unlike the less strict *Visitante Rentista* the applicant must also submit a medical health certificate and a police clearance certificate. Also, unlike the lesser plan, after five years of residence in *Immigrante Rentista* status, status, the visa holder qualifies for permanent residence and may eventually seek nationality and a passport. Citizenship is generally available after five years' official residence, but at least six months each year must be spent within the country.

Foreign nationals wishing to invest in Mexico are also eligible for special residence visas upon government approval of the proposed investment, which must be in an amount not less than 40,000 times the minimum daily wage, currently M$1,800,000 (US$162,000). The investor visa applicant must also submit a health certificate and police clearance and other documentation.

Various other Mexican one-year temporary entry permits are available for students, technical personnel, and business visitors. These do not grant official residence status and do not lead to a passport or permanent residence in five years.

Full details on all these programs can be obtained from any Mexican Consulate or Embassy.

Real Estate Laws

Mexican laws and practices regarding purchase and rental of real estate, including time-shares, are markedly different from and far more complicated than those in the United States. U.S. citizens should beware of the inherent risks involved and of the absolute need to obtain authoritative information and guidance prior to any real estate investment. Foreigners may be granted the right to own real property only under very specific conditions. The use of competent local legal assistance for any real estate or business purchase is a must. A list of local attorneys can be obtained from the U.S. Embassy or nearest Consulate in Mexico. Potential purchasers of real estate should also consider obtaining title insurance prior to investing in real property. Information on title insurance companies and investing in property, in general, can be obtained from the State Tourism Offices in Mexico. In Baja, California, information can be obtained from the State Tourism Office at Tel: +(52-55) 34-6300.

Travel to Mexico

Proof of citizenship and photo ID is required for entry by all U.S. citizens. A U.S. passport is recommended, but other U.S. citizenship documents (certified copy of a U.S. birth certificate, naturalization certificate, consular report of birth abroad, or a certificate of citizenship) are acceptable. U.S. citizens boarding flights to Mexico should be prepared to present one of these documents along with photo identification. A visa is not required for a tourist/transit stay of up to 180 days. A tourist card, issued by Mexican Consulates and most airlines serving Mexico, is required. The Government of Mexico charges U.S. citizens traveling to Mexico's interior an entry fee of US$15 per person. Minors require notarized consent from parent(s) if traveling alone, with one parent, or in someone else's custody. Mexican regulations limit the value of goods brought into Mexico by U.S. citizens arriving by air or sea to US$300 per person and by land to US$50 per person. Amounts exceeding the duty-free limit are subject to a 32.8% tax. Upon arrival in Mexico, business travelers must complete a form authorizing the conduct of business, but not employment, for a 30-day period.

Citizens of Canada, the U.K., Ireland, Australia, New Zealand, and much of Western Europe need no visa to enter Mexico as tourists for less than 180 days. Every visitor does need a valid passport and a tourist card (or *FMT - folleto de migración turística*). These cards are free, and if you're flying direct, you should get one on the airplane or from the airline before leaving. They're also issued by Mexican Consulates, in person or by post. Canadian citizens also can enter Mexico without a passport if they carry such documents plus their tourist card.

A tourist card isn't strictly necessary for anyone who only intends to visit the northern border towns and stay less than three days, though you still need a passport or photo ID. Along the U.S. border is a duty-free zone where you can come and go as you please; heading further south beyond this zone, however, there are checkpoints on every road and you'll be sent back unless you have the necessary documents and have been through customs and immigration.

For further information, contact the Embassy of Mexico at 1911 Pennsylvania Avenue, NW, Washington, D.C. 20006; Tel: (202)736-1000, or any Mexican Consulate in major U.S. cities. U.S. citizens planning to work or live in Mexico should apply for the appropriate Mexican visa (FM-2 or -3). Tourists should avoid demonstrations and other activities that may be deemed political by Mexican authorities. In 1998 and 1999, U.S. citizens and other foreigners were detained in

Chiapas and expelled from Mexico for allegedly violating their visa status or interfering in Mexican internal politics.

U.S. driver's licenses are valid in Mexico. Mexican insurance is required for all vehicles, including rental vehicles in Mexico. Travelers should obtain full coverage insurance when renting vehicles in Mexico. Travelers arriving in their own vehicle can easily obtain Mexican insurance on the U.S. side of the land border and should do so. If a traveler is involved in a vehicle accident resulting in damages or injuries to another party, the driver can be arrested and detained by Mexican authorities until a settlement is arranged with the injured party, and/or, depending upon the extent of damages or injuries to the other party, the traveler may face charges filed by the Mexican judicial authorities.

For additional information concerning Mexico driver's permits, vehicle inspection, road tax, mandatory insurance, etc., you can contact the Mexico Government Tourist Organization (MGTO) at 1-800-44-MEXICO (639426).

Contacts

United States: The U.S. Embassy is located in Mexico City at Paseo de la Reforma 305, Colonia Cuauhtemoc, telephone from the United States: 011-52-55-5080-2000; telephone within Mexico City: 5080-2000; telephone long distance within Mexico 01-55-5080-2000. You may also contact the Embassy by e-mail at ccs@usembassy.net.mx. The web site is http://www.usembassy-mexico.gov.

U.S. Consulates are located in: **Ciudad Juarez:** Avenida López Mateos 924-N, Tel: (52)(656) 611-3000; **Guadalajara:** Progreso 175, Tel: (52)(333) 825-2998; **Monterrey:** Avenida Constitución 411 Poniente 64000, Tel: (52)(818) 345-2120; **Tijuana:** Tapachula 96, Tel: (52)(664) 622-7400; **Hermosillo:** Avenida Monterrey 141, Tel: (52)(662) 217-2375; **Matamoros:** Avenida Primera 2002, Tel: (52)(868) 812-4402; **Merida**: Paseo Montejo 453, Tel: (52)(999) 925-5011; **Nogales:** Calle San José, Nogales, Sonora, Tel: (52)(631) 313-4820; and **Nuevo Laredo:** Calle Allende 3330, Col. Jardín, Tel: (52)(867) 714-0512.

U.S. Consular Agencies are located in: **Acapulco:** Hotel Acapulco Continental, Costera M. Alemán 121-Local 14, Tel: (52)(744) 484-0300 or (52)(744) 469-0556; **Cabo San Lucas:** Blvd. Marina Local C-4, Plaza Nautica, Col. Centro, Tel: (52)(624) 143-3566; **Cancun:** Plaza Caracol Two, Second level, no. 320-323, Boulevard Kukulcán, km. 8.5, Zona Hotelera, Tel: (52)(998) 883-0272; **Ciudad Acuna:** Ocampo #

305, Col. Centro, Tel: (52)(877) 772-8661; **Cozumel:** Plaza Villa Mar en El Centro, Plaza Principal, (Parque Juarez between Melgar and 5th Ave.) 2nd floor, Locales #8 and 9, telephone (52)(987) 872-4574; **Ixtapa/Zihuatanejo:** Hotel Fontan, Blvd. Ixtapa, Tel: (52)(755) 553-2100; **Mazatlan:** Hotel Playa Mazatlan, Playa Gaviotas #202, Zona Dorada, Tel: (52)(669) 916-5889; **Oaxaca:** Macedonio Alcala No. 407, Interior 20, Tel (52)(951) 514-3054 (52)(951) 516-2853; **Piedras Negras:** Prol. General Cepeda No. 1900, Fraccionamiento Privada Blanca, Tel: (52) (867) 788-0343; **Puerto Vallarta:** Zaragoza #160, Col. Centro, Edif. Vallarta Plaza, Piso 2 Int.18, Tel: (52)(322) 222-0069; **Reynosa:** Calle Monterrey #390, Esq. Sinaloa, Colonia Rodriguez, Tel: (52)(899) 923-9331; **San Luis Potosi:** Edificio "Las Terrazas", Avenida Venustiano Carranza 2076-41, Col. Polanco, Tel: (52)(444) 811-7802; and **San Miguel de Allende:** : Dr. Hernandez Macias #72, Tel: (52)(415) 152-2357 or (52)(415) 152-0068.

United Kingdom: The British Embassy in Mexico City is located at Rio Lerma 71, Col Cuauhtémoc 06500 México D.F.; Tel: (52) (55) 5242 8500; Fax: (52) (55) 5242 8517; Email: Consular.mexico@fco.gov. uk; Consular, commsec@embajadabritanica.com.mx; Commercial Web site: http://www.embajadabritanica.com.mx/.

British Consulates are located in:

Acapulco: Casa Consular, Centro Internacional Acapulco, Costera Miguel Aleman, 39851 Acapulco, Guerrero, Tel: (52) (744) 484 1735, Fax: (52) (744) 481 2533; Email: gbconsul_aca@hotmail.com;

Cuidad Juárez: Calle Fresno 185, Campestre Juárez 32460 Cuidad Juárez, Chihuahua, Tel: (52) (656) 617 5791, Fax: (52) (656) 617 5088; **Guadalajara:** Jesus de Rojas No 20, Colonia Los Pinos, 45120 Zapopan Jalisco, Tel: (52) (33) 3343 2296, Fax: (52) (33) 3343 2296; **Monterrey:** Viveca Mortenson (Vice Consul) Callejon de la Piedra 127, Col. Las Lajas Monterrey, Nuevo Leon, CP, Tel: (52) (81) 8315 204, Fax: (52) (81) 8315 2049; Email: hconsulate@terra.com.mx; **Cancun:** The Royal Sands Blvd Kukulkan Km 13.5, Zona Hotelera, 77500 Cancun, Quintana Roo, Tel: (52) 998 881 0100, Fax: (52) 998 848 8229; Email: information@britishconsulatecancun.com

Oaxaca: Hotel Xestal Blvd Chahue Lote 37 Mza 4 Sector R, 70989 Bahias de Huatulco, Oaxaca, Tel: (52) (958) 587 2372 Leave a message, Fax: (52) (958) 587 2773, Email: wolfgangww@ hotmail.com; **Tijuana:** Blvd Salinas No 1500, Fracc Aviación Tijuana, 22420 Tijuana, Baja California N., Tel: (52) (664) 686 5320, (52) (664) 681 7323, Fax: (52) (664) 681 8402; and **Veracruz:** Independencia No 349-1 Zone, (P.O. Box 724), 91700 Veracruz, Veracruz, Tel: (52) (229) 931 1285 / 931 0955, Fax: 52) (229) 931 1285.

United States of America

CAPITAL:	WASHINGTON, DISTRICT OF COLUMBIA
POPULATION:	290,342,554
LANGUAGE:	ENGLISH, SPANISH (SPOKEN BY A SIZABLE MINORITY)
CURRENCY:	U.S. DOLLAR (US$)
AREA:	9,629,091 SQUARE KM (50 STATES + WASHINGTON, D.C.; EXCLUDES TERRITORIES)
ETHNIC GROUPS:	WHITE 77.1%, BLACK 12.9%, ASIAN 4.2%, AMERINDIAN AND ALASKA NATIVE 1.5%, NATIVE HAWAIIAN AND OTHER PACIFIC ISLANDER 0.3%, OTHER 4%.
RELIGION:	PROTESTANT 56%, ROMAN CATHOLIC 28%, JEWISH 2%, OTHER 4%, UNAFFILIATED 10%

PASSPORT HIGHLIGHTS: U.S. immigration law is arguably the most complex in the world, with 53 different types of non-immigrant visas and a number of ways of gaining coveted permanent residence (the "Green Card"). There is a special visa program for investors willing to commit US$1 million to create at least ten new jobs. In certain rural areas with high unemployment, the investment level can be as little as US$500,000. It is frequently better to obtain one of the non-immigrant visas and later apply for an adjustment of status to "lawful permanent residence." Naturalization may be available after five years of residency in the U.S.

Since the terrorist attacks on September 11, 2001, the U.S. has restricted many of its formerly loose visa rules. Check for the latest visa rules at http://www.dhs.gov/.

World's Most Costly Passport

The United States is indeed "a nation of immigrants," as former

U.S. President Franklin D. Roosevelt once said. To live in the U.S. has been the goal of millions of immigrants for nearly 250 years. Originally British colonies, its founding dates to 1620 when immigrant "Pilgrims," escaping religious oppression in England landed on Plymouth Rock in what was to become the Massachusetts Bay Colony. As a country of every race and language, the U.S. continues to be a desired destination for the homeless, oppressed, and persecuted, as well as for rich individuals who want to invest or live in this "bastion of capitalism."

The immigrant's theory has always been that, in America, anyone with ambition, drive, and creativity can become wealthy. The U.S. is said to be one of the most economically free countries in the world and, with fewer restrictions on free enterprise, it's an easy place for an entrepreneur to succeed. The economy functions best with the least amount of government control, and beginning with the presidency of Ronald Reagan (1981-89), privatization and deregulation have become a deliberate government policy, although unevenly applied by both major political parties.

Wages and prices are free of most controls. In most cases, supply and demand and free market forces operate freely. Leveraged trading, real estate, and stock market investments account for many new American personal fortunes.

U.S. tax laws are highly complex, especially for foreign citizens ("resident aliens") living full or part-time in the U.S. There are special, profitable tax breaks denied by law to U.S. citizens, but freely given to foreign citizens who invest in the U.S. but live elsewhere. A few legal tax shelters exist, but a lawyer or accountant is needed to understand how they work. A wealthy American without careful tax planning can pay half or more of his/her income in federal and state income and other taxes.

Need we say that as the leading world power, the U.S. is diplomatically and militarily active worldwide and also maintains selective "foreign aid" programs. U.S. foreign policies are often highly unpopular in some countries, so if you are traveling on a U.S. passport, you may encounter hostility and even violence in some places.

American laws classify more acts as criminal than anywhere else in the world. The U.S. now has the highest percentage of its population in prison, surpassing even South Africa under apartheid and the former Soviet Union at its oppressive zenith. Two-thirds of these prisoners are serving drug-related sentences. This horrifying reality, which most Americans seem never to consider, dramatically conflicts with the personal freedom and liberty upon which the country was founded.

Economically, things are far better. The U.S. standard of living is near the top per capita and the possibility of making your fortune still exists. The U.S. is attractive to many foreign-born people as a possible part-time residence, a place of financial opportunity and perhaps even citizenship. Non-resident foreigners who invest in the U.S. can do so virtually tax-free. In fact, for non-Americans, the U.S. is one of the world's leading tax havens.

The U.S. has the most powerful, diverse, and technologically advanced economy in the world, with a 2002 per capita income of US$31,632, the largest among major industrial countries. In this market-oriented economy, private individuals and business firms make most of the decisions, and government buys needed goods and services predominantly in the private marketplace. U.S. business firms enjoy considerably greater flexibility than their counterparts in western Europe and Japan in decisions to expand capital plants, lay off surplus workers, and develop new products. At the same time, they face higher barriers to entry in their rivals' home markets than the barriers to entry of foreign firms in U.S. markets. U.S. firms are at or near the forefront in technological advances, especially in computers and in medical, aerospace, and military equipment, although their advantage has narrowed.

Long-term problems include inadequate investment in economic infrastructure, rapidly rising medical costs of an aging population, sizable trade deficits, and stagnation of family income in the lower economic groups.

U.S. Immigration Law

Legal U.S. "resident aliens" may apply for citizenship after five years of residence.

During this time, the U.S. person is subject to all applicable taxes paid by U.S. citizens. Investigation of citizenship applications used to be lax. There are severe penalties for misrepresentations, including deportation and possible incarceration prior to being deported. In the aftermath of the September 11, 2001 terrorist attacks in New York and Washington the rules governing illegal aliens have been more strictly enforced than at any time in recent history. As a result, many illegal aliens, especially those of Arab and middle Eastern origin, have been jailed and held without charges or deported.

Under U.S. law, certain groups have been excluded in the past as "undesirables," including homosexuals, drug users, HIV-infected persons, unpopular political activists, as well as controversial artists, musicians, writers, and scholars. Tax expatriates were added to this ignominious list in 1997, but none have actually been excluded.

The U.S. Immigration and Naturalization Service (INS) is a notoriously arbitrary, offensive, and high-handed government agency. It is also one of the most inefficient and poorly run agencies, according to an official report from the U.S. General Accounting Office. There has been serious discussion of abolishing the agency and transferring its duties elsewhere. Immigration regulations are subject to arbitrary interpretations that suit the prejudices of the bureaucrat involved. Corruption on the part of immigration officials is not unknown, but historically, it is the exception and not the rule. After the 9-11 attacks, the service was incorporated into the new U.S. Department of Homeland Security, but that has not improved its overall efficiency.

In recent years twenty INS staff members in the New York City area were indicted for selling official green cards and falsifying records to speed up applications for people who had paid them to do so. More recently INS officials in south Florida have been sent to jail for similar crimes. Attempted bribery of U.S. Government officials is a criminal felony, and if some government clerk solicits you for a bribe, you should seriously consider the possibility of entrapment.

A prospective new U.S. citizen is advised to hire an American attorney who specializes in immigration matters. The cost can be US$20,000 or more. Beware of "expert" immigration lawyers who make big promises, demand fees, then fail to produce. Not having a lawyer can prejudice your case, so check references and get a good lawyer. Aliens do not have the same or as many rights as U.S. citizens, and therefore, may not receive judicial review of a negative INS administrative decision.

The Immigration Process

U.S. citizenship may be acquired: 1) by birth within the United States or its territories; 2) by birth outside the U.S. to one or both U.S. parents; or 3) by the formal naturalization process. After five years of legal residence, it is possible to apply for and acquire U.S. citizenship.

But U.S. immigration law is arguably the most complex in the world, with 53 different types of non-immigrant visas and a number of ways of gaining coveted permanent residence (the "Green Card"). It is frequently better to obtain one of the non-immigrant visas and later apply for an adjustment of status to "lawful permanent residence."

Because of extreme complexity, each immigration case requires individual assessment to find the best legal path and plan for all tax implications in advance. U.S. immigration law does offer distinct possibilities for foreign persons willing to invest and they may obtain relatively quick permanent resident status. Nevertheless, until the exact impact of U.S. taxes is calculated, "green card" status well may be worth avoiding.

For a wealthy foreign national, a so-called "high net worth individual" (HNWI), obtaining U.S. permanent resident status definitely may not be the best possible step because of U.S. taxes, especially income taxes. A foreign national, who does not live in the U.S. full time, who has no need for a green card, can obtain many very beneficial investments and tax advantages under U.S. law just as well. There is an existing entry program for foreign investors willing to commit US$1 million to create at least ten new jobs. In certain rural areas with high unemployment, the investment level can be as little as US$500,000. This program has been accused of being abused and investigated for fraud and INS corruption. In any event, it has not been widely used.

The holder of a green card is entitled to work and reside in the United States on a permanent basis. However, green card status may be worth avoiding because, once granted, the U.S. views the cardholder as a "U.S. person" (as described above) for taxation purposes. A green card is a strong indication of having acquired a U.S. domicile. That means being subjected to U.S. estate and gift taxes on all worldwide income. Maximum estate and gift taxes can be as high as 55% of the value of assets passing on at death, and in some cases, even higher.

Unlike almost all other major countries, the U.S. imposes taxes on all worldwide income of its citizens and of those non-citizens with permanent U.S. resident ("green card") status, regardless of where they actually live in the world. (Many countries exempt their citizens from some or all taxes if they live abroad). U.S. Internal Revenue Code (IRC), sec. 61 states: "Except as otherwise provided . . .gross income means all income from whatever source derived . . ." The IRS and courts interpret this to include income of every nature and wherever it may be earned in the world, including offshore income. For tax purposes, the IRC defines a "U.S. person" as any individual who is a U.S. citizen, a U.S. resident alien deemed to be a permanent resident, or a U.S. domiciled corporation, partnership, estate, or trust.

Punitive Expatriate Taxes

An individual who remains a U.S. resident alien for eight years or more, then leaves, may be subject to burdensome U.S. tax expatriation laws. Punitive tax penalties come into play if the Internal Revenue Service determines that the relinquishment of long-term residence was done for U.S. tax avoidance as a principal purpose.

In 1996, U.S. expatriation tax rules were toughened considerably. The rules are aimed at "U.S. persons" who relinquish their U.S. status for tax avoidance purposes. This includes both U.S. citizens and permanent resident aliens who have lived in the U.S. for eight of the fifteen immediately preceding tax years.

If the IRS determines tax avoidance motivated expatriation has occurred, the person is subject to income, estate, and gift taxes for ten years after abandoning their U.S. status. A person is presumed to have relinquished U.S. status for tax avoidance reasons if: a) the individual's average annual U.S. federal income tax liability for the five taxable years ending before the date of the loss or termination is greater than US$100,000, or b) the individual's net worth as of the date of the loss of status is a minimum of US$500,000.

For the first time since 1952, the 1990s saw dramatic reforms in national immigration laws. Few of these changes affect non-immigrant visitors or travelers, but if you are a holder of a green card, the changes are major. However, for those seeking residence and caught on long waiting lists, new possibilities and priorities are available. Some great opportunities now exist if you want a non-immigrant visa in order to do business in the U.S., but you don't want to become a citizen.

The period spent in the U.S. as a holder of an immigrant visa — a resident alien with a green card — counts towards the five-year requirement for citizenship. Time spent in the U.S. on a non-immigrant visa does not count. A green card holder must pay U.S. taxes on all worldwide income, but a non-immigrant visa holder may avoid most U.S. taxes, even on some income earned within the U.S. In most categories of non-immigrant visas, the length of stay is at the discretion of the reviewing immigration officer at the place of entry. The applicant must not intend to abandon his home country residence, nor should the person's foreign passport have an expiration date that occurs while they will be in the U.S.

A visa applicant must be certifiably free from mental or physical disability, alcoholism, or drug addiction. They must be literate and not associated with an organization seeking to overthrow the government of the United States.

Since the terror attacks of September 11, 2001, both the provisions and enforcement of the immigration laws have been toughened considerably. Many non-citizens, including students, who overstayed their visa terms were jailed and deported. Strict compliance with all visa and other immigration laws is now a must.

Non-Immigrant Visa Categories

Type A1, 2, 3: : Diplomats, accredited foreign officials and their immediate families.

Type B1: Business visitors for less than a three-month stay, but can be up to one year.

Type B2: VVisitors for pleasure. Tourists are admitted for six months, may not take jobs and must leave at the end of their stay. A six-month extension is routinely granted upon filing a written request giving reasons.

Type C1, 2, and 3: Transit visas for immediate and continuous transit through the U.S., including to the United Nations headquarters.

Type D: For the crew of ships and aircraft who will leave on another ship or aircraft after a short stay.

Type E1, 2: Business persons and investors who will manage or work in a business with substantial trade between the U.S. and a foreign country. This visa class is permitted under bilateral U.S. trade treaties. A spouse and unmarried children under 21 also are entitled to this visa and to work in the U.S. The E-1 "treaty trader visa" is for an employee of a business in which there is "substantial trade" between the U.S. and the foreign national's home country, or for a U.S. business in which there has been substantial investment (US$50,000 or more) by a businessman from that country. These are the only non-immigrant visas that allow for indefinite extensions. This usually means at least 50% of the trade must be between the U.S. company and the foreign nation with which there is a relevant international trade agreement with the U.S.

Type F1, 2: A student visa, issued for the length of a recognized course of study, with a spouse and unmarried children. Under limited circumstances, the visa holder may be employed, usually by the educational institution attended. The student must have been accepted by an educational institution and show availability of funds to cover the educational costs.

Type G1, 2, 3, 4, and 5: Another diplomatic visa for a "designated principal resident representative" of a recognized foreign government or international organization, including staff.

Type H, 1A, 1B, 2A, 2B, 3, 4: The principal visas available for those wishing to work in the U.S. with certain desirable skills such as nurses, specialty occupations, temporary agricultural worker, non-agricultural temporary workers, trainees, and their families.

The H-1B visa for a "specialty occupation" as a "specialist knowledge worker" is usually for a graduate or graduate equivalent and it allows entry for up to six years to work for a U.S. company. The question of "graduate equivalent" is often misunderstood and many foreign non-graduates with proper documentation may be able to enter the U.S. on this basis.

The great U.S. demand for professionally trained nurses and physical therapists are evidenced by a special H-1A visa for health care personnel. This requires a license (or equivalent) to practice and certification that the applicant is fully qualified to engage in the intended employment.

The H-2B visa allows entry for both skilled and unskilled workers. The main requirement is for a "labor certification" from the prospective employer stating there are no unemployed but qualified U.S. citizens or permanent residents who can fill the vacancy. Holders of this visa usually cannot apply for permanent residence.

The H-3 visa is for training in the U.S. of a type to augment present experience and qualifications for future foreign employment, especially if this is for a U.S. employer. The H-2A visa is for agricultural workers.

In recent years all of the H type visas have come under political attack by those who allege that this category is being abused for the benefit of foreign workers at the expense of American jobs. This has led to several revisions of the category and its definitions.

Type I: For accredited representatives of foreign newspapers and broadcasting organizations.

Type J1, 2: For a student or academic on a short-term educational exchange or training program and family. This visa is used in a program to bring exchange visitors to the U.S. to acquire skills that can be used in their home country. The United States Information Agency designates which programs are available. For those who want to work in the U.S. for a short period, this is usually the easiest visa to obtain.

Type K1, 2: For a person engaged to be married to a U.S. citizen or resident alien who seeks entry solely to marry. Minor children may also qualify for entry under this category. The marriage must occur within 90 days of arrival and the couple must show they met within the last two years. After marriage, the foreign party may apply for "conditional permanent residence" in the U.S., which is valid for two years. Thereafter, the person may apply for permanent residence based on the marriage. Marriage to a U.S. citizen does not guarantee permanent residence status and marriages of this type are investigated with suspicion by the INS. If a visa is granted, the residency period for applying for U.S. nationality is reduced from five to three years.

Type L: A visa for personnel transferred to the U.S. by an international company for from five to seven years. If a U.S. company has an affiliate or subsidiary in either country, the L-1 "intra-company transferee visa" is used, mainly for a manager, executive, or an employee with specialized knowledge. It does not allow a spouse or children to work without first obtaining visas of their own. Under some circumstances, owners, stockholders, or partners in an international company may be able to qualify for this visa.

Type M1, 2: An alien coming to the U.S. for vocational study at an educational institution approved by the INS. Immediate family members may also qualify.

Type N: For a former employee of an international organization who has resided in the U.S. for long periods of time in the G-4 non-immigrant category. Granted only in very special situations.

Type O1, 2: For persons with extraordinary personal abilities in the sciences, arts, education, business, or athletics, together with their family.

Type P1, 2, 3: For entertainers or athletes who cannot qualify under the extraordinary ability standard for the O category but who are part of a group or team.

Type Q: Persons coming to the U.S. for participation in an international cultural exchange program designated by the U.S. Attorney General.

Type R1, 2: A temporary visit by a religious worker, including family.

To obtain a student visa, your place of study has to confirmed, approved in advance, and no change of school is allowed without INS approval. You are only permitted employment if it's considered necessary training in the chosen career field; such as a medical student completing a required hospital internship. F-l visa holders are also allowed to work on campus without permission from the INS. Your spouse or children may not hold jobs.

Visas other than C, D, or K categories may be extended if you apply to stay before the visa expires. When you make a visa application, you will be told of any additional documents needed, usually proof of intent to return to your home country, such as proof of property ownership. You can apply for Type B visas by letter or at a U.S. Embassy or Consulate. Visa Types A, G, H-2, H-3, as well as most I and L visas, are applied for by an employer. With H-l visas, you or your employer have to prove your case. If you go to the U.S. on an L visa and want to change jobs or are self-employed, and not eligible for an E visa, you may need an immigrant visa.

Admission to the U.S. for non-immigrants chiefly depends on the decision of the immigration officer at the place of entry. If you have a return ticket for transportation back to your home country and sufficient assets — though you need not have an American bank account — a stay for three or six months is usually automatic.

The U.S., unlike many other countries, allows you to change visa status after entering. This permits you to change your non-immigrant visa when you have established contacts to obtain an immigrant visa. If you want to immigrate and do not qualify immediately for an immigrant visa, a brief stay in the U.S. on a non-immigrant visa, say as a student enrolled in a one-year program, gives you "a foot in the door."

Terrorism Attacks Change Visa Rules

The 2001 Border Security Act enacted by the U.S. Congress calls for 27 countries who have been in the former Visa Waiver Program to issue passports with biometric data to their citizens who travel to the United States. Sixty-eight percent of all U.S. visitors come from visa waiver countries, such as Canada, Great Britain, Germany, France, Australia, New Zealand and Japan.

Under the law's congressional mandate, citizens from countries that don't meet the mandated deadline of Oct. 26, 2004 for digital passports were to have to go through the formal U.S. visa application process. This would have meant that the U.S. State Department would have to process millions of additional visa applications annually. But in 2004 the Congress loosened the requirements of this immigration law enacted to protect the country from future terrorist attacks. The new digital passport program will become effective sometime in 2005 or later.

The visa waiver issue is one of the first serious problems to emerge with new immigration policies that Congress passed in the aftermath of the Sept. 11, 2001 terrorist attacks in New York and Washington, D.C.

The requirement for digital, biometric passports from foreign nations meshes with a new U.S. border security program. This program required all visitors to photographed and fingerprinted upon arrival at U.S. ports of entry.

The U.S. Department of Homeland Security refers to the resulting documents as "laser visas," since they contain digital photographs and biometric identifiers for each person. Test runs in the U.S. began on January 5, 2004 and were to be expanded from 119 airports and seaports to an additional 50 more U.S. land ports of entry which process more than 90 percent of the foreign visitors who enter and leave the United States.

The government claims the program, known as "US-VISIT," (United States Visitor and Immigrant Status Indicator Technology) is designed to enhance security while allowing legitimate travel and trade across U.S. borders. They claim it gives U.S. Customs and Border Protection (CBP) inspectors the ability to determine whether a person seeking entry is the same person who was issued the visa by the State Department. Officials claim that the biometric and biographic data are tagged instantly to federal watch lists, to guard against the entry of terrorists to the United States.

How successful this may be is questionable. Domestic warning lists of airline passengers created by the federal government have been riddle with names of innocent people, or the names of suspect people who simply have the same names as real suspects. These blacklists, kept secret and allowing no procedure for removal of mistaken names, are now the subject of numerous court challenges.

Under the program, all visitors to the United States except those from Canada, Mexico, and 25 other exempted countries are fingerprinted and photographed when they enter the country by air.

Reaction from foreign nations has been angry and swift. Brazil instituted a similar requirement for all U.S. citizens visiting there and fined one U.S. airline pilot $10,000 when he refused to comply and detained him until he paid. Many European nations have also objected, saying the US-VISIT system treats their nationals as criminal suspects. American tourist business leaders complained bitterly that the system was already discouraging visitors to America and losing millions of dollars in travel industry income, as well as related taxes. Strong objections from the governments of Mexico and Canada resulted in the easing of the new restrictions for those who cross the border daily for work.

The European Union's 15 current members enjoy visa reciprocity with the United States, but most of the countries slated to join the EU in 2004 do not have any existing mutual visa relationship. Foreign ministers from Bangladesh and Indonesia traveled to Washington specifically to protest the measures.

Under the previous U.S. Visa Waiver program citizens from 28 countries initially were exempt from the new US-VISIT program, and could continue to enter the United States without a visa, traveling on passports for business or pleasure for up to 90 days. Over 10 million people visited the U.S. using the old Visa Waiver Program (VWP), a program for visitors from countries that allow reciprocal visits by Americans. This granted admission to the U.S. for up to 90 days as a B-l or B-2 status visitor. No extensions of stay were permitted.

The program is currently available to citizens of Andorra, Austria, Belgium, Denmark, Finland, France, Germany, Iceland, Italy, Japan, Liechtenstein, Luxembourg, Monaco, the Netherlands, New Zealand, Norway, San Marino, Spain, Sweden, Switzerland, and the United Kingdom.

As a VWP visitor, you are not allowed to change status to another non-immigrant classification without first leaving the U.S. If you are using the waiver program and wish to apply for a green card, you must do so only at a U.S. Embassy or Consulate abroad. Any evidence that you intend to seek employment, such as resumes or letters of recommendation, should be sent ahead and not brought with you personally, lest they create the wrong impression if your papers are searched upon entry.

The Visa Waiver Program is really meant as a tourist option, so avoid it if you can. If you are from a qualifying VWP country, you can just as well get a standard visitor's visa, with much more flexibility. The VWP is useful for a short holiday visit of 90 days or less and precludes extensions or changes that might be necessary.

Immigrant Visas

The U.S. has an annual worldwide maximum quota of 675,000 immigrant admissions. Applicants are considered on a first-come, first-served basis.

The two major exceptions to these numerical limits are refugees and asylum seekers. An annual political asylum quota is set by Congress, depending on disturbances in various parts of the world. The refugee category can be as high as 200,000 visas annually, but availability is for applicants from countries suffering political crisis that the U.S. Congress formally recognizes.

Family Sponsored Immigrants

The U.S. allows a maximum of 226,000 admittees annually for the purposes of family reunification; they are divided into four categories, listed here in their order of preference:

1) Unmarried sons and daughters of U.S. citizens and their children (23,400 annual total);

2) Spouses, children, and unmarried sons and daughters of lawful permanent resident aliens. At least 70% must go to spouses and children, the remainder to unmarried sons and daughters, (114,200);

3) Married sons and daughters of U.S. citizens and their spouses and children, (23,400); and

4) Brothers and sisters of U.S. citizens and their spouses and children, provided the U.S. citizens are 21 years old (65,000).

If there are insufficient applicants in any class, those numbers become available to immigrants in other family classes. Visa availability in the family-sponsored, visa preference categories varies widely depending on your country of origin. Natives of the Philippines, Mexico, India, and the Dominican Republic typically face the longest delays. First preference visas for the Philippines are backlogged more than five years. Fourth preference visas for the Philippines are backlogged more than 14 years. The waiting list for Mexicans is more than 12 years.

If you qualify for employment-based immigration and are from one of these countries, you should pursue that route rather than the family option.

U.S. Immigration Debate

The 1990 immigration reform law and subsequent restrictions, such as tightened qualifications for welfare assistance to immigrants, result from a continuing U.S. national debate about whether further immigration should be restricted, or even ended.

Labor unions and right wing isolationists have formed an unusual alliance on this issue. The unions charge that immigration causes massive job losses for Americans, although others claim they create new jobs and pay taxes. Some conservatives say the "American way of life" is threatened by non-English speakers who are changing the nation's culture. Both groups seem to forget Franklin Roosevelt's truism that only the Indians are native Americans and everyone else is descended from immigrants.

Most businesses strongly favor liberal immigration because they need qualified people and want cheap labor willing to take the low paying jobs that most Americans reject. What this means to a prospective immigrant is that great opportunities do exist if the person has desirable skills.

The 1990 reform law tripled the number of employment-based visas, making available 140,000 slots for this category divided into five preference groups, as follows:

Priority Workers: extraordinary ability in the sciences, arts, education, business, or athletics. Outstanding professors and researchers and certain multinational executives and managers are also included, (28.6%);

Members of Professions: holding advanced degrees and people of exceptional ability in the sciences, arts, and business, (28.6%);

Professional Skilled and Unskilled Workers: those holding baccalaureate degrees, skilled workers with at least two years experience, and other workers whose skills are in short supply in the U.S., (28.6%, but unskilled workers are subject to a sub-limit of 10,000);

Special Immigrants: religious workers and ministers of religion, international organization employees and immediate family members, and specially qualified current and former U.S. Government employees, (7.1%); and

Investors: people who create jobs for at least ten unrelated people by investing capital in a new commercial enterprise. Minimum capital required between US$500,000 and US$1 million, depending on unemployment rate in the geographic area — see "Investor Immigration" below, (7.1%).

How to Obtain Employment Visas

All employment preference categories described above require filing a first petition with the INS seeking classification within the specific visa preference sought. If granted, a second application for the visa needs to be filed at a U.S. Consulate.

Before filing for a visa under either the second or third preference described above, the applicant's prospective employer must apply for and obtain an approved "alien employment certification" application from the U.S. Department of Labor. (A DOL certification is not required for the first, fourth, and fifth preferences).

The DOL certification states your employer's finding that there is no U.S. worker available and qualified for the position, and that the proposed wages and working conditions offered are on par with that of other similar U.S. workers. The employer must conduct a recruitment campaign for the job at issue, advertising the position in newspapers and at its work site. With some artistic skill, the job description is usually tailored to fit these requirements.

The second step is filing the visa petition with the INS in the state where employment is to occur. Usually, an employer does this, but in cases where an applicant has "extraordinary ability," they can file their own petition.

INS acceptance of the preference petition means you are qualified for that preference category. This decision allows the filing with a U.S. Consulate of the second application, this one seeking an immigrant visa. But this filing is also contingent on a determination by the U.S. Department of State that an immigrant visa is immediately available, based on the total numbers remaining in the annual quota. Each month, the Department of State publishes a "Visa Office Bulletin" listing the latest priority dates available for immigrant visas in each preference and countries which are oversubscribed for annually allotted visas. Sometimes, a visa number is available immediately, but demand backlogs develop frequently.

Under the former system, five-year waits were common, but since the new 1990 law, major delays for employment-based visas are rare. Different problems have arisen instead, such as the 1998 quota for technical experts being far over-subscribed because of demand within the computer industry.

If you are already legally in the U.S. at the time an immigrant visa becomes available, you may apply to adjust status to permanent residence. This is useful if you entered on a business visa, found a job and want to accept it without the expense of leaving the country and then applying for a visa at a consulate. It is not possible to adjust status from an expired visa or if there is a pending complaint that you have violated your visa, such as by working on a visitor's visa.

Immigration Based on Investment

The fifth employment-based preference granted to immigrant investors has drawn the most attention, probably because it is a blatant "buying your way" into U.S. citizenship that only the wealthy can afford. Immigration lawyers specializing in this aspect of the law are making big fees from rich foreigners willing to pay them and the U.S. Government to gain quick citizenship.

Before we explain this process, carefully consider whether you want to subject your business and financial life to the scrutiny that is attached to citizenship under this investment program. It means being taxed by the U.S. on all your worldwide income, totally opening your books to the IRS, and paying taxes far above those imposed in tax haven countries. In addition, failure to comply with U.S. laws can mean huge fines, penalties, interest, and even prison. Consider, too, that your citizenship is contingent on the investment being a success. If it fails, or if you don't comply with all the rules, your citizenship status is revoked.

Having considered all of that, here's how the investor citizenship program works:

If you invest at least US$1 million in a designated "high unemployment area" or at least US$500,000 in a "targeted employment area," then citizenship can be yours. Your investment must benefit the U.S. economy and create full-time employment for at least ten qualified employees, who are NOT you — the investor, your family, or any non-immigrant visa holders; and it must be a true profit-making business. You can't set up a corporation to own a personal residence, which employs a staff of ten. The assets of the business may not be used to finance it, meaning an actual cash investment is required. You must also be prepared to document the legitimate sources of the money to be used. Multiple investors in the same enterprise are allowed, provided each investment meets the minimum requirements and creates ten jobs, meaning ten people would have to open a US$10 million business employing 100 people. The purchase of an existing business is only permitted as part of a restructuring that increases the overall capital and employment of that existing business.

As might be expected, the specific details of the program are quite extensive and require a lawyer to interpret. Among the many drawbacks to this program is that approval in this category, unlike the other permanent residence visa categories, results in a conditional visa for you for the first two years. Continued involvement with the business and proof of its success are necessary to have your visa renewed. If your business fails during the first two years, regardless of the reason, your visa will be revoked. There are no exceptions. Proof of having made your best effort will only be ignored.

Refugees

There may be circumstances in which you can gain U.S. residence as a political refugee or asylum seeker. However, if you fit better into another visa category, you should do so. Refugee and asylum seeker status is politically controversial in the U.S. and is actively opposed by immigration authorities. So-called "economic refugees" are generally rejected. To qualify as a political refugee, a person must demonstrate that they are fleeing from their home country because of past persecution or have a well-founded fear of future persecution. Refugees must apply outside the U.S. and have a financial sponsor in the U.S.

Retired Foreign Persons

A major attraction for foreigners is lower cost U.S. real estate. A non-immigrant B-2 visa allowing a stay of up to six months is not difficult to obtain. However, realize that a U.S. stay in excess of 122 nights makes a foreign visitor liable for U.S. income taxes. A foreign person who wants to retire permanently to the U.S. might better obtain a non-immigrant H-2 visa and open a small business. That will not bring U.S. citizenship, but it can assure continued permanent residence.

Illegal Immigrants

It is estimated that as many as 10% of the 290 million U.S. population may be illegal aliens, mainly from Mexico and Latin America. Until recent years, U.S. land borders have been largely unguarded and unfortified. Coastal surveillance by air has been more vigilant because of the "war on drugs," but entry by small boat from Mexico, Cuba, Haiti, or Central America is a common occurrence.

Increased U.S. citizen concern about international terrorism and drug smuggling has produced massive new government spending on border patrols and fences. Much greater surveillance of the land border with Mexico and coastal waters is in place. New walls and fences have been erected, and inspections at all border crossings with Mexico have been stepped up, causing long traffic backups. The number of INS and customs officers has been increased, and for the first time, U.S. military forces patrol remote border areas.

One of the glaring discontinuities in U.S. law is that although illegal aliens are subject to capture and instant deportation, many welfare and social services agencies cannot withhold benefits from them while they are otherwise illegally in the country. Typically, one government agency fails or refuses to communicate with another, thereby creating this paradox.

As a result, many illegal aliens openly receive welfare benefits for months or years without the INS being informed. This, plus assistance from organized church groups makes the U.S. a very attractive destination for Mexicans, Haitians, and Central Americans who seek education, medical benefits, and subsistence until they find a job or start a business.

As we go to press, President George W. Bush has proposed an amnesty and resident alien status for many millions of persons now in the United States illegally. This proposal has met with considerable opposition in the U.S. Congress and its eventual acceptance is in doubt.

Immediate Passports

Only U.S. citizens or key alien employees of the U.S. Government can obtain instant U.S. passports legally, and then only with proper proof and documentation.

The most important requirement is a certified copy of a birth certificate issued by the state of birth. This must show a file or reference number, the date of birth, and the official certification of the issuing office. Passport offices rarely check authenticity with birth certificate issuing offices, but they might check if a passport application looks suspicious. Hospital birth certificates will not suffice for a U.S. passport application. Notification of Birth Registration forms filed with U.S. Consulates abroad may be accepted without birth certificates on a case-by-case basis, but the original birth certificate plus a translation certified by a U.S. Consulate abroad is usually required.

When applying for a passport, a U.S. citizen born abroad, with at least one parent who was a U.S. citizen, and has been a recent U.S. resident, must submit a certified copy of a "Consular Report of Birth" or Certification of Birth. Naturalized U.S. citizens must submit either a Certificate of Naturalization or Certificate of Citizenship.

To prove identity, a passport applicant must show a valid U.S. current photo ID, such as an expired U.S. passport, a driver's license, or any Government Issue photo ID card. Alternatively, a business card or school/college ID with a photograph and name on it can be accepted at the discretion of a passport officer.

The U.S. requires a passport application to be accompanied by two identical pictures, either color or black and white taken within the previous six months. Photo size is 2 x 2 inches, full front view, with plain white or off-white background. Image size between 1-inch and 1 3/8 inches measured from top of head — including hair and bottom of chin. Dark glasses that hide eyes are not acceptable, hats or other headgear must not be worn, and photos from coin-operated booths are not acceptable.

Any passport applicant 13 years or older must appear in person and sign the application in the presence of a U.S. passport agent or consular official. Parents can sign for younger children. Previous U.S. passport holders can renew by mail using standard Form DSP-82.

Summary

Web site of the U.S. Immigration and Naturalization Service (INS): http://www.ins.usdoj.gov/graphics/index.htm

INS Forms on Line; Visas and Applications: http://www.ins.usdoj.gov/graphics/formsfee/forms/index.htm

INS services available including citizenship, asylum, lawful permanent residency, employment authorization, refugee status, international adoptions, replacement immigration documents, family and employment-related immigration, and foreign student authorization: http://www.ins.usdoj.gov/graphics/services/index.htm

For a pdf downloadable file of the official "U.S. Guide to Naturalization," go to: http://www.ins.usdoj.gov/graphics/services/natz/insfnl.pdf

For information about obtaining permanent residence status: http://www.ins.usdoj.gov/graphics/services/residency/index.htm

For a list of all INS offices in the U.S., including ports of entry: http://www.ins.usdoj.gov/graphics/fieldoffices/index.htm

How to Apply for U.S. Passport Renewal

Web site: http://travel.state.gov/passport_services.html

U.S. citizens can apply for passport renewal by mail if they already have a passport, it is their most recent one, it was issued within the past 12 years, and if the person was over age 16 when it was issued. U.S. citizens who are residents abroad should renew their passports at the nearest U.S. Embassy or Consulate. Passports renewed by mail can only be forwarded to U.S. addresses. If your passport has been mutilated, altered, or damaged, you cannot apply for renewal by mail. You must apply in person using Form DSP-11, present evidence of U.S. citizenship, and have acceptable identification.

Obtain a Form DSP-82, "Application For Passport By Mail." Fill it out, sign and date it. Attach to it: 1) your most recent passport; 2) two identical passport photographs; and 3) a US$85 fee for age 16 and over and for under age 16 a US$70 fee. Passport renewal isUS$55. If applicable, an additional, US$60 fee for urgent service.

If your name changed since your previous passport was issued, enclose a certified copy of the court order, adoption decree, marriage certificate, or divorce decree specifying another name for you to use. (Photocopies are not acceptable.) If your name has changed by other means, you must apply in person. Mail (if possible, in a padded envelope) the completed DSP-82 application and attachments to: National Passport Center, P.O. Box 371971, Pittsburgh, PA 15250-7971.

Your previous passport will be returned to you with your new passport. If you wish to use an overnight delivery service, include the appropriate fee for overnight return delivery of your passport. Please note that overnight service will not speed up processing time unless payment for expedited service is also included. If the service of your choice will not deliver to a post office box, send it to: Passport Services, Lockbox, Attn: Passport Supervisor 371971, 500 Ross Street, Room 154-0670, Pittsburgh, Pennsylvania 15262-0001.

United Kingdom Contacts: The British Embassy is located at 3100 Massachusetts Avenue, NW, Washington; D.C. 20008; Tel: (202) 588-6500; Fax: (202) 588-7870; Web site: http://www.britainusa.com/ embassy/

British Consulates are located in New York, Atlanta, Miami, Orlando, Boston, Chicago, Dallas, Los Angeles, Nashville, Phoenix, Pittsburgh, Salt Lake City, Seattle, St. Louis, San Diego, and Puerto Rico.

Section 2
Central America and
the Caribbean

UNITED STATES
OF AMERICA

BERMUDA

BAHAMAS

TURKS & CAICOS

C U B A

MEXICO

DOMINICAN
HAITI REPUBLIC

VIRGIN ISLANDS

BELIZE

JAMACIA

ST. KITTS
& NEVIS

GUATEMALA HONDURAS

ST. VINCENT &
THE GRENADINES

EL SALVEDORE NICARAGUA

GRENADA

COSTA RICA

PANAMA

VENEZUELA

COLOMBIA

Commonwealth of The Bahamas

CAPITAL:	NASSAU, NEW PROVIDENCE ISLAND
POPULATION:	297,477
LANGUAGE:	ENGLISH
CURRENCY:	BAHAMIAN DOLLAR (B$)
AREA:	13,939 SQUARE KM
ETHNIC GROUPS:	AFRICAN 85%, EUROPEAN 12%, ASIAN & HISPANIC 3%
RELIGION:	BAPTIST 32%, ANGLICAN 20%, ROMAN CATHOLIC 19%, METHODIST 6%, CHURCH OF GOD 6%, OTHER PROTESTANT 12%, NONE OR UNKNOWN 3%, OTHER 2%

PASSPORT HIGHLIGHTS: Although naturalization to Bahamian citizenship is reserved for those who marry Bahamian nationals, permanent residency status is available, and even encouraged, for high-net-worth foreigners and those who invest in approved projects or support business operations there.

The Bahamas is the haven country nearest to the U.S. — just min utes from Miami by airplane or a few hours by boat, 744 air miles from New York City.

The nation consists of over 700 islands, only 22 inhabited. The main islands are Grand Bahama, Andros, Eleuthera, Abaco, and New Providence Island (where about two thirds of the nation's population resides), site of the capital, Nassau. The second largest city is Freeport, on Grand Bahama. Eighty-five percent of the Bahamian population is of African heritage. Many Bahamians' ancestors arrived in the Bahama Islands when they served as a staging area for the slave trade in the early 1800s. Others accompanied thousands of British loyalists who fled the American colonies during the Revolutionary War.

Arawak Indians inhabited these islands when Christopher

Columbus arrived in 1492, but they remained largely unexplored by

Europeans until 1717 when they came under control of the British Crown. Because of the American Revolution, in 1776, the islands were briefly in American hands, followed by Spanish control in 1781. In 1783, they again became British territories, remaining so until independence was declared on July 10, 1973. The Bahamas is a member of the British Commonwealth and a parliamentary democracy based on the Westminster model. Since independence, the nation has acquired a deserved reputation for official corruption and government venality, although this has lessened markedly in recent years.

Low-lying limestone or coral islets with sandy beaches, the Bahamian archipelago provides year-round recreational opportunities on land and in the water. The varieties of its marine habitats assure a broad range of prospects for enthusiasts of deep-sea and reef fishing, diving, and sailing. Some of the islands' regattas and powerboat races draw participants and spectators from around the globe. The subtropical climate, warmed by the Gulf Stream, allows dry-land activity around the calendar as well, including golf, polo, cricket, and tennis.

Over a quarter of a million people live in this archipelago, the oldest offshore money haven in the Americas. An independent nation since 1973, its origins as a money haven date to 1908 when the Royal Bank of Canada opened a branch in Nassau. Today, tourism, hotel, resort, and convention industries are booming and the islands are a retirement haven for the very wealthy, many of them prominent U.S. expatriates.

Being close to the U.S. has advantages, but also can cause problems for offshore business and banking, especially if privacy is a major concern. The U.S. and Bahamian dollar are equal in value. There are many banks and trust companies chartered in The Bahamas. Bahamian banks with U.S. branches find it difficult to avoid U.S. government pressures when Washington wants information.

Keeping Money Clean

The Banks and Trust Companies Act of 1965 requires close bank inspections by the government and reports of "suspicious activities." All cash deposits of US$5,000 or more must be reported if made by "unknown persons." New account applicants must show a valid passport and other official identification as well as business references, and banks have a legal duty to identify "beneficial owners" of accounts.

The Drug Trafficking Act of 1986 outlaws money laundering and makes it an extraditable offense. The U.S.-Bahamian "Mutual Legal Assistance Treaty" (MLAT), requires cooperation between Washington and Nassau in all financial investigations. The Bahamas has similar treaties with Canada and the U.K. A new Tax Information Exchange Agreement (TIEA) with the U.S. takes effect in 2005, ending financial privacy if the IRS is interested in a U.S. person with business in The Bahamas.

The Bahamas levies no taxes on capital gains, corporate earnings, personal income, sales, inheritance, or dividends. Tax freedom is available to all resident corporations, partnerships, individuals, and trusts. The International Business Companies Act of 1990 permits cheap, fast incorporation. Incorporation costs include registered agent, nominee directors, and nominee officers, which can total up to US$1,500-$2,400. (Keep in mind that the U.S. and Bahamian dollar are equal in value). Corporations can also be formed with bearer shares. The Bahamas are one of the few jurisdictions in which a company can act as a nominee director.

Bahamas politicians of both parties in recent years have adopted laws that radically tightened banking practices, financial reporting and "know your customer" requirements. As a result, many thousands of banking licenses were revoked, corporation charters yanked andmassive capital flight has occurred.

Bahamian Residency Status

Although a Bahamian resident alien passport is available, full citizenship usually is allowed only after marriage to a Bahamian national. In most cases, it's best not to be a citizen of the place in which you actually live most of the time. That gives your home place government more control over you than you want or need. Thus, becoming a Bahamian national could spoil a potentially beautiful home base for your international operations.

Since 1990, "The Bahamas Investment Promotion Program" have allowed wealthy foreigners to obtain instant permanent residence in one of three categories:

Category I: Individual Investor. TThis status is available for those who have a proven personal net worth of US$2 million, reside in The Bahamas, and make a minimum investment of at least US$500,000, which cannot be repatriated from the country for at least ten years. The principal applicant must invest US$500,000 either in securities or a business the government approves, with an additional required US$250,000 expenditure to purchase or build a business place. This achieves permanent residence, but not Bahamian citizenship. A non-citizenship travel document is issued.

Category II: Group Investor. This status is easiest to obtain, requiring a minimum US$150,000 investment in a government-approved project, a plan similar to Canada's investor citizenship law. The exact amount depends on the individual project, usually a tourist-related development, such as rental town houses or vacation resorts.

Category III: Entrepreneur. This requires an agreed upon investment in a government-approved program for a period of at least ten years.

Agency fees for help in qualifying for any of these categories averages US$20,000. In addition, a foreign retired person of independent means who purchases Bahamian real estate valued of at least US$500,000 will also be granted residency.

Contacts

Henley and Partners Carribean, PO Box 481, 3 Church Street, Basseterre, St. Kitts, West Indies, Tel: +1 869 465 1711 Fax: +1 869 465 1711 Contact Mr. Vernon S. Veira vernon.veira@henleyglobal.com

Visas are not required for U.S. citizens for stays up to eight months, but U.S. citizens must carry original documentation proving U.S. citizenship (valid or expired passport, certified U.S. birth certificate, or Certificate of Naturalization), photo ID, and an onward/return ticket. U.S. voter registration cards are not accepted as proof of citizenship. There is an airport departure tax of US$15 for travelers age six years and older. In Freeport the departure fee is $18.00.

United States: Embassy of the Commonwealth of The Bahamas is located at 2220 Massachusetts Avenue, NW, Washington, D.C. 20008; Tel: (202) 319-2660. The Bahamas has Consulates in Miami and New York City. The U.S. Embassy in The Bahamas is located next to McDonald's restaurant on Queen Street in downtown Nassau; Tel: (242) 322-1181 or after hours (242) 328-2206. Consular Section hours are 9:00 a.m. - 12:00 noon and 2:00 p.m. - 4:00 p.m. Monday-Thursday and 10:00-12:00 on Fridays. The Embassy is closed on local and U.S. holidays. You may wish to contact the Consular Section by e-mail at acsn@state.gov. Additional information is available via web site http://www.bahamas.com, by telephone at 1-800-422-4262, and on the official web site of the Government of The Bahamas, http://www.bahamas.com.bs/.**United Kingdom:** The British High Commission is located at Ansbacher House, 3rd Floor, East Street, P.O. Box N7516, Nassau, Bahamas; Tel: (242) 325-7471; Fax: (242) 323-3871. Email: bhcnassau@fco.gov.uk.

Belize

CAPITAL:	BELMOPAN
POPULATION:	266,440
LANGUAGE:	ENGLISH (OFFICIAL), SPANISH (30%)
CURRENCY:	BELIZE DOLLAR (Bz$); SINCE 1976
AREA:	22,963 SQUARE KM
ETHNIC GROUPS:	MESTIZO 48.7%, CREOLE 24.9%, MAYA 10.6%, GARIFUNA 6.1%, OTHER 9.7%
RELIGION:	ROMAN CATHOLIC 49.6%, PROTESTANT 27% (ANGLICAN 5.3%, METHODIST 3.5%, MENNONITE 4.1%, SEVENTH-DAY ADVENTIST 5.2%, PENTECOSTAL 7.4%, JEHOVAH'S WITNESSES 1.5%), NONE 9.4%, OTHER 14%

PASSPORT HIGHLIGHTS: Although abuses brought an end to Belize's economic citizenship program, the country still offers significant tax incentives to retirees, who can become permanent residents if they show a minimum of US$2,000 monthly income from sources outside Belize.

Belize is the only English-speaking country in Central America. Its mixed population of 200,000 includes descendants of native Mayans, Chinese, East Indians, and Caucasians. Independent since 1981, its language came from its colonial days when it was called British Honduras. Situated south of Mexico and to the east of Guatemala, Belize is on the Caribbean seaboard. It has the largest barrier reef in the Western Hemisphere and great deep sea diving. Inland, visitors and residents enjoy eco-tourism in lush tropical rain forests and exploration of countless Mayan architectural sites and sacred caves, with many yet to be discovered. To the east, there's a sprinkle of Caribbean tropical islands included within the nation's borders providing access to sport fishing in the lagoons and open sea.

A member of the British Commonwealth, Belize retains many of the colonial customs and features familiar in places like the Cayman Islands and Bermuda. The first settlers were probably British woodcutters, who in 1638 found the valuable commodity known as "Honduran mahogany." Bananas, sugar cane, and citrus fruit are principal crops. Like many small countries dependent on primary commodities, Belize recently recognized the benefits of introducing tax haven services to boost its income.

In 1992, the Belize National Assembly enacted up-to-date legislation seeking to make the country a competitive offshore financial center. Drafters combed tax haven laws worldwide and came up with a series of minimal corporate and tax requirements, which could well fit your business needs. The new laws include the Trust Act, which allows a high level of asset protection, great freedom of action by the trustee, and no taxes on income earned outside Belize. There is also a statute allowing the creation of international business companies. These corporations can be formed in less than a day for about US$700. You only need one shareholder and/or director, whose name can be shielded from public view.

Since 1990, when the International Business Companies Act became law, foreigners have registered about 4,000 IBCs. That's a relatively small number compared to a place like the Cayman Islands, but the number is growing. There are no local income taxes, personal or corporate, and no currency exchange controls.

Belize City, the main center for business, has also seen major growth in the shipping registry business. A new law also encourages this. Now in the works are laws favoring offshore insurance companies, limited liability partnerships, and banking. There are no anti-money laundering laws.

So far, the Belize banking sector is tiny, but very secret by force of law. Deposits could have soared as even more new laws made this subtropical paradise the next hot international tax and asset haven. But recent official cooperation with the United States government, especially the IRS, has dampened the enthusiasm of foreign privacy seekers.

Belize Bank, Ltd. owned by BHI Corporation, a holding company with banking and financial services in Belize issues visa credit cards. BHI also has major stakes in local electricity, hotels, citrus, and other industries. The principal owner of BHI is Michael Ashcroft, a British multi-millionaire member of the House of Lords, described by the *Wall Street Journal* as an "unconventional and sometimes controversial deal maker." BHI stock is publicly traded in the U.S. on the NASDAQ stock exchange. The Belize Bank is the largest commercial banking operation in Belize and is a correspondent of Bank of America.

Belize's investment policy is codified in the Belize Investment Guide, which sets out the development priorities for the country. A country "Commercial Guide for Belize" is available at: http://www.state.gov/www/about_state/business/com_guides/1999/wha/belize99.html.

Checkered Passport History

Two decades ago, it was easy to obtain a genuine Belize passport by fraudulent means. This was done by paying a few hundred American dollars to local police, a government official, or a lawyer with connections. They, in turn, would certify to passport authorities that they knew the "applicant" as having been a Belize resident for at least five years. Poor or non-existent official record keeping also lent itself to the widespread use of fake Belize birth certificates to obtain passports.

In December 2001, the nation's cabinet officially ended the Central American tax haven's economic citizenship program, effective March 31, 2002. A constitutional reform commission had urged the change, but pressure from the U.S. and Canadian governments undoubtedly was also a factor. In 2004 a former cabinet minister was refused a U.S. visa based on accusations that he sold Belize passports to selected individuals for thousands of dollars each.

Qualified Retired Persons Program

In 1998, the Retired Persons Incentives Act was enacted with hopes of making Belize a retirement haven for foreign citizens, while bringing foreign currency into the country. It establishes a residency program for "qualified retired persons" (QRPs), offering them significant tax incentives to become permanent residents (but not citizens) of Belize. The program is aimed primarily at residents of the United States, Canada, and the United Kingdom, but is open to all.

A qualified retired person is exempted from all taxes on income from sources outside Belize. QRPs can own and operate their own international business based in Belize, which will be exempt from local taxes. Local income is taxed at a graduated rate of 15-45% and QRPs need a work permit in order to earn local income. For the QRP, import duties are waived for personal effects, household goods, and for a motor vehicle or other transport, such as an airplane or boat.

There is no minimum time required to be spent in Belize and QRPs can maintain that status so long as they maintain a permanent local residence.

To qualify for the QRP program, the applicant must be 45 years of age or older and prove personal financial ability to support oneself and any dependants. A spouse and dependants (18 years and younger) qualify along with the head of household. Initial fees for the program are US$700 for the qualified retiree and US$350 for each dependant, plus US$100 for an ID card upon application approval.

Minimum financial requirements include an annual income of at least US$24,000 (or equivalent) from a pension, annuity, or from other sources outside Belize. By the 15th of each month, at least US$2,000 must be deposited in the QRP's Belize account, or by April 1 annually US$24,000 must be placed in deposit.

For more information about the QRP Program, contact the following agencies:

The Belize Tourist Board, New Central Bank Building, Level 2, Gabourel Lane, P.O. Box 325, Belize City, Belize; Tel: 011-501-223-1913; Fax: 011-501-223-1943; Tollfree: 1-800-624-0686, E-mail: info@travelbelize.org. Web site: }http://www.travelbelize.org/

The Ministry of Tourism & Youth, Constitution Drive, Belmopan, Belize; Tel: 08 - 23393, 08 - 23394; Fax: 08 - 23815; E-mail: }tourismdpt@btl.net. Web site: http://www.belize.gov.bz/cabinet/m_espat/welcome.shtml

Contacts

United States: Belize Embassy, 2535 Massachusetts Avenue, N.W., Washington, D.C. 20008; Tel: (202) 332-9636; Fax: (202) 332-6888. There is a Belize Consulate in Miami, Los Angeles, Chicago, New Orleans, Detroit , San Juan (Puerto Rico), Dallas, Houston, San Francisco, and Belleville, IL, or at the Belizean Mission to the UN in New York and Belize travel information office in New York City at (800) 624-0686. Web site: http://www.embassyofbelize.org/home.html.

U.S. Embassy in Belize City is located at the intersection of Gabourel Lane and Hutson Street in Belize City; Tel: 011 (501) 227-7161/62/63. The Embassy is open from 8:00 a.m. to 5:00 p.m. Monday through Friday, except for the 12:00 noon to 1:00 p.m. lunch hour.

United Kingdom: British High Commission, P.O. Box 91, Belmopan or BFPO 12; Tel: (501) 822 2146; Fax: (501) 822 2761; E-mail: }brithicom@btl.net. Web site: }www.britishhighbze.com

Bermuda

CAPITAL:	HAMILTON
POPULATION:	64,482
LANGUAGE:	ENGLISH (OFFICIAL), PORTUGUESE
CURRENCY:	BERMUDIAN DOLLAR (BD$)
AREA:	50 SQUARE KM
ETHNIC GROUPS:	BLACK 61%, WHITE AND OTHER 39%
RELIGION:	ANGLICAN 28%, CATHOLIC 15%, AFRICAN METHODIST EPISCOPAL (ZION) 12%, SEVENTH-DAY ADVENTIST 6%, METHODIST 5%, OTHER 34%

PASSPORT HIGHLIGHTS: Permanent accommodation in Bermuda is scarce and land for development practically non-existent. Qualified non-Bermudans may apply for permits to reside there, but housing prices are extremely high for the fortunate few who are selected.

So far as local population, Bermuda is the largest remaining colonial possession of Great Britain, a self-governing overseas territory of the U.K., 750 miles southeast of New York City and 3,445 miles from London. Although self-governing, it is ultimately under British law and often under pressure from London. In 2004 the incumbent government called for a national debate on whether the island should declare independence from the U.K., as it has the right to do. Even if independence is eventually supported, it would not occur for a period of some years.

Based on a remote archipelago that makes up a landmass of only 21 square miles, Bermuda has one of the world's most unusual and enviable economies. Gross domestic product exceeds US$2.3 billion, growth is running at about 4%, and inflation hovers around 2%. The territory has a healthy balance of payments surplus, employment levels are high among the population of 62,000, and the average wage is more than US$660 per week.

Renowned for its pink, sandy beaches and moderate climate

warmed by the Gulf Stream, Bermuda has long been a favored playground of affluent tourists from both sides of the Atlantic. At least three publicly managed golf courses and more than a dozen private courses crowd the islands' scanty land area. Aquatic activities of all kinds are another major attraction of Bermuda. Renowned yacht races both in the archipelago and with Bermuda as a goal draw thousands of sailors and boaters annually. Snorkeling, whale-watching, and other kinds of eco-tourism round out the pleasures awaiting visitors and residents.

It enjoys one of the highest per capita incomes in the world, having successfully exploited its location and political status by providing financial services for international firms and luxury tourist facilities for 360,000 visitors annually. The tourist industry, which accounts for an estimated 28% of GDP, attracts 84% of its business from North America. The industrial sector is small, and agriculture is severely limited by a lack of suitable land. About 80% of food needs are imported. International business contributes over 60% of Bermuda's economic output. It has a long history as a tax and banking haven. This is a world-class financial outpost, not to mention a very pleasant place to visit or live in any season.

Bermuda imposes no corporate income, gift, capital gains, or sales taxes. The income tax is extremely low, just 11% on income earned from employment in Bermuda. More than 10,500 international business corporations call Bermuda home. They are drawn by the island's friendly, tax-neutral environment, established business integrity, and minimal regulation. Over 60% of these companies operate as "exempted," meaning their business is conducted outside Bermuda (except for the minimal contacts needed to sustain an office on the island).

Residency

The "jewel of the Atlantic" is also a great place to live, but a word about real estate restrictions. Demand is high and supply short. And you have to be very wealthy.

In general, non-Bermudians are permitted to own only one local property. Acquisition is allowed only after careful background checks (at least one bank reference and two or more personal references). Purchase licenses are issued by the Department of Immigration and take six months or more for approval. A real estate tax based on the total purchase price is payable at settlement: 22% for detached homes, 15% for condominiums.

Out of 20,000 residential units on the island, only 256 detached homes and 480 condominiums qualify for non-Bermudian purchasers based on government set values. The price for a single home starts at US$1.5 million, US$375,000 for condominiums. In 1999, over US$40 million was spent by non-Bermudans for the few available properties.

The buyers tend to be rich and famous. The mayor of New York City, Michael Bloomberg and David Bowie own homes on the island, while Silvio Berlusconi, the Italian prime minister and Ross Perot, the erstwhile U.S. presidential candidate, are neighbors. International celebrities can pass almost unnoticed on the island, a luxury they don't have on the streets of Manhattan or London.

Canadians currently have a special interest in buying on the island because Canadian tax laws make living abroad particularly attractive. The Immigration Department reports that citizens of more than 80 different countries work on the island, with the U.K. providing the most, followed by Canada, Portugal, the U.S., the Philippines, and workers from the Caribbean. In 1999, there were 8,100 work permit holders on the island, a large number out of so small a population. Employers must apply to the Department of Immigration when they want to hire a non-Bermudian, showing proof that no suitably qualified islander is available.

Such extensive worldwide finance and insurance activity requires a highly sophisticated banking system. Bermuda provides this with up-to-date services and fiber optic connections to the outside world. The three local banks clear over US$3 billion daily.

Bermuda's three banks follow very conservative, risk-averse policies. They hold an average of 85% of customer liabilities in cash and cash equivalents. For example, the Bermuda Commercial Bank recently had a weighted "risk-asset ratio" of 32%. Eight percent is the minimum required by Basle International Banking Agreement standards. Butterfield Bank (founded in 1859) also has offices in all of those havens, except the Caymans. The Bank of Bermuda, founded in 1889, has assets exceeding US$5 billion and offices in George Town, the Cayman Islands, Guernsey, Hong Kong, the Isle of Man, Luxembourg, and an affiliate in New York City.

In 2004 the island was stirred by a short debate on whether the global banking giant, HSBC, should be permitted to acquire control of the Bank of Bermuda. The question was answered when stockholders overwhelmingly approved the merger.

The Bermudian dollar circulates on par with the U.S. dollar. U.S. currency is accepted everywhere. There are no exchange controls on foreigners or on exempt companies, which operate freely in any currency except the Bermudian dollar.

Unlike the Cayman Islands or The Bahamas, Bermuda has no bank secrecy laws officially protecting privacy, but bank and government policy make it difficult to obtain information in most cases. To do so requires a lengthy judicial process. Bermuda now has in place a Tax Information Exchange Agreement (TIEA) with the U.S. that allows for exchange of financial and tax information with the IRS upon formal request. Bermuda does have strict anti-drug and general money laundering laws. On a comparative 1-to-10 international bank privacy scale, Bermuda ranks about five.

Of interest to U.S. expatriates, Bermuda residents have visa-free entry into the United States.

If you are interested in residency on Bermuda, we recommend contacting attorney: Gordon L. Hill, QC, Cox, Hallet & Wilkenson, Milner House, 18 Parliament Street, P.O. Box HM 1561, Hamilton HM FX, Bermuda; Tel: (441) 295-4630; Fax: (441) 292-7880; E-mail: cw@cw.bm. Or contact Henley & Partner, Inc., Haus zum Engel, Kirchgasse 24 8001 Zurich, Switzerland. Tel: +41 1 267 60 90 Fax: +41 1 267 60 91 E-mail: zurich-office@henleyglobal.com

Contacts

Henley and Partners Carribean, PO Box 481, 3 Church Street, Basseterre, St. Kitts, West Indies, Tel: +1 869 465 1711 Fax: +1 869 465 1711 Contact Mr. Vernon S. Veira vernon.veira@henleyglobal.com

U.S. citizens entering Bermuda must present a U.S. passport or a certified U.S. birth certificate, and photo identification. The Consulate strongly recommends that visitors travel with a valid passport at all times. A U.S. driver's license or a voter registration card is not sufficient for entry into Bermuda. For additional information on entry requirements, travelers may contact the British Consulate in New York, Tel: (212) 745-0273/3206/0281, or the British consulate in Atlanta, Boston, Chicago, Dallas, Los Angeles, New York or San Francisco; Web site: http://www.britain-info.org or http://www. immigration.gov.bm. For additional entry requirements, contact Bermuda Department of Tourism, 310 Madison Avenue, Suite 201, New York, N.Y., telephone (212) 818-9800, or via the Internet at http://www.bermudatourism.com.

United States: In Bermuda, the U.S. Consulate General is located at Crown Hill, 16 Middle Road, Devonshire DV03, telephone 1-441-295-1342, where they may also obtain updated information on travel and security in Bermuda. Office hours for American Citizens Services are 1:30-3:30 Monday-Wednesday and 8:30-10:30 on Thursdays, except Bermudian and U.S. holidays. American citizens in need of after-hours emergency assistance may call the duty officer at telephone 1-441-235-3828.

United Kingdom: In Bermuda, Government House is located in Hamilton; Tel: (441) 292-3600, (441) 292-2587 Deputy Governor; Fax: (441) 295 3823; E-mail: depgov@ibl.bm.

Republic of Costa Rica

CAPITAL:	SAN JOSÉ
POPULATION:	3,896,092
LANGUAGE:	SPANISH (OFFICIAL), ENGLISH
CURRENCY:	COSTA RICAN COLÓN (C)
AREA:	51,100 SQUARE KM
ETHNIC GROUPS:	WHITE (INCLUDING MESTIZO) 94%, BLACK 3%, AMERINDIAN 1%, CHINESE 1%, OTHER 1%
RELIGION:	ROMAN CATHOLIC 76.3%, EVANGELICAL 13.7%, JEHOVAH'S WITNESSES 1.3%, OTHER PROTESTANT 0.7%, OTHER 4.8%, NONE 3.2%

PASSPORT HIGHLIGHTS: Retirees with fixed incomes of over US$600 per month and others with fixed monthly incomes of more than US$1,000 may qualify for residency status in Costa Rica. There is also a program granting residency in return for substantial investments in approved, key forest or other types of development projects. Naturalization as a Costa Rican national is available after seven years' residency.

Located between Nicaragua to the north and Panama to the south, Costa Rica straddles Central America, bordered by the Caribbean Sea on the east and the Pacific Ocean on the west.

It has been called "The Switzerland of the Americas" because of its impressive terrain marked by a rugged, mountainous interior. The highest peak in the region is Chirripo Grande, rising to 3,800 meters. Not far north of the Equator, the nation enjoys a lush, tropical climate, low cost of living, low taxes, high-quality medical care, educated citizens, as well as highly developed agricultural and tourist industries. In 1502, Columbus made a landfall in this area and gave it the name "Costa Rica" which means "Rich Coast."

Perhaps nowhere in the Western Hemisphere is the tension between conservation of natural assets and the drive for development so readily apparent as in Costa Rica. The Ticos, as the inhabitants call themselves, take great pride in the extensive marine and beach environments, lowland and highland forests, and cultural attractions their country offers. Acutely conscious of the stress that tourists, retirees, and industrialists put on Costa Rica's delicate natural and human resources, the government has instituted guidelines for "sustainable tourism" aimed at minimizing visitors' impact on the country's parks and resort areas.

The nation has a strong democratic tradition. Costa Rica declared its independence from Spain in 1821. After a turbulent beginning, it inaugurated an era of peaceful democracy in 1889, interrupted only twice, by a dictatorial interlude in 1917-19 and an armed uprising in 1948.

Increasing the role of the private sector while maintaining the government's social safety net, and keeping under control the budget deficit, unemployment, and inflation are important current issues. In the 1990s, unemployment has been high, and despite subsidies to coffee and banana growers, the two basic industries, the economy has been at a virtual standstill.

Costa Rica is still considered one of the more stable democracies in Latin America. It has a high literacy rate (95%) and a good health care system. The cost of living there is reasonably low and with about US$1,000 a month an individual could live an expatriate lifestyle in a modern studio apartment, complete with a swimming pool.

Crime Problems

The U.S. State Department has issued periodic warnings about crime in Costa Rica. Tourists as well as the local populace have been frequent victims. Most crimes are non-violent, including pickpocketing, house burglaries, and car break-ins, but violence does occur. Travelers are warned to purchase theft insurance when renting vehicles, to never leave valuables in a vehicle, and to park in paid lots whenever possible. Criminals have reportedly used skeleton keys to break into cars, particularly rental cars. Car jackings have occurred, with motorists confronted at gunpoint while stopped at traffic lights or upon arrival at their homes. There have been several kidnappings, including those of foreigners, in recent years.

Incidents of crime commonly occur in downtown San José, at beaches, the airport, and at national parks and other tourist attractions. There have been assaults on tourist buses in recent years. Travelers who stay in a group, keep valuables out of sight, do not wear jewelry, and travel during daylight hours lessen their risk. Local law enforcement agencies have limited capabilities. People offering money exchange on the street pass off counterfeit U.S. dollars and local currency. Credit card fraud is also growing.

Passport Problems

In recent years, Costa Rica has been plagued with scandals involving "honorary" consular and diplomatic appointments. Authorities also broke up a criminal group, including a former director of Immigration and Security that was selling visas. It was also discovered that "humanitarian and cultural visas" were granted to expatriate Cubans in return for cash payments of US$5,000 - $7,000. The illegal sale of passports appears to be a continuing problem. For these reasons, carrying a Costa Rican passport can subject a person to close scrutiny at border points, resulting in delays and questioning.

Permanent Residence and Citizenship

Costa Rica has a checkered history of official programs for foreign persons wishing to become citizens. A repealed law offered citizenship for non-nationals who purchased both a home in Costa Rica and a US$30,000 government bond. Only after five years did a permanent resident qualify for citizenship and a passport that was renewable and allowed visa-free travel to most countries. Because the nation then had few extradition treaties, several wealthy U.S. fugitives took advantage of the program, became permanent residents and lived openly in the country. Under U.S. pressure, the program was eventually closed down.

Now, another residence program is in place that requires no up-front investment. Instead, the foreign applicant must guarantee to bring a certain amount of hard currency into the country each month to be exchanged for the colón at the official rate.

The program recognizes two categories, *pensionados* (retired persons) and *rentistas* (recipients of passive income). *Pensionados* must import at least US$600 per month from an established pension source for a term of at least five years. *Rentistas* must get at least US$1,000 per month for five years, generally, from a guaranteed source such as certificates of deposit at a recognized bank. All applicants must stay in the country for at least four months or 120 days annually, but this need not be continuous.

All applicants receive the same rights and privileges. They can reside in Costa Rica and are not taxed on foreign source income. They are not allowed to work in the country, but can conduct business there for the purpose of receiving dividends rather than a salary. Local income is subject to a 17% flat tax. Imported motor vehicles are hit with a whopping duty of 100%, with household goods subject to duties from 25-100%.

A spouse and dependants can be included on a single application, and after seven years residence, you qualify for nationality. The Costa Rican Association of *Pensionados* and *Rentistas* says that two people who own a house can live quite comfortably here on US$1,000 a month.

In the past, Costa Rica did not allow dual nationality and required surrender of other passports upon naturalization. In 1995, the right to hold dual nationality was recognized in law.

Environmental Citizenship

The government has launched an unusual residence program for foreigners willing to invest in reforestation projects qualified under Costa Rica's environmental law No. 7575. Individuals who invest in Forestales Alegría, S.A. (Melina Farm) can qualify for Investor Residency Status, similar to a U.S. green card, which allows permanent residence and most rights and privileges of citizenship. Investors receive registered title to a designated parcel of land, a return on investment and tax-free income. This program stems from the government's strong environmental policies that have made the nation a leader in forestry conservation. Over 90% of remaining forests are protected and the nation has the world's largest percentage of land dedicated to national parks.

Under this program, a person must live in Costa Rica only four months a year to maintain residency status, but persons who wish to live permanently in Costa Rica, either for retirement or business can do so. They are granted title to and management of one hectare (2.47 acres) of mature farmed trees, their own local corporation, a return on investment, legal services, tax advantages, and assistance in getting settled. Full information about this project is available on the Internet at http://www.melina.co.cr. E-mail inquiries can be sent to: info@ melina.co.cr.

Be cautious about your inquiries into this program. We have heard numerous stories of difficulties with the Melina Farm Project. One American investor, who has 20 years personal experience in Costa Rican forestry projects, says that the Melina Farm's one-hectare plots are too small to produce income from tree harvesting that would pay off the US$115,000 investment. He also says it is extremely difficult to obtain logging permits. Permits often cost several thousand dollars with no guarantee they will be issued, and the process can take many months. "In my experience," he advises, "an individual owner with just a few trees on a one-hectare lot doesn't stand a chance against the Costa Rican bureaucrats."

In the years since the inauguration of the Melina Farm program, the government has expanded its granting of residence permits in recognition of approved development investments from abroad. In general, an investment of US$100,000 in reforestation projects, US$50,000 in tourism or export development, or US$200,000 in other types of activity will allow the investor to live in Costa Rica with his or her family.

Land Investment Cautions

Notwithstanding this new program, foreign investors should exercise extreme caution before investing in real estate. Costa Rica has a long history of investment and real estate scams and frauds perpetrated against foreign visitors. U.S.-style land title insurance is generally unavailable and there have been numerous instances of duly registered properties reverting to previously unknown owners who possess clear title and parallel registration. Due to irregular enforcement of property rights, existence of unresolved expropriation claims, and squatter invasions, property protections are uncertain, particularly in rural areas.

Some U.S. citizen landowners have long-standing expropriation disputes with the Government of Costa Rica. Claims from the 1970s to the present day remain unresolved, with the landowners uncompensated. Existing unenforced government expropriation decrees cloud land titles even when owners remain in possession.

Organized squatter groups against which the government has been reluctant to act have invaded real estate throughout the country. These groups, often supported by politicians and their political organizations, take advantage of legal reforms allowing people without land to claim title to unused agricultural property. This is common in rural areas, where local courts show considerable sympathy for squatters. The squatters regularly resort to threats and actual violence and often are able to block U.S. citizen landowners from entering their property. In November 1997, a U.S. citizen was killed in a confrontation with squatters in the southern region of Pavones.

Contacts

Henley and Partners Carribean, PO Box 481, 3 Church Street, Basseterre, St. Kitts, West Indies, Tel: +1 869 465 1711 Fax: +1 869

465 1711 Contact Mr. Vernon S. Veira vernon.veira@henleyglobal.com

United States: A valid passport is required to enter Costa Rica. At the discretion of Costa Rican authorities, travelers 17 years of age or older are sometimes admitted with a certified copy of their U.S. birth certificate and valid photo ID for tourist stays up to 90 days. U.S. citizens under the age of 17 are not admitted without a valid passport. Information may be obtained from the Consular Section of the Embassy of Costa Rica at 2114 S Street, NW, Washington, D.C. 20008; Tel: (202) 234-2945/46, Fax: (202) 265-4795 or from a Costa Rican Consulate in Atlanta, Chicago, Denver, Honolulu, Houston, Las Vegas, Los Angeles, Miami, New Orleans, New York, St. Paul, San Diego, or San Francisco. The Costa Rican Embassy maintains a web site: http://www.costarica.com/embassy.org/

The U.S. Embassy maintains a web site at http://sanjose.usembassy.gov/ Americans visiting Costa Rica are encouraged to inform the Embassy of their itineraries and contact information via the web site. This can also be accessed through the Department of State's web site at http://www.state.gov. The U.S. Embassy in Costa Rica is located in Pavas, San Jose, Tel: (506) 220-3050/3939; the extension for American Citizen Services is 2453. The Embassy is open Monday through Friday, and closed on Costa Rican and U.S. holidays. For emergencies arising outside normal business hours, U.S. citizens may call Tel: (506) 220-3127 and ask for the duty officer.

United Kingdom: The British Embassy in Costa Rica is located at Apartado 815, Edificio Centro Colóon, 11th Floor, Sane José 1007; Tel: (506) 258 2025; Fax: (506) 233 9938; E-mail: britemb@racsa.co.cr.

Dominican Republic

CAPITAL:	SANTO DOMINGO
POPULATION:	8,715,602
LANGUAGE:	SPANISH
CURRENCY:	DOMINICAN PESO ($RD)
AREA:	48.3 SQUARE KM
ETHNIC GROUPS:	WHITE 16%, BLACK 11%, MIXED 73%
RELIGION:	ROMAN CATHOLIC 95%

PASSPORT HIGHLIGHTS: Although "instant citizenship" in the Dominican Republic is a thing of the past, residency requirements for obtaining citizenship are among the most lenient in the world. As noted below, however, the desirability of obtaining a second passport from the Dominican Republic without actually establishing domicile there is questionable.

A Word of Caution

When it comes to acquiring second passports, the problem with the Dominican Republic is its decidedly bad reputation.

Unless you make it your residence and live there, we do not recommend that anyone acquire Dominican Republic citizenship, not even legally. In 1999, a Russian national was arrested at London's Heathrow International Airport with a suitcase full of Dominican Republic passports. In recent years, there have been several similar scandals in which people with government connections apparently sold quantities of DR passports. Although the stolen passports involved were official, the fact that they were being sold on the black market called into question everyone traveling on DR passports. The customs and immigration services of every major nation knew this and acted accordingly, much to the chagrin of the legal DR passport holders.

By some estimates, almost 10,000 passports were sold illegally, for as little as US$5,000 and for as much as US$18,000. The sellers claimed that the passports were valid for six years with automatic renewal at any DR Consulate. Needless to say, they were not renewed.

At the present time, there is no "instant" DR passport program available, regardless of what you may be told. Yet, one continues to see numerous advertisements in international publications promising quick "official" DR passports, always at inflated prices.

There are too many legitimate second passport possibilities without having to chance it with a DR passport. Stay away unless you make your second home or business there.

About the Dominican Republic

The Dominican Republic is the second largest nation in the Caribbean, with a population of over 8 million descended from Spanish settlers and their African slaves. Two million live in the greater Santo Domingo capital area. There are an estimated one million expatriate Dominicans in the U.S., with which the DR has close economic ties and trade.

The DR's tropical latitude gives it a moderate year-round climate and its extensive beaches make it a popular tourist destination. Santo Domingo is accessible by air from New York (three hours), Miami (under two hours), and San Juan (45 minutes). The terrain is varied and includes Lake Enriquillo, the lowest point in the Caribbean, and Pico Duarte, the highest. Watershed areas contain many rivers and streams, and the economy traditionally has been agricultural. Mining of silver, gold, nickel, and bauxite is also significant.

Historically, the Dominican Republic, the eastern two-thirds of the island of Hispaniola, was the seat of the original capital of the Spanish New World. The French ruled Haiti as a colony on the western third of the island where a successful slave revolt in 1804 brought independence. Control of the island was divided between Haitians and the Spanish until 1916, when U.S. troops occupied it for eight years to ensure debts were paid to U.S. and European banks. In 1930, dictator Rafael Trujillo gained power in the DR, ruling until his assassination in 1961. In 1965, the U.S. Marines were sent in to end civil war and democracy was introduced. Quadrennial elections produced repeated re-election of the corrupt, aging Joaquin Balaguer until 1996. In that year a reform president, Leonel Fernandez Reyna, a U.S.-educated attorney and former resident of New York City, was elected. Since then regular democratic elections have been held without incident.

The 1966 Constitution guarantees free enterprise and individual freedoms. The legal system is much like that of Napoleonic Code civil law countries and Dominican courts apply French judicial precedents.

The Dominican economy has undergone reform in the 1990s. Tourism and business-free zones are bright spots. There are 1.5 million foreign visitors annually occupying 32,000 (and growing) hotel rooms, leading all Caribbean countries. Tourism accounts for 17% of the GNP and provides 50% of the DR's hard currency. Industrial-free zones allow duty-free passage of raw materials and finished products, employing over 164,000. These free zones are for exports, mostly to the U.S., and over 250 companies now operate in free zone industrial parks, with major textile and electronics segments. The special free zones allow owners to operate a business free from corporate income tax for up to 20 years. Offshore business based here is also tax-free for its foreign earnings. In 2004 the failure of a major bank, linked to government corruption, caused a serious downturn in the national economy.

Transportation and communication infrastructure is extensive, with two major international airports and a good domestic highway system. Telecommunications are good and the DR is part of the U.S. direct-dialing phone network. The phone company is owned by GTE and service is excellent. The greatest handicap to economic activity has been the serious shortfall in electricity generation.

Visas

DR visas is of several kinds: diplomatic, official, courtesy, business, tourist, residency, or student. Applications for business or tourist visas can be made at any Dominican Consulate. Most tourists can enter without a visa for a period of 90 days if they have a valid passport. Consular fees are charged on business, dependant, tourism, residency, and student visas. The Ministry of Foreign Affairs can revoke visas without prior notice. Residency visas require a great deal more documentation and must be submitted at the Dominican Consulate nearest the applicant's actual residence. If a residency visa is granted, the recipient must arrive in the DR within 60 days, then apply to the Immigration Department for a provisional residency card, which is valid for one year and renewable annually.

Citizenship

Although "instant" DR passports are definitely no longer a legal possibility, legal citizenship is available. (From time to time reports of the illegal sale of citizenship surfaces). Dual citizenship is permitted.

To qualify for naturalization, one of the following conditions must be satisfied: 1) authorization from the Chief Executive to establish and maintain a DR domicile for not less than six months; 2) continuous DR residency for at least two years; 3) continuous DR residency for at least six months and either having founded/currently operating a DR business or owning real estate; 4) continuous residency for at least six months and marriage to a Dominican at the time application is submitted; 5) authorization from the Chief Executive to establish domicile, and, within three months, owning at least 30 hectares of land under cultivation; or 6) continuous residency for six months and having performed technical or special services for the armed forces.

A spouse need not fulfill residency requirements for naturalization if applications are made jointly. Children over the age of 18 may obtain citizenship after one year of residency if the application is made jointly with the mother. The naturalization process takes between 12 and 18 months to complete.

All DR residents are subject to income tax on global income and residents' estates, excluding real estate located abroad which is not subject to DR inheritance tax. Above US$4,800, the income tax rate is applied progressively. Those with a net income in excess of US$12,000 are taxed at a rate of 25%. For corporations, foreign or domestic, and for dividends, a single rate of 30% is taken for income tax.

Contacts

Henley and Partners Carribean, PO Box 481, 3 Church Street, Basseterre, St. Kitts, West Indies, Tel: +1 869 465 1711 Fax: +1 869 465 1711 Contact Mr. Vernon S. Veira vernon.veira@henleyglobal.com

United States: Diplomatic representation in the U.S.: Embassy of the Dominican Republic, 1715 22nd St. N.W., Washington, D.C. 20008, tel. (202) 332-6280. There are also Dominican consulates in, Miami, New Orleans, New York, Chicago, and San Juan. Travelers may obtain further information via the Internet at http://www.domrep.org.

The Consular Section of the U.S. Embassy is located at the corner of Calle Cesar Nicolas Penson and Avenida Maximo Gomez. The American Citizens Services Unit can be reached by Tel: (809) 731-4294, or on the Internet at http://www.usemb.gov.do/Consular/ACS/acsindex.htm. Consular office hours are 7:30 a.m. to 12:00 p.m. and 1:00 p.m. to 2:00 p.m., Monday through Friday, except U.S. and Dominican holidays. The Chancery of the U.S. Embassy is located a half-mile away from the Consular Section, at the corner of Calle Cesar Nicolas Penson and Calle Leopoldo Navarro in Santo Domingo. The telephone numbers are: (809) 221-2171; after hours (809) 221-8100. There is a Consular Agency in the north coast city of Puerto Plata at

Calle Beller 51, 2nd floor, office 6, Tel: (809) 586-4204; office hours are 9:00 a.m. to 12:00 p.m., and 2:30 p.m. to 5:00 p.m., Monday through Friday, except holidays. The consular agency has a secondary office in Sosua, also on the north coast. That office may be reached at: "Sea Horse Ranch Project" Administrative Office, Carretera Sosua - Cabarete, Sosua, D.R., Tel: (809) 571-3880, Fax (809) 571-2374.

United Kingdom: The British Embassy is located at Ave 27 de Fabrero No. 233, Edificio Corominas Pepin, Santo Domingo; Tel: (809) 472 7111 Embassy, (809) 472-7905 Commercial, (809) 472 7671/ 7373 Consular, (809) 399 7599 Emergencies outside office hours (mobile), Fax: (809) 472 7190, (809) 472-7574 Chancery; E-mail: brit.emb.sadom@codetel.net.do. The British Consulate is located at Calle Beller 51, Puerto Plata, RD; Tel: (809) 586-4244, (809) 586 8464; Fax: (809) 586-3096.

Republic of Guatemala

CAPITAL:	GUATEMALA CITY
POPULATION:	13,909,384
LANGUAGE:	SPANISH 60%, AMERINDIAN 40% (23 OFFICIALLY RECOGNIZED AMERINDIAN DIALECTS)
CURRENCY:	QUETZAL (Q)
AREA:	108,000 SQUARE KM
ETHNIC GROUPS:	MESTIZO 55%, AMERINDIAN OR PREDOMINANTLY AMERINDIAN APPROXIMATELY 43%, WHITES AND OTHERS 2%
RELIGION:	ROMAN CATHOLIC, PROTESTANT, TRADITIONAL MAYAN

PASSPORT HIGHLIGHTS: The Guatemalan government is willing to receive immigrants as new citizens if they "contribute to the country." Naturalization can normally be obtained by those who establish a two-year residency in Guatemala.

Guatemala is one of the Central American Republics with two coastlines, on the west, the Pacific Ocean, and on the east, the Caribbean Sea. Its northern border is with Mexico and to the east is Belize. Honduras and El Salvador border it to the south.

There are indications that ancient peoples existed here as long ago as 1500 B.C. But, by 1520 AD, and the arrival of the Spanish, these civilizations had largely disappeared and Guatemala became the center of Spanish rule in Central America. In 1821, Guatemala achieved independence from Spain. After suffering under dictators for a century, Guatemala became a democracy in 1944. Its history since then, marked by civil war, communist and leftist guerilla insurgency, has been turbulent, to say the least.

Still rebuilding from the last episode of civil strife, Guatemala poses challenges for those traveling outside the major urban or resort areas. Lush tropical forests, mountain lakes, and major Mayan ruins attract visitors from around the world. However, infrastructure is poor throughout most of the country, and crime against foreigners is a major problem in most rural areas.

The agricultural sector accounts for one-fourth of GDP and two-thirds of exports, employing more than half of the labor force. Coffee, sugar, and bananas are the main products. Manufacturing and construction account for one-fifth of the GDP. Since 1996, the government implemented a program of economic liberalization and political modernization. The signing of the peace accords in December 1996, which ended 36 years of civil war, removed a major obstacle to foreign investment.

Contributors Welcome

Guatemala does not officially market and sell citizenship, but the government is willing to receive immigrants as new citizens if they "contribute to the country." For those interested, this requires a personal visit to Guatemala and obtaining two responsible local sponsors to vouch for an applicant's character and good standing. Naturalization can be obtained by those who establish a two-year residence in Guatemala. With the right local connections, this waiting period can be reduced or waived. As in many Latin American nations, the sale of official passports is certainly not unknown in Guatemala.

A Guatemalan passport is good for travel to most countries in Europe without a visa, and dual citizenship here is common. Most upper-class Guatemalans hold U.S. and Spanish passports. Spain gives special consideration to Guatemalans, who by treaty need only two years of residence in Spain to acquire Spanish citizenship or vice-versa. (See the chapter on Spain for details).

Upon a grant of citizenship, a person receives a passport valid for five years, a national ID card, a driver's license and a naturalization certificate. Name changes to make a foreign name sound more like that of a Guatemalan national are not uncommon. Guatemala does not inform a new citizen's home country about the naturalization event.

Contacts

Henley and Partners Carribean, PO Box 481, 3 Church Street, Basseterre, St. Kitts, West Indies, Tel: +1 869 465 1711 Fax: +1 869 465 1711 Contact Mr. Vernon S. Veira vernon.veira@henleyglobal.com

United States: A valid U.S. passport is required to enter and depart Guatemala, but U.S. citizens do not need a visa for a stay of 90 days or less, a period that can be extended upon application. An exit tax equivalent to US$30 must be paid, in either U.S. dollars or Guatemalan quetzals when departing Guatemala.

The Guatemalan Embassy is located at 2220 R Street, NW, Washington, DC 20008; Tel: (202) 745-4952, extension 102; Fax (202) 745-1908; E-mail at info@guatemala-embassy.org Web site: http://www.guatemala-embassy.org or contact the nearest Guatemalan consulate (Chicago, Denver, Houston, Los Angeles, Miami, New York, or San Francisco).

U.S. Embassy in Guatemala City is open from 8:00 a.m. - 12:00 noon and 1:00 - 3:00 p.m. weekdays, excluding U.S. and Guatemalan holidays. The U.S. Embassy is located at Avenida la Reforma 7-01, Zone 10; Tel: (502) 331-1541 during business hours (8:00 a.m. - 5:00 p.m.) or (502) 331-8904 for emergencies during non-business hours; Fax: (502) 331-0564. Web site: http://usembassy.state.gov/guatemala.

United Kingdom: The British Emabassy in Guatemala is located at Avenida La Reforma y 16 Calle 0-55, Zona 10, Edificio Torre Internacional, Nivel 11, Guatemala City; Tel: (502) 367-5425,6,7,8,9; Fax (502 367-5430; E-mail: embassy@intelnett.com

Republic of Panama

CAPITAL:	PANAMA CITY
POPULATION:	2,960,784
LANGUAGE:	SPANISH (OFFICIAL), ENGLISH 14%; MANY PANAMANIANS ARE BILINGUAL
CURRENCY:	U.S. DOLLAR, BALBOA (PAB)
AREA:	78,200 SQUARE KM
ETHNIC GROUPS:	MESTIZO 70%, AMERINDIAN AND MIXED (WEST INDIAN) 14%, WHITE 10%, AMERINDIAN 6%
RELIGION:	ROMAN CATHOLIC 85%, PROTESTANT 15%

PASSPORT HIGHLIGHTS: Permanent residency in Panama (with naturalization possible after five years) is available to many classes of investors, retirees or pensioners with US$1,000 or more monthly income from outside the country.

When you think of Panama, you think of one of the great technical wonders of the world, the Panama Canal. Located in southern Central America, Panama is bordered by both the Caribbean Sea and the Pacific Ocean, situated with Colombia on the south and Costa Rica on the north. It holds a major world strategic position on the isthmus that forms the land bridge connecting North and South America, including the location of the Panama Canal linking the Atlantic Ocean via the Caribbean Sea with the Pacific Ocean.

Important in the days of the Spanish conquest, Panama gained independence from Spain in 1821 but then was incorporated into Colombia. In 1903, with the open connivance of U.S. President Theodore Roosevelt, Panama declared its independence and immediately gave the U.S. the concession to build the Panama Canal. Completed in 1915, the Canal became the focal point of the U.S.-Panama love-hate relationship for the rest of the century.

Along with the old millennium, 96 years of official United States presence in Panama officially ended at midnight, December 31, 1999. Panama finally had what its nationalistic politicians had demanded —

full control over its famous Canal.

Major World Center

The country is not so well-known for what it has become in the last 20 years. After Miami, it's Latin America's second largest international banking and business center, with ties to Asia, Europe, and a special relationship with the United States that's likely to continue.

Panama's economy is should grow at a brisk rate of about 6% in 2004, thanks mostly to growing U.S. demand for its exports, plus a boom in construction fueled by tax breaks the government offers for builders. Panama City is dotted with scores of new high rise condos and office buildings. South of Miami, it's the leading banking and financial center in South America with over 80 banks, many local branches of global banks such as HSBC, Barclays and Dresdener. Between 1955 and 2003, inflation averaged 2.4%, and, for the decade of the 1990's barely exceeded 1% per year. Annual inflation has averaged 1.7% for the past 30 years, lower than in the U.S.

Then, there is the wealth represented by the Panama Canal, generating more than US$900 million in tolls every year (most of which must be plowed back into constant maintenance), and the thousands of acres of land from former U.S. military installations, prized real estate with an estimated value of US$4 billion. As of this writing the government and the people have an historic decision to make: should Panama launch a multi-billion dollar canal expansion project to keep the waterway competitive? Expansion will cost untold billions and will require a national referendum.

A recent first-time American visitor to Panama City came back marveling at the modern skyscrapers, first-class hotels and restaurants, excellent Internet and other communications, and the thoroughly American ambiance. He reported on the availability of fabulously low priced buys on condos and other real estate, a byproduct of the official U.S. canal exodus. Downtown Panama City, the balmy, tropical capital on the southern, Pacific end of the Canal, suggests Los Angeles or Miami, except arguably more locals speak English here than in some parts of south Florida.

Panama is a renowned tourist destination, with attractions ranging from the Canal to natural parks in many different topographic zones offering some of the most fascinating "eco-tourism" in the Western Hemisphere. The country offers a wide variety of prospective places to settle or retire in, each seemingly more attractive than the last. From island chains on both the Caribbean and Pacific coasts to lush, temperate highland regions, the country offers a broad range of options as to scenery, climate, and level of development. As an example of the latter, advertisements for the increasingly popular Bocas del Toro islands off the north coast on the Caribbean side solicit financial aid for infrastructure improvements as well as offering plots of beach-front property.

Yes, Panama also has a long history of government corruption that continues to this day. This hasn't seemed to affect the largely unregulated banking sector, but bribery, cronyism, nepotism, and kick-backs in government dealings regularly make headlines here.

In 2004 Panamanians went to the polls in the first national election since the Panama Canal was returned to that nation by the United States at the end of 1999. The clear victor was Martin Torrijos, the son of the late dictator, Omar Torrijos, who died in 1981. The son admires the father, but has made clear he wants no dictatorship and is very much pro-business and free market in his policies and views. A Torrijos victory "should mean a considerable improvement in the outlook for policy in Panama, and a generally more pro-business stance by the government," Wall Street brokerage Morgan Stanley said at the time.

Big Banking

In many ways, the Republic of Panama is ideally suited for the offshore investor who wants strong financial privacy and no taxes, corporate or personal. Its proximity to the growing Latin market makes it a natural as a base for world business operations and, in spite of its history, it isn't directly under the thumb of either the U.S., or, like Bermuda and the Cayman Islands, that of the U.K.

The major players here are the multinational banks representing 30 countries. They hold 72% of a reported total US$72 billion in assets. Doing business primarily in the offshore market, foreign banks account for about 70% of all deposits that now exceed US$26 billion. Banking alone accounts for about 11% of the nation's gross domestic product. Nearly every major world bank has a full-service branch office in Panama.

Slow But Sure

Admittedly, it's taken time for the banking sector's reputation to recover from the aftermath of the brutal 1989 U.S. military invasion ordered by President George Bush. That left nearly every financial institution in Panama under suspicion of drug money activity. Under the direction of U.S. Drug Enforcement Agency and FBI agents, invading U.S. troops hauled away bank records alleged to show criminal conduct by the deposed president, Noriega, and his regime accused of major drug trafficking.

Since then, Panama's bankers have been anxious to reassert the sanctity of their banking secrecy laws. Only students of banking history realize that, along with Luxembourg and Liechtenstein, Panama adopted specific tax haven legislation as far back as the 1920s.

A central part of that long tax haven tradition has been statutory guarantees of financial privacy and confidentiality. Violators can suffer civil and criminal penalties for disclosure. There is no requirement to reveal beneficial trust or corporate ownership to Panamanian authorities and no required audit reports or financial statements. Bearer shares still are permitted. Panama has no double taxation agreements and no tax information exchange agreements (TIEA) with other countries. The United States has pressed for a TIEA but so far Panama has ignored these demands.

Offshore banking and IBCs were major revenue sources in the past. The economic health of Panama depends on financial facilities with safeguards sufficient to ensure legal compliance. However, to claim Panama has cleaned up its dirty money act would be too optimistic. In U.S. government circles, a bank account in Panama raises immediate suspicion about the account holder. But that's also true of accounts in Bermuda, the Cayman Islands, Nevis, the Channel Islands, and anywhere else in the world the IRS can't readily stick its official nose into private financial activity.

While "dollarization" is debated as a novel concept elsewhere in Latin America, since 1904 the U.S. dollar has been Panama's official paper currency. (The local equivalent is the balboa, and there are Panamanian coins that circulate along with U.S. coins).

Service by many international airlines, excellent communications, telephone, mail, and telex all make travel and living here first rate. Local laws and customs encourage free trade and there are minimal import or export duties, especially if the Colon Free Trade Zone is used. Ship registration is cheap and consequently, the growing Panamanian merchant marine of registered commercial ships is now second only to that of Liberia.

However suspect it may have been in the past, Panama is fast becoming one of the major financial crossroads of the world. Base your business there and you're connected everywhere.

Residence & Citizenship

Panamanian immigration policies favor both the wealthy and the moderately rich. Anyone who can meet the following criteria is welcome as a resident: employment with an international corporation in an executive capacity; a proven income of US$1,000 or more per month from foreign sources.

Permanent residency, followed by naturalization in five years, is available to foreigners opening a one-year CD with at least US$100,000 (plus US$5,000 for each dependant) in principal. Similarly, investors of at least US$40,000 in teak plantations or small businesses employing at least three Panamanians are eligible for permanent residency. Approved investments in agriculture (seven year minimum commitment) and free trade zones may also confer resident status on the investor.

As a foreigner, you may obtain the special status of "pensioner" if you can prove a steady and guaranteed income of at least US$1,000 a month. For this purpose, a deposit of US$12,000 must be made at the National Bank of Panama, which pays high monthly interest on a fixed five-year CD. The immigration authorities will approve permanent residency within 30 to 90 days and after a five-year residence, you are eligible for citizenship.

In order to make these arrangements, it is best to travel personally to Panama. Local agent's fees range from US$20,000 to $30,000, depending on the urgency and a client background. However, see the end of this section for contacts that provide much lower fees for legal services of this nature.

Foreign ownership of property is encouraged in the desirable resort areas, but is restricted within ten miles of national borders. Property ownership is not required before or after obtaining residence, citizenship, and a passport.

Passport Problems

The Government of Panama has a liberal history of appointing numerous honorary consuls. Anyone interested in Panamanian social life, as well as partial diplomatic immunity when traveling abroad, should make inquiries. The nearest Panamanian Consul is a good place to start. Nevertheless, be cautious.

In recent decades, Panama's immigration service has often been a corrupt cash machine peddling visas and passports. Secret documents from the regime of deposed dictator Manuel Noriega revealed a vast network of passport sales that brought a flood of refugees to Panama's shores from Cuba and Hong Kong. The going price was US$2,500 for entry visas and US$12,000 for passports. During the late 1980s, before the U.S. invasion, an estimated 30,000 Cubans, 11,000 Hong Kong Chinese, and 2,500 Libyans moved to Panama. Millions of dollars may have been paid to Noriega and his cronies for passport deals alone. Eight former immigration agency officials were prosecuted for corruption.

In spite of this unsavory history, a Panamanian passport now guarantees visa-free travel to most Spanish or English-speaking countries worldwide. The only annoying drawback is that traveling to the U.S. on a Panamanian passport may mean a search upon entry on the general supposition that all Panamanians may be drug dealers, money launderers, or currency

Contacts

U.S. citizens are encouraged to obtain a U.S. passport before traveling to Panama. Although entry into Panama is permitted with any proof of U.S. citizenship, such as a certified birth certificate or a naturalization certificate, and an official photo ID, such as a driver's license, there may be difficulties returning to the U.S. without a valid U.S. passport. Panamanian law requires that travelers must either purchase a tourist card from the airline serving Panama or obtain a visa from a Panamanian Embassy or Consulate before traveling to Panama.

United States: Embassy of Panama, 2862 McGill Terrace, NW, Washington, D.C. 20009, Tel: (202) 483-1407, Consulates are located in Atlanta, Chicago, Houston, Los Angeles, Miami, New Orleans, New York, Philadelphia or Tampa.

U.S. citizens living or visiting Panama are encouraged to register at the Consular Section of the U.S. Embassy in Panama and obtain updated information on travel and security within Panama. The Consular Section of the U.S. Embassy is located in Building 520, in the Clayton section of Panama City (formerly Fort Clayton). The international mailing address is Apartado 6959, Panama 5, Republic of Panama. The U.S. mailing address is U.S. Embassy Panama, Department of State, Washington, D.C. 20521-9100. The telephone number of the Embassy (Consular Section) is 011-507-207-7030 or 011-507-207-7000 (for after hour emergencies, 011-507-207-7200); Fax 011-507-207-7278; Web site: http://usembassy.state.gov/panama or E-mail: Panama-ACS@state.gov

United Kingdom: The British Embassy is located at Torre Swiss Bank, Calle 53 (Apartado 889) Zona 1, Panama City, Panama; Tel: (507) 269-0866; Fax: (507) 223-0730; E-mail: britemb@cwpanama.net

General Contacts

Trust companies:

Trust Services SA. PO Box 0832-1630 World Trade Centre, Panama, Republic of Panama. Edificio Balboa Plaza, Oficina 522, Avenida Balboa Panama, Repulic of Panama. Tel.: +(507) 269-2438 or +(507) 263-5252. Fax: +(507) 269-4922. E-mail: marketing@trustserv.com Link: www.trustserv.com Licensed in Panama since 1981, this respected firm specializes in offshore corporations and trust formation. Derek R. Sambrook, a member of the Sovereign Society Council of Experts, is director of the firm.

Attorneys:

Rainelda Mata-Kelly, P.O. Box 9012, Panama 6 (Bethania), Republic of Panama. Office Address: No. 414, 4th Floor, Balboa Plaza, Balboa Avenue, Panama 6, Republic of Panama. Tel.: +(507) 263-4305. Fax: +(507) 264-2868. E-mail: rmk@mata-kelly.com Link: www.mata-kelly.com Ms. Mata-Kelly specializes in Panamanian administrative, commercial and maritime law and assists clients with immigration, real estate, contracts, incorporation and other legal issues. She is a member of the Sovereign Society Council of Experts.

Panamanian residency & real estate:

Greg Geurin, c/o International Living (Panama), 17 Avenida Jose Gabriel Duque, La Cresta, Panama, Republic of Panama. Tel.: +(507) 264-2204. Mr. Guerin directs the operations of International Living in Panama and has excellent contacts in the Panamanian legal and real estate communities.

Henley & Partners, Panama office: Galindo, Arias and Lopez, Scotia Plaza,18 Ave. Federico Boyd & 51st St., Floors 9, 10, 11 - P.O. Box. 8629, Panama 5, Rep. of Panama. Telephone: (507) 263-5633 Facsimile: (507) 263-5335 E-mail: gala@gala.com.pa Web: http://www.henleyglobal.com/panama

On the Web:

List of Panamanian embassies and consulates. Link: www.embassyworld.com

General Information on Panama. Link: www.panamainfo.com/english/index.htm

Pensionados for retirees. Link: www.internationalliving.com/contadora/whypanama.html

Turks & Caicos Islands

CAPITAL:	GRAND TURK (COCKBURN TOWN)
POPULATION:	19,350
LANGUAGE:	ENGLISH
CURRENCY:	U.S. DOLLAR (US$)
AREA:	430 SQUARE KM
ETHNIC GROUPS:	BLACK 90%, MIXED, EUROPEAN, OR NORTH AMERICAN 10%
RELIGION:	BAPTIST 40%, METHODIST 16%, ANGLICAN 18%, CHURCH OF GOD 12%, OTHER 14%

PASSPORT HIGHLIGHTS: Under a program begun in 1996, investors in the Turks and Caicos are entitled to apply for and receive a Permanent Residency certificate, which costs US$50,000 for self-employed persons, US$30,000 for skilled workers, US$15,000 for retired persons, and US$8,000 for unskilled workers. Qualifying investments vary according to the status of the applicant and the location of the investment, but US$250,000 is the usual capital input required for start-ups or acquisitions on the main island of Providenciales (US$125,000 for investments in the other inhabited islands)..

The Turks and Caicos Islands are an archipelago of eight major, inhabited islands and numerous uninhabited cays. They lie in the Atlantic Ocean nearest to the larger island of Hispaniola (shared by Haiti and the Dominican Republic). The Islands are 575 miles southeast of Miami at the southern end of the Bahamas chain. The Turks and Caicos are called the "Isles of Perpetual June" because they enjoy a year-round comfortable climate cooled by trade winds, but with abundant sunshine. The islands are graced with 230 miles of sandy beaches, and are becoming a major stopover for eco-tourists, divers who have begun to discover some of the finest coral reefs and walls in the world. From the walls of Grand Turk, West Caicos and Providenciales's Northwest Point to the historic wrecks south of Salt Cay, a dozen world-class coral walls have become a magnet for serious scuba enthusiasts.

From late December through April, the entire Atlantic herd of 2,500 humpback whales pass on their annual migration to the Mouchoir bank, some 20 - 30 miles southeast of the islands. During this period divers can listen to an underwater concert of the whales' songs. In summer, divers can swim among manta rays cruising the faces of the walls. Encounters with dolphin are not uncommon.

In 1512, Europeans first visited these uninhabited islands but no settlement resulted. In the late 17th Century, British settlers from Bermuda came in search of salt. Gradually, over many years, the area also was settled by some U.S. planters and their slaves. With the local abolition of slavery in 1838, these planters left. Until 1848, the Islands were under the jurisdiction of the Bahamas. In 1873, they became a dependency of Jamaica and remained so until 1959. In 1962, Jamaica gained independence and the Turks and Caicos became a Crown colony. Since 1976, it has had local autonomy. In ensuing years, there has been a continuing political struggle between the islands on one hand and the colonial governors and the Foreign Office in London on the other. This was partially due to a strong pro-independence move-ment, but also because of alleged drug smuggling in the TCI. A low-keyed but persistent movement has been afoot for some years seeking to have Canada annex the Turks and Caicos. Despite having adherents in both jurisdictions, it appears not to have gained any serious momentum. The legal system is based upon English common law and the law of Wales, with some laws from Jamaica and The Bahamas.

The Turks and Caicos Islands are an English-speaking British over-seas territory that combines tax-free status, an idyllic climate, and close proximity to the United States. They enjoy freedom from income, corporate, and estate taxes. There are no exchange controls and the U.S. dollar is the country's legal tender. There is a wide range of financial and other professional services readily available.

The local economy is based on tourism, fishing, and offshore financial services. Most capital goods and food for domestic consump-tion are imported. The U.S. was the leading source of tourists, in 1996, accounting for more than half of the 87,000 visitors. Major sources of government revenue include fees from offshore financial activities and customs receipts. Most tourist facilities are located on Providenciales (Provo) and Grand Turk Islands.

If maximum financial privacy is important to you, keep in mind that the TCI are a British Overseas Territory and, ultimately, under the police and political control of the Government of the United

Kingdom.

Tax-Free Permanent Residency

TIn early 1996, the TCI Government coupled the Islands tax-free attraction with a statutory program granting qualified foreign citizens full-time residency. A TCI permanent residence certificate is valid for life and covers the family head, spouse, and dependent children. A one-time fee of $50,000 for self-employed persons, $30,000 for skilled workers, $15,000 for retired persons, or $8,000 for unskilled workers is charged for issuance.

The program does not confer full citizenship or a right to a TCI passport. It requires a US$250,000 investment in a development enterprise in the Island of Providenciales, or US$125,000 in the islands of Grand Turk, Salt Cay, South Caicos, Middle Caicos, or North Caicos. In return, the investor is granted a "Permanent Residence Certificate." Certain other foreign individuals may qualify by investing at least US$50,000 in government authorized investments. Aiming to stimulate the economies of the less developed islands, since 1996, the government has allowed up to 50 permanent residence certificates for family heads and dependants in return for a purchase of US$40,000 worth of shares in the Grand Turk-based airline, Sovereign TCI, Ltd., which operates as "Sovereign Air."

The following documents must be submitted with an application for TCI permanent residence: 1) four passport-style photographs of you and any dependants; 2) a medical certificate for each applicant and each dependant, dated no more than one month prior containing a negative HIV test; 3) a birth certificate for each person; 4) marriage and divorce certificates, where appropriate; 5) a copy of passports; 6) a bank reference showing good financial standing; 7) a certificate of no criminal convictions; 8) a character reference from an attorney/ solicitor or other professional; 9) a letter declaring the investor has sufficient means to support him/herself and any dependants and has obtained a local residence; and 10) the formal application for a permanent residence certificate. Other information may also be required.

A permanent residence certificate can be revoked but only in certain limited circumstances, such as conviction of serious crimes or an act of disloyalty to the British Crown.

Contacts

For permanent residence information: Henley & Partner AG, Kirchgasse 22 8001 Zurich, Switzerland. Tel: +41 44 266 22 22. Fax: +41 44 266 22 23 91. E-mail: zurich-office @henleyglobal.com Web site: http://www.henleyglobal.com

For tourist stays up to 30 days, U.S. citizens need a passport, naturalization certificate, or original certified birth certificate as well as photo identification, onward or return tickets, and sufficient funds for their stay. A $23 departure tax is required of all persons 12 years of age and older. In order to arrange for longer stays or obtain work permits in the Turks and Caicos, travelers should contact the Turks and Caicos Immigration Department at (649) 946-2939.

United States: For information regarding entry and customs requirements of the Turks and Caicos, U.S. citizens may contact the British Embassy, 3100 Massachusetts Avenue, N.W., Washington, D.C. 20008; Tel: (202) 462-1340; or the nearest British consulate in Atlanta, Boston, Chicago, Dallas, Los Angeles, New York or San Francisco. Web site: http://nsi.org/travel/british-west-indies.txt or http://www.britain-info.org. Travelers may also contact the Turks and Caicos Tourism Office at 11645 Biscayne Boulevard, Suite 302, Miami FL 33181; Tel: (305) 891-4117 or download information from the Turks and Caicos tourist board's web site: http://www.turksandcaicostourism.com.

There is no U.S. embassy, consulate or consular agency in the Turks and Caicos. U.S. citizens living in or visiting Turks and Caicos may wish to register at the Consular Section of the U.S. Embassy in Nassau, Bahamas, which has consular responsibilities over the territory. The Embassy is located next to the McDonald's Restaurant on Queen Street in downtown Nassau, and may be reached Monday-Friday at telephone (242) 322-1181; after-hours (242) 328-2206; fax (242) 356-7174. Office hours are from 9:00 a.m. to 12:00 noon Monday-Friday (except for U.S. and Bahamian holidays).

United Kingdom: Governor's Office, Waterloo, Grand Turk, Tel: (649) 946-2309, (649) 946-2702 Chief Secretary's Office; Fax: (649) 946-2903; E-mail: Governor_Office@gov.tc

U.S. Virgin Islands

CAPITAL:	CHARLOTTE AMALIE, ST. THOMAS ISLAND
POPULATION:	124,778
LANGUAGE:	ENGLISH (OFFICIAL), SPANISH, CREOLE
CURRENCY:	U.S. DOLLAR (US$)
AREA:	352 SQ KM
ETHNIC GROUPS:	BLACK 78%, WHITE 10%, OTHER 12% NOTE: WEST INDIAN 81% (49% BORN IN THE VIRGIN ISLANDS AND 32% BORN ELSEWHERE IN THE WEST INDIES), US MAINLAND 13%, PUERTO RICAN 4%, OTHER 2%
RELIGION:	BAPTIST 42%, ROMAN CATHOLIC 34%, EPISCOPALIAN 17%, OTHER 7%

PASSPORT HIGHLIGHTS: As a Territory of the United States, the U.S. Virgin Islands are subject to the same restrictive immigration laws as the mother country. Nonetheless, those already possessing U.S. permanent residency or citizenship may move freely to the U.S. Virgin Islands and benefit from the Islands' exemption from estate and gift taxes for residents, as well a tax holiday program for businesses established there.

The Virgin Islands of the United States, as their name is officially styled, constitutionally, are "an unincorporated territory" of the U.S. With the Caribbean Sea to the south and the Atlantic Ocean to the north, the Virgin Islands offer a variety of deep sea and coastal fishing. Their tropical climate and minimal industrial development assure an abundance of unspoiled reefs for divers and snorkelers, with sandy beaches ringing deep coves. The large number of isolated, secure anchorages in the U.S. Virgin Islands and the British Virgins just to the east has made the chain a cebter for yachting. A thriving charter-boat industry in the Virgin Islands draws tens of thousands of visitors annually for crewed or "bare-boat" sailing adventures.

After their discovery by Columbus in 1493, the islands passed through control by the Dutch, English, and French. In 1666, St.

Thomas was occupied by Denmark, which five years later founded a colony there to supply the mother country with sugar, cotton, indigo, and other products. By the early 17th Century, Danish influence and control were established and the islands became known as the Danish West Indies. That political status continued until Denmark sold the islands to the U.S. for US$25 million in 1917.

The islands — St. Croix, St. Thomas, and St. John — have a strategic value for the U.S. since they command the Anegada Passage from the Atlantic Ocean into the Caribbean Sea as well as the approach to the Panama Canal. U.S. citizenship status was conferred on the islands' inhabitants in 1927. Although they do not vote in U.S. presidential elections, residents are represented by a non-voting delegate in the U.S. House of Representatives.

A Low Tax Residence

The islands are administered by the U.S. Department of the Interior under the Basic Organic Act of 1954 and earlier statutes dating back to the Naval Service Appropriations Act of 1922 (48 USC 1397). The 1922 law provides, in part, that "the income tax laws in force in the United States shall be likewise in force in the Virgin Islands of the United States, except that the proceeds of such taxes shall be paid to the treasuries of said islands."

It is not widely known, but under a unique federal income tax arrangement applying only to the Virgin Islands, it is possible for U.S. nationals who make the islands their main residence to enjoy substantially reduced taxes compared to other Americans. This makes the islands an offshore tax haven option for wealthy U.S. citizen-entrepreneurs and for foreign nationals seeking U.S. citizenship.

Unlike all other U.S. taxpayers, islands' residents and corporations pay federal taxes on their worldwide income to the Virgin Islands Internal Revenue Bureau (IRB), not to the U.S. Internal Revenue Service. Legal residents of the islands, those who are born there, or those who become naturalized U.S. citizens in the V.I., for purposes of U.S. federal gift and estate taxes, are not treated as residents of the U.S. Since the V.I. levies no estate or gift taxes, this means that upon death, the estates of such persons owe zero federal/state estate or gift taxes.

Special Business Incentives

To attract investment, the Virgin Islands Industrial Development Commission grants generous tax relief in the form of a 90% exemption on corporate federal taxes on all worldwide income. This tax holiday package, usually offered for a period of 10 to 15 years, with a possible five-year extension, is available to V.I. chartered corporations, partnerships, and limited liability companies.

Here's an example of how valuable this tax break can be, using a V.I. corporation we'll call "Worldwide, Inc."

Worldwide, Inc. has a US$10 million international portfolio with a wide range of investments. Last year, Worldwide, Inc. did well and ended with net taxable income after all possible deductions of US$2 million.

U.S. mainland corporate tax computations based on US$2,000,000 taxable income:

15% x US$50,000 = US$7,500

25% x US$25,000-= US$6,250

34% x US$25,000-= US$8,500

37% x $1,900,000 = US$703,000-

Total tax liability without exemption = US$725,250

-90% V.I. Exemption = -US$675,000-

Worldwide income net taxes owed = US$50,250

If the principal shareholders of Worldwide, Inc. are V.I. residents, the V.I. tax laws allow each of them a 90% individual income tax exemption on income derived from corporate dividends.

If Worldwide, Inc. is a subchapter "S" corporation, owned by a single individual, the total income tax liability on US$2,000,000 at the maximum U.S. income tax rate would be US$79,200 (39.6% x 90% exemption). Because the V.I. imposes no territorial or local income taxes, the individual can keep US$1,920,800. In sharp contrast, if this investor was a U.S. mainland resident, he/she would owe the IRS US$792,000 in U.S. income taxes, plus any applicable state and local taxes which could amount to another US$200,000.

For the last 40 years, a few knowledgeable U.S. investors, with business activities ranging from petroleum production, aluminum processing, hotel and other tourism activities, banking, insurance, and other financial services have taken advantage of-these very liberal V.I. tax laws. In 1998, 68 V.I. corporations with over 3,500 employees enjoyed these tax benefits.

The V.I. Government recently established a new precedent by granting the 90% tax exemption to a financial management company.

The investing partners established a V.I. corporation to manage their worldwide assets. Each owner established bona fide V.I. residence by renting or buying a home or condominium, registering to vote in the V.I., and designating their stateside home as their secondary residence. The investors confirmed their new principal residence by canceling their stateside voter registration, their state and county homestead exemptions, and moving their business and personal affairs to the V.I.

There is no restriction against maintaining a second home elsewhere, either in or outside of the U.S., as long as a V.I. resident maintains a principal residence in the V.I. These fortunate people can live in a second home anywhere in the United States during spring, summer, and fall, then come home to the Virgin Islands for the winter, where they play golf, tennis, sail and swim, all under protection of the U.S. flag. In addition, they enjoy the unique and legal privilege of paying only 10% of what they would otherwise owe in federal income taxes.

Moving your residence to the V.I. is no more difficult then moving from one U.S. State to another. The V.I. has a well-developed infrastructure and judicial and legal system under the U.S. Constitution. The islands are served by the U.S. court system, postal service, currency, customs and immigrations laws. For any wealthy person considering U.S. naturalization, or any current U.S. citizen willing to relocate to a warmer climate to legally avoid burdensome taxes, this little known tax "loophole" certainly is worth exploring.

Contacts

Henley and Partners Carribean, PO Box 481, 3 Church Street, Basseterre, St. Kitts, West Indies, Tel: +1 869 465 1711 Fax: +1 869 465 1711 Contact Mr. Vernon S. Veira vernon.veira@henleyglobal.com

USVI Government Web site: www.usvi.net/usvi/tax.html

Attorneys:

Marjorie Rawls Roberts, PC, LLB, JD, AB, PO Box 8809, St. Thomas, U.S. Virgin Islands 00801, Tel: +1 340 776 7235 Fax: +1 340 776 7496, E-mail: jorieroberts@worldnet.att.net Web site: www.lawyers.com/ robertslaw

Denis Kleinfeld, JD, CPA, The Kleinfeld Law Firm, Suntrust International Building, One SE 3rd Avenue, Suite 1940, Miami, Florida 33131, Tel: (305) 375-9515, Fax: (305) 358-6541, E-mail: denis_ kleinfeld@kleinfeld.com

For residency information for foreign nationals contact: Henley & Partner AG, Haus zum Engel, Kirchgasse 24 8001 Zurich, Switzerland. Tel: +41 1 267 60 90. Fax: +41 1 267 60 91. E-mail: zurich-office@henleyglobal.com Website:http://www.henleyglobal.com

Section 3.
South America

PANAMA

VENEZUELA

COLOMBIA

GUYANA

SURINAME

FRENCH GUIANA

ECUADOR

PERU

BRAZIL

BOLIVIA

PARAGUAY

CHILE

ARGENTINA

URUGUAY

FALKLAND ISLANDS

Republic of Argentina

CAPITAL:	BUENOS AIRES
POPULATION:	38,740,807
LANGUAGE:	SPANISH (OFFICIAL), ENGLISH, ITALIAN, GERMAN, FRENCH
CURRENCY:	ARGENTINE PESO (ARS)
AREA:	2,766,890 SQ KM
ETHNIC GROUPS:	WHITE (MOSTLY SPANISH AND ITALIAN) 97%, MESTIZO, AMERINDIAN, OR OTHER NONWHITE GROUPS 3%
RELIGION:	ROMAN CATHOLIC 92%, PROTESTANT 2%, JEWISH 2%, OTHER 4%

PASSPORT HIGHLIGHTS: Two years after admission as an immigrant, not all of which need be spent in the country, residents of Argentina may receive naturalization. Dual nationality is allowed.

The Argentine Republic is the second largest country in Latin America and occupies most of the southern part of the continent. Five countries form its borders; Chile to the east, Bolivia and Paraguay to the north, Brazil and Uruguay to the northeast. The Rio Colorado flows east and divides the country in two. Argentina is home to a wide variety of terrain, including jungle, pampas, infertile plain, and South America's highest mountain, Mount Aconcagua.

Like most South American countries, Argentina is a former Spanish colony. It declared its independence from Spain in 1816 and became a republic in 1852. During the 20th Century, the nation's political course has veered from military dictatorship to fledgling democracy, and full development of its enormous economic potential has suffered as a result.

Part of the Spanish Empire until independence in 1816, Argentina subsequently experienced many periods of internal political conflict between conservatives and leftists and between civilian and military factions. Thanks to rich natural resources and foreign investment, a modern agriculture, and a diversified industry were gradually developed. After World War II, a long period of dictatorship under Juan Perón and his Peronista Party was followed by military junta rule. Since 1983, Argentina has had a democratically -elected president as head of government.

Argentina is a cosmopolitan country with a population of 33 million, many of Spanish, German, Italian, and English descent. Buenos Aires, the capital, is one of the largest cities in the world with a population of 11 million. Its elegant architecture and broad avenues justify its local nickname, the "Paris of the New World." Fun-loving and generous, the Porteños – the capital's residents – describe themselves as "Italians who speak Spanish and pretend to live like English lords." The dramatic, sensuous tango developed among Buenos Aires' working classes and has come to symbolize city's life, alternately vibrant and tragic. Elsewhere in Argentina, visitors enjoy excellent hunting and fishing, pleasant beaches, outstanding ski resorts, huge ranches where the old Gaucho traditions linger, and eco-tourism in the Paraná-Iguazú Falls region, the Andes, Patagonia, and Tierra del Fuego.

The country is one of the more highly developed countries in the Western Hemisphere. Its people are among the most educated in South America, with a literacy rate of 90%. Its economy has gradually shifted from an exclusive dependence on large-scale livestock and agriculture production to one in which service and industrial sectors are dominant. Since the 1950s, it has been one of the 20 largest trading countries in the world. However, until recently, economic growth has been hampered by excessive inflation. The nation had one of the highest Latin American standards of living at the turn of the century, and it is anxious to regain its past glory. An economic recession precipitated by Argentina's default on International Monetary Fund and private debt obligations in 2000-2001 has led to high unemployment and sporadic civil disorders. At the same time, kidnapping, robbery, and other crimes against persons and property have surged dramatically, requiring travelers there to exercise caution.

Residence and Citizenship

Argentina accepts up to 100,000 immigrants a year, with particular interest in trained professionals. Residence can be arranged by submission of a birth certificate, police certificate of good conduct or lack of criminal record, and a marriage certificate, if applicable. Proof of adequate education and/or work experience are also required. People of independent means or the self-employed are favored, and those with firm business proposals may receive a reduced residency requirement.

Exact guidelines applicable to foreign nationals seeking residence are unclear, which is not unusual in Latin America, and decisions are made on a case-by-case basis. Two years of bona fide residence is required for naturalization, but not all that time need be in the country. An Argentinean passport is valid for five years. As a travel document, the Argentinean passport allows visa-free travel to over 100 countries, including most of Europe and nearly all of South and Central America. The Argentinean passport is also the first in South America that entitles its holder to visa-free entry into the U.S. Argentineans also qualify for a reduced residence period when seeking Spanish nationality.

Argentinean law recognizes dual nationality. Dual citizens, who are also considered to be citizens of Argentina and who remain in Argentina for more than 60 days, are required to use an Argentine passport to depart the country. Argentineans who use a second passport experience no problems with the nation's customs service. If you have dual nationality, when entering the country, a customs official may stamp "Argentino" on the entry page of your other passport, as recognition of dual nationality status. The 1995 Mercosur Agreement allows individuals holding Argentinean passports to have free access to other Latin American member states.

Contacts

United States: A passport is required for entry into Argentina. U.S. citizens do not need a visa for visits up to 90 days for tourism and business. The Argentine Embassy is located at 1600 New Hampshire Ave., N.W., Washington, D.C. 20009, Tel: (202) 238-6401. Web site: http://www.embajadaargentinaeeuu.org Travelers may also contact the nearest Argentine consulate in Los Angeles, Miami, Atlanta, Chicago, New York, or Houston.

Americans living in or visiting Argentina are encouraged to register at the Consular Section of the U.S. Embassy in Buenos Aires and obtain updated information on travel and security within Argentina. American Citizens may also register by fax by sending your full name, contact information, passport number and the name and phone number of a relative/friend the Embassy can contact in an emergency. The U.S. Embassy is located at Avenida Colombia 4300 in the Palermo neighborhood of Buenos Aires (near the Plaza Italia stop on the "D" line subway).

The main Embassy switchboard telephone is (011)(54)(11) 5777-

4533. Recorded consular information, including instructions on whom to contact in case of an American citizen emergency, is available at Tel: (54)(11) 4514-1830. The main embassy fax is (54)(11) 5777-4240. The Consular Section fax is (011)(54)(11) 5777-4293. Additional information on Embassy services available to U.S. citizens is available on the Internet at http://buenosaires.usembassy.gov or by e-mail:BuenosAires-ACS@state.gov

United Kingdom: The British Embassy is located at: Dr Luis Agote 2412, 1425 Buenos Aires; Tel: (54) (11) 4808 2200 Switchboard; Fax: (54) (11) 4808 2274 General, (54) (11) 4808 2283 Commercial, (54) (11) 4808 2228 Press & Public Affairs, (54) (11) 4808 2316 Chancery (54) (11) 4808 2221 Defense Section. E-mail: askconsular.buenosaires@fco.gov.uk askcommercial.baires@fco.gov.uk or askinformation.baires@fco.gov.uk

Republic of Bolivia

CAPITAL:	LA PAZ
POPULATION:	8,586,443
LANGUAGE:	SPANISH, QUECHUA, AYMARA (ALL OFFICIAL)
CURRENCY:	BOLIVIANO ($B)
AREA:	1,098,580 SQUARE KM
ETHNIC GROUPS:	QUECHUA 30%, MESTIZO (MIXED WHITE-AMERINDIAN) 30%, AYMARA 25%, WHITE 15%
RELIGION:	ROMAN CATHOLIC 95%, PROTESTANT (EVANGELICAL METHODIST)

PASSPORT HIGHLIGHTS: Ownership of real estate or investment in Bolivia entitles a person to a residence visa, with naturalization authorized after five years' residency. Persons making grants to certain public or semi-public development projects may qualify for immediate Bolivian citizenship.

"Unspoiled," "a place for adventuresome nature lovers," "slow-paced" — Bolivia's advocates alert the potential immigrant that this landlocked country cascading down the eastern slopes of the Andes though rain forests and onto a high plain is not likely to satisfy cravings for modern conveniences and exciting urban experiences. The country's only golf club, at 4,000 meters above sea level in La Paz, is the highest in the world. Lake Titicaca is the world's highest navigable body of water. Anacondas and jaguars feature more prominently in travelogues about Bolivia than spas and night clubs. Because of the climatic and topographical diversity of its regions and the high proportion of its Spanish colonial architecture still extant, Bolivia can indeed be endlessly rewarding for ecological explorers, anthropological tourists, and those seeking out its rich cultural heritage.

Bolivia broke away from Spanish rule in 1825. Its subsequent history has been marked by a seemingly endless series of coups, counter-coups, and abrupt changes in leaders and policies. Comparatively democratic civilian rule was established in the 1980s, but the leaders have faced difficult problems of deep-seated poverty, social unrest, strikes, and drug dealing. Current issues include encouraging and negotiating the terms for foreign investment, strengthening the educational system, continuing the privatization program, pursuing judicial reform and an anti-corruption campaign.

With its long history of semi-feudal social controls, dependence on mineral exports, and bouts of hyperinflation, Bolivia has remained one of the poorest and least developed Latin American countries. However, it has experienced generally improving economic conditions since the 1980s, when market-oriented policies reduced inflation from 11,700% in 1985 to about 20% in 1988. Bolivia has entered into a free-trade agreement with Mexico and the southern Latin American common market (Mercosur) and is privatizing numerous state-owned businesses, airline, telephone company, railroad, electric power company, and oil company. A powerful positive consequence of Bolivia's early stage of development is its extremely low cost of living. A comfortable existence can be maintained for less than US$20,000 per year, with housing costs at a small fraction of the figures for equivalent lodging in the developed world. On the other hand, underdevelopment means that infrastructure and amenities lag considerably behind those expected in industrialized countries.

Residence and Citizenship

Permanent residency is available in Bolivia for foreigners and their dependants who own property or invest in the country and to retirees and their families showing adequate means of support, from whatever source. Residence visas must be renewed every two years. Absence from Bolivia for more than three months without authorization of the Foreign Ministry is grounds for revocation of a residence visa. Permanent residents are eligible for naturalization after five years in Bolivia.

Bolivia has had a loose program under which quasi-government corporations seek private grants from foreign nationals of approximately US$25,000. Donors are recognized as a "benefactor to Bolivia" and this serves as the basis for conferral of citizenship. Some variations on this program have had quoted prices as low as US$10,000. The US$25,000 package includes a *cédula* or identity card, a driver's license, and certificate of citizenship. The single contribution includes the main applicant, spouse, and dependent children under 18. No visit to Bolivia is necessary. Bolivian passports, although valid for five years, are renewable every two years while in the country. The passports allow travel to most European countries without visas, although this passport is causing concern. As you can imagine, this arrangement has led to the illegal sale of official passports, which appears to continue, making foreign nations wary.

Civil marriage in Bolivia of a resident foreign national to a Bolivian requires certain documentary evidence. A Bolivian potential spouse should check with the Office of the Civil Registry in La Paz at Tel: +(591) 2-316-226 to determine what documents are required.

Contacts

United States: A valid U.S. passport is required to enter and depart Bolivia. U.S. citizens do not need a visa for a stay of one month or less (that period can be extended upon application to 90 days). Visitors for other purposes must obtain a visa in advance. U.S. citizens whose passports are lost or stolen in Bolivia must obtain a new passport and present it, together with a police report of the loss or theft, to the Bolivian government immigration office in La Paz, Cochabamba, or Santa Cruz in order to obtain permission to depart. An exit tax must be paid at the airport when departing Bolivia. Travelers who have Bolivian citizenship or residency must pay an additional fee upon departure. For further information regarding entry, exit, and customs requirements, travelers should contact the Consular Section of the Bolivian Embassy at 1819 H Street, N.W, Suite 240, Washington, DC 20006; Tel: (202) 232-4828; Or the Bolivian consulate in Houston, Los Angeles, Miami, New Orleans, New York, San Francisco, or Seattle.

U.S. citizens living in or visiting Bolivia are encouraged to register at the Consular Section of the U.S. Embassy in La Paz and obtain updated information on travel and security in Bolivia. The Consular Section is open for citizen services, including registration, from (8:45 a.m. to 12:noon) weekdays, excluding U.S. and Bolivian holidays. The U.S. Embassy is located at 2780 Avenida Arce in La Paz; Tel: (591-2) 2433-812. Business hours 8:30a.m.-5:30p.m., or (591-2) 2430-251 for after-hours emergencies; Fax: (591-2) 2433-854; Questions should be directed to the e-mail address: consularlapaz@state.gov or for further information visit the web site: http://bolivia.usembassy.gov

There are also U.S. Consular Agencies in Santa Cruz and Cochabamba, which are open weekday mornings from 9: 00a.m.-12:00noon, excluding U.S. and Bolivian holidays. The consular agency in Santa Cruz is located at Calle Guemes 6, Barrio Equipetrol; Tel: (591-3) 3363-842 or 3330-725; Fax: (591-3) 3325-544. The consular agency in Cochabamba is located at Avenida Oquendo 654, Torres Sofer, room 601; Tel: (591-4) 4256-714; Fax: (591-4) 45 26-714.

United Kingdom: The British Embassy in Bolivia is located at Avenida Arce No. 2732 Casilla (PO Box) 694, La Paz; Tel: (591) (2) 2433424; Fax: (591) (2) 2431073. E-mail: ppa@megalink.com Embassy, dfid@zuper.net.

Note: Prior to visiting high altitude locations over 10,000 feet above sea level, such as La Paz, travelers may wish to discuss the trip with their personal physician and request advice concerning medication and activity at high altitudes.

Brazil

CAPITAL:	BRASILIA
POPULATION:	182,032,604
LANGUAGE:	PORTUGUESE (OFFICIAL), SPANISH, ENGLISH, FRENCH
CURRENCY:	REAL (BRL) PRONOUNCED "REE - AL"
AREA:	8,511,965 SQUARE KM
ETHNIC GROUPS:	WHITE (INCLUDES PORTUGUESE, GERMAN, ITALIAN, SPANISH, POLISH) 55%, MIXED WHITE AND BLACK 38%, BLACK 6%, OTHER (INCLUDES JAPANESE, ARAB, AMERINDIAN) 1%
RELIGION:	ROMAN CATHOLIC (NOMINAL) 80%

PASSPORT HIGHLIGHTS: Those investing at least US$200,000 in Brazil's economy are eligible for registration in the country's official economic investment permanent residence program. Investments must be to establish commercial or industrial activities that create new jobs. Permanent residency may also be obtained through normal immigration channels, a relatively easy task if procedures are duly followed. Naturalization is then available after four years.

It can be big, brassy, bawdy, and balmy, as in Rio or São Paulo. It can be the deepest, darkest jungle, as in the Amazon. But with all its attractions, Brazil, one of the world's most diverse and potentially rich countries, is often overlooked as an offshore home for expatriates. It is also one of the most "high crime" nations in Latin America, especially in the major cities.

The nation of Brazil will unquestionably play a major role in the 21st Century. It is rich in natural resources and produces a vast array of sophisticated goods including jet aircraft and computers. Brazil is actually the fifth largest country in the world and has the seventh largest economy. It has a population of over 170 million, 60% under the age of 18.

Brazil could be a perfect second home. It is very democratic, without all the rules and regulations most industrialized countries insist upon. With 4,800 kilometers of ocean beaches, you can wile away time and enjoy an average annual temperature of 24° C (75° F). Many wealthy Americans and Europeans move to Brazil to get away from the cold weather, high taxes, government controls and regulations, law suits, divorces, and even prosecution.

Brazilians are a friendly and fun-loving people who possess a refreshing "live and let live" attitude to life. They enjoy soccer, good food, and, of course, a good carnival! Some figures which might surprise you: 75% of all Brazilians are home owners, whether it be a mansion or a more simple affair, with 78% owning their furniture and household appliances. Ninety percent of all automobiles are paid for and 87% of these run on alcohol, helping to reduce the level of pollution, maintain the environment, and, thus, increase the standard of living available in the country.

The national language is Portuguese but German, English, Japanese, Korean, and African communities are already well-established in this cosmopolitan South American country.

Possessing large and well-developed agricultural, mining, manufacturing, and service sectors, Brazil's economy outweighs that of all other South American countries and is expanding its presence in world markets. Prior to the institution of a major stabilization plan, Plano Real (Real Plan) in mid-1994, stratospheric inflation rates had disrupted economic activity and discouraged foreign investment. Since then, tight monetary policy has brought inflation under control; consumer prices increased by 2% in 1999 compared to more than 1,000% in 1994. At the same time, GDP growth slowed from 5.7% in 1994 to about 3.0% in 1998 due to tighter credit.

Investment Residence Program

Brazil has an official economic investment permanent residence program. Those wishing to qualify must invest at least US$200,000 in Brazil's economy. Investments must be to establish commercial or industrial activities that create new jobs. Brazil, not surprisingly, is an attractive place for would-be immigrants with wealth. If you move the money out of Brazil once the residence process is complete, you still retain your permanent residence visa for yourself and your family. Many use the US$200,000 to start companies to convince authorities that they plan to reside in Brazil.

Permanent Residence Visa

North Americans and Europeans can normally obtain permanent residency in 60-90 days if they use a reputable and honorable Brazilian immigration firm that knows how to cut through red tape. Without qualified professional help, the process can be prolonged.

An application for residence is submitted to government officials in the capital, Brasília, for approval. Once an application is approved, the Brazilian Consulate nearest to where the applicant currently resides will be notified and, in turn, notify them.

The applicant then takes the notification and his/her existing passport to the Brazilian Consulate and a permanent visa will be stamped into your home country passport. The approved applicant then has 60-90 days to enter Brazil and apply for a Brazilian national ID card (also known as the green card), and a national banking number.

Once this procedure is complete, you are free to live, work, or invest in Brazil, or alternatively, you can return to your country of origin. If you want your visa to remain valid, however, you must enter Brazil every two years or it will be rescinded. The administrative fees for this whole procedure are usually in the region of US$31,000 for a single applicant or US$36,500 for a family consisting of husband, spouse, and all children under 18 years of age.

Once permanent residence visas are obtained, the holder is free to exercise all rights of a Brazilian national except voting, running for public office, or purchasing land in certain restricted areas adjacent to military bases and international border areas.

Permanent residence visas can also be obtained through employment if the potential resident has a local employer submit the necessary paperwork on his behalf to the Ministry of Labor.

Naturalization

Permanent residents in Brazil become eligible for naturalization and the Brazilian passport after four years. One need not live in Brazil during this interim period. As long as you enter Brazil at least once every two years in order to keep your permanent visa valid, you can spend the remainder of the time wherever you wish.

Naturalization can be achieved in one year from the date of issue of a resident permit should you marry a Brazilian or father a Brazilian child. Your name must appear on the birth certificate for you to qualify, but fathering a child need not mean marriage. A child born outside of wedlock still qualifies you for naturalization within a year. It is also possible to achieve naturalization after one year through marriage to a

Brazilian.

Naturalization brings with it the all important Brazilian passport. This travel document permits visa-free travel to all western European countries and over 130 other countries worldwide. Brazilians do still have to obtain a B1 or B2 visa for travel into the U.S.; similar visa restrictions apply to Canada and Mexico.

The South American Mercosur agreement in force since 1995 allows those with a Brazilian passport free entry into Argentina, Paraguay, Uruguay, and Chile. This free transit was instituted to increase trade opportunities and cross-border business ventures.

Brazilian citizen status can also provide a faster back door into the European Union. If a Brazilian applies for and receives permanent residence in Portugal, he/she will only have to wait three years, half the usual time, before being granted Portuguese citizenship and the rights of an EU citizen. This unique situation prevails because Brazil is a former Portuguese colony. More Portuguese nationals live in Brazil than live in Portugal.

Dual nationality is allowed in Brazil due to a revision of the constitution in 1994. As long as you profess loyalty to Brazil, you are entitled to hold on to any other nationality you possess.

Brazilian authorities generally respect personal privacy and freedom of action. They do not inform authorities in a foreign national's home country about naturalization. During the naturalization process, the applicant is offered the option of changing his/her name to make it sound more Portuguese.

Applicants for naturalization must be able to speak some Portuguese. A naturalization judge may ask questions related to the impending action. Don't let the language requirement daunt you. Brazil has been a popular destination for Americans since the U.S. Civil War (1860-65) when many thousands, mostly from the defeated Confederacy, sought refuge there. We would rate Brazil as a top place for a passport as well as a great place to live.

A passport and visa are required for U.S. citizens traveling to Brazil for any purpose. Brazilian visas must be obtained in advance from the Brazilian Embassy or consulate nearest to the traveler's place of residence. There are no "airport visas," and immigration authorities will refuse entry to Brazil to anyone not possessing a valid visa. All Brazilian visas, regardless of the length of validity, must initially be used within 90 days of the issuance date or will no longer be valid. Immigration authorities will not allow entry into Brazil without a valid visa. The U.S. Government cannot assist travelers who arrive in Brazil without proper documentation.

In response to the introduction of the US-VISIT program, on January 1, 2004 the Government of Brazil began fingerprinting/photographing all U.S. citizens arriving in Brazil. U.S. citizens can expect long delays, up to several hours, in being processed through immigration at Brazil's other airports. U.S. travelers to Brazil should avoid planning tight transit connections due to the expected delays. For current entry and customs requirements for Brazil, travelers may contact the Brazilian Embassy at 3009 Whitehaven St. NW, Washington, D.C., 20008; Tel: (202) 238-2818, E-mail daw@wilson.com.br.

Contacts

A passport and visa are required for entry into Brazil. Brazilian visas must be obtained in advance. Immigration authorities will not allow entry into Brazil without a valid visa. Contact: Brazilian Embassy at 3009 Whitehaven Street, N.W., Washington, D.C. 20008; Tel: (202) 238-2700; Web site: http://www.brasilemb.org. Brazilian Consulates are located in Boston, Houston, Miami, New York, Chicago, Los Angeles, and San Francisco. Web site: http://www.brasilemb.org/consular/visainfo.html.

United States: The U.S. Embassy is located in Brasília at Avenida das Nações, Lote 3; Tel: 011-55-61-312-7000, after-hours telephone 011-55-61-312-7400; Web site: http://www.embaixada-americana.org.br.

There are Consulates in **Rio de Janeiro**Avenida Presidente Wilson 147, Tel: 011-55-21-2292-7117, after-hours 011-55-21-2220-0489, Web site:http://www.consulado-americano-rio.org.br; in **Sao Paulo** at Rua Henri Dunant, 500 Barrio Chacara Santo Antonio, Tel: 011-55-11-5186-7000, after hours telephone 011-55-11-5181-8730, Web site: http://www.amcham.com.br/consulate; and **Recifeat**: Rua Gonçalves Maia 163, Tel: 011-55-81-3421-2441, after-hours telephone 011-55-3421-2641; Web site: http://www.consulado-americano.org.br/. There are also U.S. Consular Agencies located in: **Belem**: Edificio Sintese 21, Av. Conselheiro Furtado 2865, Rooms 1104/1106; Tel: 011-55-91-259-4566; **Manaus**: Rua Franco de Sa, 230 Sao Francisco, Edificio Atrium, Rm. 306; Tel: 011-55-92-611-3333; **Salvador da Bahia**: Av. Tancredo Neves, 1632, Rm. 1401 - Salvador Trade Center - Torre Sul, Caminho da Arvores; Tel: 011-55-71-3113-2090/2091/2092; **Fortaleza**: The Instituto Cultural Brasil-Estados Unidos (IBEU), Rua Nogueira Acioly 891, Aldeota; Tel: 011-55-85-252-1539; and **Porto Alegre**: The Instituto Cultural Brasil-Norteamericano, Rua Riachuelo, 1257, Centro; Tel: 011-

55-51-3226-3344.

United Kingdom: The British Embassy in Brazil is located at SES Quadra 801 Lote 8 Cj K, Av das Nações 70408-900, Brasilia – DF; Tel: (55) (61) 225-2710; Fax: (55) (61) 225-1777; E-mail: mailto:britemb@zaz.com.br Web site: http://www.reinounido.org.br

British Consulates are located in:

Belem: Av Governador J. Malcher, 815 Ed Palladium Center Cj 410/411, Belem - Pará 66035-900, Tel: (55) (91) 222-5074, (55) (91) 223-0990, Fax: (55) (91) 212-0274;

Manaus: Swedish Match da Amazônia S.A Rua Poraquê, 240 Distrito Industrial, Manaus–AM 69075 –180, Tel: (55) (92) 613-1819, Fax: (55) (92) 613-1420, E-mail: vincent@internext.com.br;

Rio de Janeiro: Praia do Flamengo 284/2 andar, 22210-030, Rio de Janeiro-RJ, Tel: (55) (21) 2555 9600, (55) (21) 2555 9640; Fax: (55) (21) 2555 9670, E-mail: britishconsulaterio@terra.com.br or consular.section. riodejaneiro@fco.gov.uk;

Belo Horizonte: Rua dos Inconfidentes 1075 Sala 1302, Savassi, Belo Horizonte - MG 30140-120, Tel: (55) (31) 3261 2072, Fax: (55) (31) 3261 0226, E-mail: britcon.bhe@terra.com.br;

Fortaleza: Rua Leonardo Mota, 501 Meireles - CEP: 60170-040 - Fortaleza/Ceará, Tel: (55) (85) 242 0888, Fax: (55) (85) 242 9222, E-mail: consulado@emitrade.com.br;

Salvador: Av Estados Unidos 18-B 8º andar, Comercio edificio, Estados Unidos Comercio 40010-020, Salvador – BA, Tel: (55) (71) 243 7399, Fax: (55) (71) 242 7293, Email: adcos@allways.com.br;

São Paulo: British Consulate-General, Rua Ferreira de Araujo, 741 Pinheiros, 05428-002, Sao Paulo-SP, Tel: (55) (11) 3094 2700, Fax: (55) (11) 3094 2717, E-mail: saopaulo@gra-   bretanha.org.br; Web site: http://www.gra-bretanha.org.br;

Rio Grande: Wilson Sons, Rua Riachuelo, 201 Térreo, CEP, 96200-390, Rio Grande-RS, Tel: (55) (53) 233 7700, Fax: (55) (53) 233 7701, E-mail: rjg@wilson.com.br;

Santos: Rua Tuiutí 58 2º andar, Caixa Postal 204, 11101-220, Santos-SP, Tel: (55) (13) 3211 2300, Fax: (55) (13) 3219 5250, E-mail: daw@wilson.com.br.

Republic of Chile

CAPITAL:	SANTIAGO
POPULATION:	15,665,216
LANGUAGE:	SPANISH
CURRENCY:	CHILEAN PESO (CH$)
AREA:	756,950 SQUARE KM
ETHNIC GROUPS:	WHITE AND WHITE-AMERINDIAN 95%, AMERINDIAN 3%, OTHER 2%
RELIGION:	ROMAN CATHOLIC 89%, PROTESTANT 11%, JEWISH 1%

PASSPORT HIGHLIGHTS: Permanent residency is available for an investment of US$30,000, and can lead to citizenship after five years in the country.

Chile is located in southwest South America. It shares a common border with Peru to the north, and Bolivia and Argentina to the east. Its west coast meets the Pacific Ocean, and its southernmost point ends at the tip of the South American continent. Several islands and archipelagos are included in the country's overall area of 292,258 square miles (756,945 square kilometers). Chile is a narrow country, extending north and south along the west coast of South America. Its length is about 2,650 miles (4,270 kilometers) and its width is less than 110 miles (180 kilometers). Its climate ranges from the frigid, stormy sub-Antarctic rigors of Tierra del Fuego to the blistering aridity of the Atacama Desert in the north. In between, from west to east, is a temperate land with a gamut of terrain and ecosystems starting at the seashore and culminating in one of the highest mountain ranges on earth. In its center is the thriving, modern metropolis of the capital, Santiago. Chile is a land of spectacular scenery, inviting recreational opportunities, and vast natural resources, populated by an energetic people of various European, Asian, and Amerindian ethnic groups, all of them proud to live in one of the world's most beautiful countries.

Chile is a stable democratic country whose constitution of 1833 is the second oldest in the Americas. Its industrial growth has doubled in recent years, and its government welcomes foreign investors with inducements seen nowhere else. Chile is a country where the future means economic opportunity. Already well known among international investors for its open trade policies, encouragement of investment, and pro-business outlook, Chile is on the rise.

Outstanding investment opportunities abound in many sectors including: manufacturing, forestry products, software design and production, fisheries, farming, mining, paper production, infrastructure expansion, and energy production. In an environment of certainty and ample guarantees, foreign investment has made a significant contribution to economic development. With an annual GDP growth rate of 6% in recent years (one of the world's highest rates), direct foreign investment accounted for an average of 20% of GDP. Exports generated by foreign investment projects currently represent 25% of the total.

Chile has a prosperous, essentially free market economy. Civilian governments, which took over from the military in March 1990, have continued to reduce the government's role in the economy while shifting the emphasis of public spending toward social programs. Growth in real GDP averaged more than 7.0% in 1991-97 but fell to about half of that average in 1998 because of spillover from the global financial crisis. Inflation has been on a downward trend and hit a 60-year low in 1998. Chile's currency and foreign reserves also are strong, as sustained foreign capital inflows, including significant direct investment, have more than offset current account deficits and public debt buybacks.

For half a century after 1900, Chile's economy centered on the mining and export of copper. In the late 1940s, the government finally began to encourage industrial growth and diversification. Today, Chile is one of the leading industrial countries in Latin America, and still remains one of the continent's largest mineral producers.

Chile's financial system is fully equipped with services, investors, and entrepreneurs required to establish a business. The Central Bank of Chile has extensive powers to regulate monetary policy. The country also has a state bank, commercial and development banks, and financial services companies.

Since 1974, the Foreign Investment Statute has been a principal attraction for foreign capital. This law created a framework of confidence and credibility in the international economic community, so that today persons from over 60 countries have investments in Chile. The Foreign Investment Statute offers a framework of special guarantees. The investor signs a legally binding investment contract with the government, which cannot be changed except by mutual consent.

Companies or investors with commercial operations in Chile's remote areas are eligible for exemptions on income tax, VAT, custom duties, and similar charges. Special subsidies and fiscal bonuses may also be available.

Forestry Sector Incentives: Investors and companies with commercial activity within the forestry sector, and those that own land deemed suitable for forestry, may be eligible to benefit from specific incentives, including: 1) a 75% subsidy of costs of forestry projects; 2) specific properties deemed suitable for forestry are exempt from real estate taxes; or 3) a 50% reduction in personal progressive income taxes on income gained from commercial forestry activities.

In and around urban areas, Chile's culture is quite cosmopolitan. Santiago is a modern city by any standards, and its residents have access to all the wonders of our technological age. The city is filled with parks and wide streets, excellent hotels and fine restaurants that offer world class menus. During Chile's winter—from June to September—Santiago's people may wish to ski in the mountains to the east, or, throughout the year, they may visit marvelous beaches that lie an hour and a half to the west.

In the more isolated areas, the culture is dominated by a mixture of Spanish and Indian heritage. Life here is slower and centers around the land. It may be said that Chile has something to offer everyone. Indeed, many investors find that to be true in the country that has been called South America's land of opportunity.

Residence and Citizenship

Permanent residence is available for an investment of US$30,000, and can lead to citizenship after five years in the country.

Contacts

Chile maintains several agencies to assist investors. ProChile is the Chilean Trade Commission within the Ministry of Foreign Affairs, and has 35 commercial offices worldwide. ProChile New York, 866 United Nations Plaza, Suite 302, New York, New York 10017, U.S.A.; Tel: (212) 207-3266; Fax: (212) 207-3649. Email: info@chileinfo.com; Web site: www.chileinfo.com/ Consul General of Chile in Canada, 801-2 Bloor Street West, Toronto, Ontario, Canada, M4W 3E2; Tel: (416) 924-0106; Fax: (416) 924-2627. Office hours: 09:00 to 13:00 hrs E-mail: consulate@congechiletoronto.com

United States: Beginning in February 2004, the government of Chile instituted enhanced security checks for all arriving passengers.

These security checks include the taking of photographs and, in some cases, inkless fingerprints. Entry to Chile requires a passport, but U.S. citizens need no visa for a stay of up to 90 days. At the international port-of-entry, a "processing fee" of US$45 is levied on U.S. citizen visitors. The fee is payable in dollars only upon arrival in Chile, and the receipt is valid for multiple entries during the validity of the traveler's passport.

The Chilean Embassy is located at 1732 Massachusetts Avenue, N.W., Washington, D.C. 20036; Tel: (202) 785-1746; Web site: http://www.chile-usa.org/. Chilean consulates are located in Chicago, Houston, Los Angeles, Miami, New York, Philadelphia, San Francisco, and San Juan. Contact details for each of the Chilean Consulates is available on the Chilean Embassy's Internet web site.

The U.S. Embassy is located at Avenida Andres Bello 2800, Santiago, Tel: (56) (2) 335-6550 or 232-2600, after-hours Tel: (56) (2) 330-3321. The Consular ACS section is open to the public 8:30am-11:30pm, Monday-Friday, except American and Chilean holidays. The Embassy's mailing address is Casilla 27-D, Santiago; the Consular fax number is (56) (2) 330-3005 and the E-mail address is santiagoamcit@state.gov. Web site: http://santiago.usembassy.gov/ is where Americans may also register on line.

United Kingdom: The British Embassy in Chile is located at Avda. El Bosque Norte 0125, Casilla 72-D, Santiago, Tel: (56) (2) 370-4100; Fax: (56) (2) 335-5988; E-mail: consular.santiago@fco.gov.uk or embsan@britemb.cl; Web site: http://www.britemb.cl. The British Consulate is located at Cataratas del Niagara 01325, Punta Arenas; Tel: (56) (61) 211535; Fax: (56) (61) 239880. E-mail: reesking@tie.cl

Republic of Ecuador

CAPITAL:	QUITO
POPULATION:	13,183,978
LANGUAGE:	SPANISH (OFFICIAL), AMERINDIAN (ESPECIALLY QUECHUA)
CURRENCY:	SUCRE (S/)
AREA:	283 SQUARE KM
ETHNIC GROUPS:	MESTIZO (AMERINDIAN-SPANISH MIX) 55%, AMERINDIAN 25%, SPANISH 10%, BLACK 10%
RELIGION:	ROMAN CATHOLIC 95%

PASSPORT HIGHLIGHTS: Visas of indefinite duration are available to individuals with monthly incomes of US$1,000 or investments of US$15,000 in Ecuador. Alternatively, permanent residency is available for individuals making an approved investment of $25,000, plus an additional US$5,000 for each dependant. Naturalization may be obtained after five years' residency.

Ecuador is located on the northwestern Pacific Ocean coast of South America with Colombia and Peru forming its borders. A magnet for eco-tourists, Ecuador also includes the Galápagos Islands some 100 kilometers to the west in the Pacific, as well as unspoiled Amazonian jungles in the eastern regions. Highly mountainous with several active volcanoes, the Equator passes through the country, which is tropical, hot and humid along the coast, but less oppressive in the Andean highlands. Ecuador is very much still a developing, third-world country. Travelers to the capital city of Quito may require some time to adjust to the altitude (close to 10,000 feet), which can adversely affect blood pressure, digestion, and energy level.

Ancient Indian tribes inhabited the highland areas around Quito thousands of years ago. Perhaps, the best known are the Incas, a highly sophisticated society. The Incas were overwhelmed by the Spanish Conquistadors, who, by 1534, solidified colonial rule of the area. By 1810, the country was in the hands of an elite class of landowners of

Spanish descent. There followed 200 years of governmental instability that continues to this day, including a border war with Peru.

Recent governments have been marked by continued corruption and incompetence. In early 2000, Ecuador experienced continued political unrest and demonstrations against government economic policies, especially by indigenous Amerindian groups. A national state of emergency was declared allowing the military to assist the police in maintaining order.

In spite of all these problems, land and homes sell here for a fraction of the price in the U.S. and even lower than in other Latin American countries. Wages are very low and a retired foreign national can live very comfortably here for a third or less of what a comparable living standard would require in the U.S.

Residence and Citizenship

While Ecuador has a reputation of being hospitable to foreign visitors, it has no formal economic citizenship program as does its neighbor, Bolivia. There are no restrictions on foreign investment or ownership of real estate, except in a few areas such as mining and the electronic media. There are no exchange controls. Foreign nationals do pay a 25% tax on local income, compared to 15% for Ecuadorians.

For foreign nationals wishing to do business in Ecuador, an initial six-month business visa is offered. The applicant must show availability of investment funds and provide a business plan. Visas are also available for foreign national executives, managers, or workers with a valid local employment contract.

Class I Visa: This visa is issued for those who prove a monthly income of US$1,000 or, alternatively, make an investment in Ecuador Bonds, local bank deposits, or real estate. The visa is for an indefinite period.

Class II Visa: This is issued for an investment in government bonds or real estate. Tailored opportunities exist for investments in the agricultural sector or in manufacturing for export. These visas also allow dependants to be included for an additional investment. This visa is also issued for an indefinite period.

After five years residency, application for naturalization can be made, but proficiency in Spanish is required for approval. With citizenship comes a passport that is renewed after five years. The Ecuadorian constitution has been amended to accept dual nationality

As in other Latin American nations, the illegal sale of passports has been and continues to be a problem in Ecuador.

Contacts

United States: A valid U.S. passport is required to enter and depart Ecuador. Tourists must also provide evidence of return or onward travel. U.S. citizens do not need a visa for a stay of 90 days or less. Those planning a longer visit must obtain a visa in advance. An exit tax must be paid at the airport when departing Ecuador.

The Ecuadoran Embassy is located at 2535 15th Street, N.W., Washington, D.C. 20009; Tel: (202) 234-7166; Web site: http://www.ecuador.org. Ecuadorian Consulates are located in **Chicago**: Tel: (312) 329-0266; **Houston**: Tel: (713) 622-1787; **Jersey City**: Tel: (201) 985-1700; **Los Angeles**: Tel: (323) 658-6020; **Miami**: Tel: (305) 539-8214; **New Orleans**: Tel: (504) 523-3229; **New York**: Tel: (212) 808-0170; and **San Francisco**: Tel: (415) 957-5921.

The U.S. Embassy in Quito is located at the corner of Avenida 12 de Octubre and Avenida Patria (across from the Casa de la Cultura); Tel: (011) (593) (2) 256-2890, ext. 4510, during business hours (8:00 a.m. to 5:00 p.m.) or 256-1749 for after-hours emergencies; Fax (011) (593) (2) 256-1524; Web site: http://usembassy.state.gov/guayaquil/.

The Consulate General in Guayaquil is located at the corner of 9 de Octubre and Garcia Moreno (near the Hotel Oro Verde); Tel: (011) (593) (4) 232-3570 during business hours (8:00 a.m. to 5:00 p.m.) or 232-1152 for after-hours emergencies; Fax (011) (593) (4) 232-0904. Consular services for U.S. citizens in the Galapagos Islands are provided by the Consulate General in Guayaquil. Travelers or prospective residents in Guayaquil's consular district may register on-line at web site: http://usembassy.state.gov/quito/, which also has an e-mail service to the Consulate General.

United Kingdom: The British Embassy in Quito is located at Citiplaza Building, Naciones Unidas Ave. and Republica de El Salvador 14th Floor (Consular Section 12th floor), PO Box 17-17-830, Quito; Tel: (593) (2) 970-800/801; Fax: (593) (2) 970-809; Web site: http://www.britembquito.org.ec/, E-mail: Britembq@interactive.net.ec.

British Consulates are located in **Guayaquil**: C/o Agripac General Córdova 623 y Padre Solano, Castilla 09-01 8598, Tel: (593) (4) 2 560-400 ext. 318; Fax: (593) (4) 2 562-641; E-mail: carmstrong@ agripac.com.ec; and **Galapagos**: c/o Etica Office, Barrio Estrada Peurto Ayora, Isla Santa Cruz, Tel: (593) (5) 526157, (593) (5) 529159; Fax: (593) (4) 687 113.

Republic of Paraguay

CAPITAL:	ASUNCIÓN
POPULATION:	6,036,900
LANGUAGE:	SPANISH (OFFICIAL), GUARANI (OFFICIAL)
CURRENCY:	GUARANÍ (PYG)
AREA:	406,752 SQUARE KM
ETHNIC GROUPS:	MESTIZO (MIXED SPANISH-AMERINDIAN) 95%, WHITE + AMERINDIAN 5%
RELIGION:	ROMAN CATHOLIC 90%, MENNONITE AND OTHER PROTESTANTS

PASSPORT HIGHLIGHTS: Applicants for permanent residency – leading to naturalization after three years – must show financial self-support by proven assets, employment, or other income. Evidence of good moral standing and a capacity for work is also required.

Paraguay is a small, landlocked country in central South America surrounded by Bolivia, Brazil, and Argentina. The Paraguay River runs north/south through the country forming an excellent commercial trade route. Its relatively flat terrain (much of its area is a featureless plain called the Chaco) lends Paraguay a reputation for uninteresting visual dullness that has discouraged potential tourists, although the land's fertility has attracted farmers from across the globe. In the national parks mainly located in the northern and western sections of Paraguay large populations of native cats – jaguars, ocelots, and pumas – survive, while visitors to the east of the country are find a wide array of Indian lace and other handicrafts offered for sale.

Paraguay was on the edge of the Inca Empire for centuries prior to the arrival of the Spanish in 1536. Independence from Spain was declared on May 14, 1811. Unlike most of its neighbors, Paraguay's culture retains a strong coloration of the indigenous population, and the Guaraní language is taught in schools and spoken among the urban elite. The country's history is marked by numerous border wars with its neighbors with great loss of life. Military regimes and dictatorships have been a more recent facet. Since 1989, democratic elections have been held, but problems continue with periodic military coups.

Paraguay has a market economy marked by what the U.S. State Department diplomatically describes as "a large informal sector." This black market, off the books economy abounds in both re-exporting of foreign imported consumer goods (electronics, whiskeys, perfumes, cigarettes, and office equipment) to neighboring countries. It also includes thousands of service-oriented micro-enterprises and urban street vendors. A large percentage of people make a living from agricultural, many on a subsistence basis. The formal economy has grown an average of about 3% over the past six years, but GDP declined in 1998.

There is no personal income tax in Paraguay. Revenues are derived principally from tariffs and the sale of hydroelectric power to neighboring countries. Smuggling is a major industry. Along with Uruguay and Ecuador, Paraguay is one of the few Latin American countries that imposes no currency controls.

Paraguay prides itself upon its independence from influence by foreign powers. Extradition demands aimed at a resident foreign national are commonly ignored if the person sought has curried favor with Paraguay's establishment. Paraguay does not recognize tax or currency crimes and has a reputation as a haven for political and tax refugees. The prevailing attitude towards immigrants seems to be, that as long as they stay out of local politics, they are quite welcome. There are colonies of Koreans, Japanese, Germans, and one three of Mennonite religionists. This is one of the few Latin America nations that has not exploited its native Indian population. The government promotes the local Guaraní culture and language in all schools. The population is largely a mix of native Indian and European, known as Mestizo.

Decent housing goes for as little as US$50,000, but luxury living is the real bargain. In Asunción, whole neighborhoods resemble Palm Springs, California. A drive through the Villa Mora section will reveal huge mansions with swimming pools, tennis courts, and staff quarters.

Residence and Citizenship

The Paraguayan Constitution is very liberal in granting rights to foreigners. It proclaims all inhabitants have the right to develop their personal inclinations, trade and business. Nationals and foreigners are equal before the law, without discrimination. There are also no restrictions on property ownership by foreign nationals.

Permanent residence leading to naturalization is fairly easy, requiring the applicant to show financial self-support by proven assets, employment, or other income. Evidence of good moral standing and a capacity for work is required.

Documents submitted for consideration must include: 1) a passport from the country of origin, with photograph; 2) birth and marriage certificates, if applicable; 3) a certificate from an administrative, judicial authority, or employer evidencing occupation, academic degrees, diplomas, and/or guaranteed retirement income; 4) a certificate from a medical doctor or institution in Paraguay evidencing good health; and 5) a certificate from the police or judicial authorities of the country of residence evidencing no criminal record. Any documents not issued in Paraguay must be translated into Spanish and certified by a Paraguayan Consulate.

After about 30 days of processing in Paraguay, a Certificate of Residence will be issued, including a cédula or identity card. After three years of residence, a resident foreign national qualifies for naturalization. Paraguayan passport holders benefit from the 1995 Mercosur Agreement, which allows free entry to other member states, currently Argentina, Brazil, Chile, and Uruguay.

Passport Past

What we described above is the only legal route to acquire citizenship in Paraguay. That observation is made with good reason.

Some in the Government of Paraguay may well have been the inventors of instant passports as an easy income source from foreign nationals seeking second passports. It is an established fact that, during recent decades, large numbers of this nation's official passports were sold illegally. As a result, border officials look closely at North Americans or Europeans who speak no Spanish and travel using a Paraguayan passport. With a change in government, in 1993, illegal "official" passports became more difficult to acquire and investigations began into "irregularities in the issuance of passports." Since the nation's passport must be renewed in person every two years at a Paraguayan Consulate, past issues are being scrutinized more carefully.

Unfortunately, the same situation exists in almost all Latin American nations, with the possible exceptions of Argentina, Brazil, and Chile.

Contacts

United States: A passport and visa are required. U.S. citizens traveling to Paraguay must submit completed visa applications in person or by mail to the Paraguayan Embassy or one of the consulates and pay a fee. Application forms are available from the Paraguayan

Embassy or Consulate by email or fax. Tourist visa applicants must present with their application a passport with at least six months validity from the date of the application; one passport photograph; a bank statement or other evidence of financial solvency; and a round-trip ticket or a printed trip itinerary prepared by a travel agency. Persons traveling on business must also submit a company letter. Applicants under 18 years of age traveling alone must appear with parents or a legal guardian. In case of a guardian, an original and one copy of proof of legal guardianship is required. A document of authorization from parents/guardian will be accepted only if it is notarized and certified by the county clerk. There is an airport international departure tax of US$18. Transit passengers and children under 2 years of age are exempt. (No credit cards or checks accepted). The Paraguayan Embassy is located at 2400 Massachusetts Avenue NW, Washington, D.C. 20008, Tel: (202) 483-6960, E-mail: embapar.usa@verizon.net or web site: http://www.embassy.org/embassies/py.html; Paraguayan consulate are located in Los Angeles, Miami or New York. The Paraguayan consulates in Kansas City, New Orleans, Detroit, and Puerto Rico are not authorized to issue visas

Americans living in or visiting Paraguay are encouraged to register at the Consular section of the U.S. Embassy in Asuncion and obtain updated information on travel and security in Paraguay. The U.S. Embassy is located at 1776 Mariscal Lopez Avenue; Tel: (011) (595) (21) 213-715, Fax (011) (595) (21) 213-728; Web site: http://asuncion.usembassy.gov.py. The Consular Section is open for U.S. citizen services, including registration, Monday through Thursday from 1:00 p.m. to 5:30 p.m. and Friday from 7:30 a.m. to 11:30 a.m., except for U.S. and Paraguayan holidays.

United Kingdom: The British Embassy is located at Avda. Boggiani 5848, C/R.I.6 Boquerón, Asunción, Paraguay; Tel: (595) (21) 612-611; Fax: (595) (21) 605-007; E-mail: brembasu@rieder.net.py.

Republic of Uruguay

CAPITAL:	MONTEVIDEO
POPULATION:	3,413,329
LANGUAGE:	SPANISH, PORTUNOL, OR BRAZILERO (PORTUGUESE-SPANISH MIX ON THE BRAZILIAN FRONTIER)
CURRENCY:	URUGUAYAN PESO (UYU)
AREA:	176,200 SQUARE KM
ETHNIC GROUPS:	WHITE 88%, MESTIZO 8%, BLACK 4%, AMERINDIAN, PRACTICALLY NONEXISTENT
RELIGION:	ROMAN CATHOLIC 66% (LESS THAN HALF OF THE ADULT POPULATION ATTENDS CHURCH REGULARLY), PROTESTANT 2%, JEWISH 1%, NON-PROFESSING OR OTHER 31%

PASSPORT HIGHLIGHTS: Naturalization as an Uruguayan citizen can be obtained three years after establishing a bona fide, full-time residence in the country. Placement of US$70,000 into approved investments, currently including ten-year government bonds or Central Bank CDs, entitles the investor to an investor passport and tax-free income on the instruments.

Uruguay is bordered by Brazil, Argentina, and the Atlantic Ocean to the east. Lying low on South America's coast, Uruguay lacks most of the natural scenic extremes that might draw visitors to many of the continent's other countries. Its highest mountain just tops 500 meters, and its temperate climate sustains broad grasslands suitable for ranching. Excellent beaches along the Río de la Plata where it meets the sea attract a wealthy crowd fleeing urban congestion in nearby Buenos Aires and São Paulo to Punta del Este during the austral summer, but tourism in Uruguay is otherwise comparatively underdeveloped.

In spite of Spanish and Portuguese claims based on early exploration and trade, immigration from all over Europe during the 19th Century reached massive proportions. By 1880, European migrants, British, Germans, Italians, made up 40% of the population. In spite of military dominance of government early in the 20th Century, more recent democratic governments have not fared much better due to corruption and graft. Banks and currency dealers selling gold and foreign currency were once commonplace in Montevideo, the country's capital. Until recently, strikes, terrorism, high inflation, and emigration of professionals and skilled workers damaged the nation's reputation.

However, once a foreign national becomes assimilated into the large expatriate community of Punta del Este, Uruguay's answer to Newport, Rhode Island, life can be quite pleasant. Bridge nights and cocktail parties are part of the routine. Many people of wealth make their home here. Elsewhere in the country, Uruguay's infrastructure is fair, and declines in quality in proportion with distance from the south coast. Montevideo, the capital, is an attractive, modern city -– among the safest in the world. Political stability has been outstanding in recent decades, and Uruguay's position at the center of the Mercosur regional trade bloc has begun to show signs of stimulating economic growth.

Uruguay imposes no personal income or estate taxes and still has one of the highest standards of living in Latin America. There is a high annual wealth tax of up to 3% on capital owned and domiciled within the country.

Residence and Citizenship

Until recently, naturalization in Uruguay followed three years after purchase of a home property, with occasional visits to the country serving to fulfill the time obligation. Now, actual bona fide residence is a condition for granting nationality.

Since 1990, Uruguay has had an official government investor passport program, attractive except for one very important detail; it grants official permanent residence status, but not full citizenship. Under Decree 289/90, the program provides an investor with a Uruguayan travel document that looks very much like a passport. This less than full citizenship does not entitle the holder to special consideration in applying for accelerated Spanish citizenship.

The principal requirement is an investment of a minimum of US$70,000 in certain programs approved by the Uruguayan Government. Currently, these include: 1) Ten-year Reforestation Bonds issued by the Central Bank of Uruguay; and 2) Ten-year Certificates of Deposit placed in escrow at the Bank of Uruguay. Both of these investments are U.S. dollar denominated and the interest is tax-free in

Uruguay. Additional passports for your spouse or children under 21 years of age require an additional investment of US$10,000 per person. Additional total fees can amount to as much as US$55,000.

Applicants must provide a clean police record; health certificates; professional references; marriage certificate, where appropriate; and bank references. Within 90 days, the Ministry of Interior rules on the application.

One problem with the Uruguay investment passport is that United Kingdom immigration rules specifically require an entry visa for these travel documents. Under the 1995 Mercosur agreement, a Uruguayan passport carrier is entitled to free travel access to other South American countries that are party to the pact.

Contacts

United States: A passport is required. U.S. citizens do not need a visa for a visit of less than 90 days. Embassy of Uruguay is located at 1913 "Eye" Street, N.W., Washington, D.C. 20006, Tel: (202) 331-1313; E-mail: uruwashi@uruwashi.org; Web site: http://www.embassy.org/uruguay/. Travelers may also contact the Consulate of Uruguay or the Honorary Consul in Boston, Chicago, Honolulu, Los Angeles, Miami, New Orleans, New York, Reno, Salt Lake City, San Francisco, San Juan, Puerto Rico or Seattle.

Americans living in or visiting Uruguay are encouraged to register at the Consular Section of the U.S. Embassy in Montevideo and obtain updated information on travel and security within Uruguay. The U.S. Embassy in Montevideo is located at Lauro Muller 1776; Tel: (598)(2) 418-7777; Fax: (598) (2) 418-4110 or –8611. Web site: http://uruguay. usembassy.gov/. Consular Section hours are Monday, Wednesday, and Friday, 9:00 a.m. to 11:00 p.m. and 2:00 p.m. to 4:00 p.m., except U.S. and Uruguayan holidays.

United Kingdom: British Embassy is located at Calle Marco Bruto 1073, 11300 Montevideo, PO Box 16024; Tel: (598)(2) 622-3630, -3650; Fax: (598)(2) 622-7815. E-mail: bemonte@internet.com.uy; Web site: http://www.britishembassy.org.uy.

Section 4.
Europe

Preface

On May 1, 2004, the fifteen nation European Union expanded with the addition of ten eastern European nations. The combined population of this enlarged EU exceeds 400 million.

Since 1992, the number of immigrants into the European Union countries has fallen by half. During that period, millions of people, including refugees from what was once Yugoslavia, sought a European haven. Countries that bore the migration brunt include Austria, France, Italy, and Germany. The French and the British have kept immigration to a minimum and the "immigrant-refugee" issue has been raised in many national elections, even in tiny Denmark. Based on total numbers alone, Germany is easily the favorite destination. It took in over 4 million foreigners by 1999, followed by Switzerland, the Netherlands, and France.

In 1998, Austria and Italy joined the so-called "Schengen" countries, which by common agreement allow free cross-border travel among themselves. In theory, this means movement without document checks or border guards. However, most European governments have cut the immigration inflow and refuse to cede total power to the EU over which immigrants and refugees each country will accept. Another restrictive device has been to require residency permits for EU citizens who seek to move in from other EU nations. The outer borders of the Schengen area countries are ringed with guards and sensors. Data on asylum-seekers, including fingerprints, are logged in computers to which all EU countries have access.

About one million people enter the European Union legally each year, mostly to join family members or by dodging police long enough to become eligible for amnesties that let them stay. That's about the same annual number as is admitted to the U.S. and Canada combined. Another 200,000 or so come to Western Europe as asylum-seekers. By some estimates, as many as 6 million people may be living in European countries illegally. Compared to 18 million unemployed across the EU, those numbers have caused much popular opposition to free immigration.

So much so, that in early 2000, both Belgium and Luxembourg opted out of the Schengen Agreement and reintroduced border controls for citizens of other EU nations. The move, designed to cope with an influx of illegal immigrants, undermines the dream of a passport-free European Union. In 2004 Switzerland agreed to join the Shegen agreement, but only with restrictions.

Eventually, the EU goal is to allow free immigration in and out of its collective borders, but individual EU countries are refusing to go along with what they consider a much too liberal immigration policy.

Principality of Andorra

CAPITAL:	ANDORRA LA VELLA
POPULATION:	69,150
LANGUAGE:	CATALAN (OFFICIAL), FRENCH, CASTILIAN, PORTUGUESE
CURRENCY:	EURO (€)
AREA:	468 SQUARE KM
ETHNIC GROUPS:	SPANISH 43%, ANDORRAN 33%, PORTUGUESE 11%, FRENCH 7%, OTHER 6%
RELIGION:	ROMAN CATHOLIC (PREDOMINANT)

PASSPORT HIGHLIGHTS: Anyone may take up residence in Andorra without formalities, but the granting of "passive residence" permits, the first step on the road to permanent installation, is subject to a quota of 200 such permits annually. After 20 years of "passive" residence, an individual can become a privileged resident, a status allowing commercial activity on behalf of one trading company, but not conferring the right to vote. Under current law, any person in residence more than 25 years may acquire Andorran nationality after renouncing his/her previous nationality.

It lies right in the center of the continent, down in a secret valley in one of the most stunning mountain ranges in Europe. It's a secluded medieval principality not governed by any European bureaucracy. For the few in the know, this picturesque valley in the Pyrenees between France and Spain, almost forgotten by the rest of the world, offers affordable crime-free, tax-free European living. The big secret is... you don't even need a permit to live there... you can just move in! Andorra's duty-free shopping and virtually tax-free living would be potent lures to almost any place on Earth. Add in the spectacular scenery of the eastern Pyrenees, abundant skiing (with epic night life in the resorts), and this mini-state embedded within increasingly homogenized Europe could fit many people's definition of paradise.

Andorra is an accident of geography. The mountaintop principality is hours away from the nearest airport in Barcelona. Andorra's 65,000 inhabitants speak Catalan at home, although French, Castilian, and English are widely spoken in the principality's capital, Andorra la Vella, and in resort areas. Andorra is also a blissful tax haven — no income, capital gains, or inheritance taxes. No sales taxes or customs duties. There is a small local residence tax charged in most "parishes," as the unit of local government is called.

As we might deduce for a country covering an area less than half the size of New York City, available tracts for newcomers are few. Foreigners (defined as non-Andorrans or those resident in the country less than 20 years) are restricted to a single property, either an apartment or a plot of land, improved or not, covering no more than 1,000 square meters. Thus, although average realty prices in Andorra are somewhat lower than the European norm, a residence in one of the more attractive villages or resorts could cost more than a similar dwelling in the center of Paris.

A parliamentary democracy since March 1993, Andorra retains as its heads of state a co-principality; the two princes are the President of France and Bishop of Seo de Urgel, Spain, who are represented locally by officials called veguers. Andorra is governed by a legislative Council General whose electors are the 11,500 plus native-born citizens with Andorran parents. This electorate constitutes less than one-sixth of the total Andorran population. The total population includes 30,000 Spanish, with sizeable communities of Portuguese, French, and English speakers.

Under Andorra's old constitution, what are called "passive residence permits" were handed out by designated personal representatives of the Spanish and French. Andorrans, with no control over this process, resented the permits given arbitrarily to politicians' friends and cronies. After the 1992 constitution, the new Council General blocked permits by refusing to pass on applications to the co-princes' representatives until a stricter immigration law was adopted. A tougher law on passive residence permits became final on June 30, 1995, and beginning again in 1997, permits again were issued.

Passive Residence

Residence, under Andorran law, is defined as a person's permanent principal residence. A second residence in Andorra does not alter an individual's domicile of origin for the purposes of home nation inheritance or estate taxes.

Those granted a passive residence in Andorra have the right to protection under the law, certain benefits from the health and social security system, the right to a driver's license and to own and register vehicles with resident plates. Residence does not confer the right to vote, either in local or national elections, nor does it allow local commercial activity, such as owning or running a business.

An individual who is not a resident is considered a tourist. But there is no legal limit on the period of stay and tourists are permitted to rent or purchase a property for personal use for as long as they wish. Thus, it is easy to live in Andorra perpetual traveler-style even without an official residence permit. In addition, there are ways to benefit from Andorran tax advantages, depending on the tax laws in your home nation or place of legal domicile. Questions on tax issues should be directed to your attorney, the financial services firm Servissim, or Henley & Partner. (See below for contact details).

There are two categories of residence permits, both difficult to obtain: 1) those that give the holder the right to work in Andorra; and 2) those that do not allow work. Residence permits are issued for periods of four years and are renewable. Applications for permits should be submitted to the Office of Immigration in Andorra la Vella, the capital city (telephone: +376-826222).

A holder of a permit should spend at least six months annually in Andorra and have documented proof of that fact. Failure to meet this requirement can result in revocation of the permit. The annual maximum quota for issuance of passive, non-work permits (passive residency permits) is now 200. The earlier each year one applies, the better the chance of obtaining one. Applications are considered without regard to nationality, race or religion, but the person must be at least 18 years of age.

Applicants must also show that they and their family have "sufficient economic means" to reside in the Principality of Andorra without any professional or work activity on their part throughout the period of his/her passive residence. How much cash or assets does "sufficient economic means" require? An applicant must be able to demonstrate income of US$24,000 per annum. A couple must be able to demonstrate combined income of US$38,000. There is an additional income requirement if children are included on the application. Proof of annual income is sometimes waived if the applicant's net worth, as declared in a required confidential financial statement, is at the very high end. Obviously, the more wealth declared, the better the chance for a permit.

An applicant for passive residence must be able to prove he/she has in force public or private health insurance to cover illness, incapacity, and old age for him/her and those in his/her charge for the duration of passive residence. Private insurance purchased from an Andorran insurer is more likely to be acceptable; the usual route since insurance can only be procured after a residence permit is granted.

The applicant must be able to show documentary evidence that he/she is the owner or tenant of a house or apartment. The applicant must also show that he/she has initiated the process of acquiring or renting a dwelling within the Principality, which process must be concluded within a period of one-year from the date of application. He/she must be able to prove neither he/she nor those in his/her charge have any previous penal criminal convictions. Some countries, including the U.K., do not issue such certificates, but a reference from a professional person of standing, such as a solicitor or attorney, usually is sufficient.

Each applicant must supply a non-interest bearing deposit of US$24,000 for the principal applicant and US$6,000 for each additional applicant (spouse/child) to the Institute National de Finances, the financial control office. Deposits are returned in full at the end of residence. In addition, a new resident must pay an annual fee to cover the benefits he/she and the family receive from residence in the Principality.

Andorran Citizenship

After 20 years of residence, whether passive or working, an individual can become a privileged resident. This stepped-up status allows activity in commercial matters on behalf of a maximum of one trading company, but does not confer the right to vote.

Under current law, any person in residence more than 25 years may acquire Andorran nationality after renouncing his/her previous nationality. Children born in Andorra of resident foreign parents may opt for Andorran nationality when they become 18 if they and their parents are still officially resident in Andorra. These applicants also must renounce any previous nationality.

Newly restrictive residency laws, adopted in 1995, produced something unusual in Andorra; a national political debate involving residents and organizations that represent the major nationality groups on one side, and the politicians on the other. Complainers see the law as pushing many residents to leave and keeping others out. They cited Andorra's then-sluggish summer property market, blaming the slump on the new residence laws.

Local politicians, not used to public criticism, were unsettled by the protests, and revisions in the law produced the present annual quota of 200 available residency permits.

Contacts

Henley & Partner, Inc., Kirchgasse 22, 8001 Zurich, Switzerland; Tel: +(41)44-266-2222; Fax: +(41) 44-266-2223; E-mail: zurich@henley-global.com; Web site: http://www.henleyglobal.com

Servissim, Edifici Areny, Baixos, Carretera General, Arinsal, La Massana, Principat d´Andorra. Tel: +376 737800 Fax: +376 737804 Web site: http://www.servissim.ad/index_servissim.htm E-mail: services@servissim.ad Servissim is a dependable relocation agent that provides a free newsletter with information about residency laws and changes that may occur.

Embassy of Andorra, 51bis, rue de Boulainvilliers – 75016 Paris, France; Tel: (01) (40) 03 – 30; E-mail: ambiaxada@andorra.ad

Andorra Tourist Delegation, 63 Westover Road, London SW18 2RF, U.K.; Tel: (44) (01) 81-874-4806.

United States: Andorra is a highly developed and stable democracy with a modern economy. A passport is required for Andorra, but a visa is not required for tourist or business stays up to 90 days. Individuals who enter Andorra without a visa are not authorized to work. For further information concerning entry requirements for Andorra, travelers should contact the Embassy of Spain at 2375 Pennsylvania Avenue NW, Washington, D.C. 20037, Tel: (202) 728-2330, or the nearest Spanish consulate in Boston, Chicago, Houston, Los Angeles, Miami, New Orleans, New York, San Francisco, or San Juan. Spanish government websites with information about entry requirements (in Spanish) can be found at http://www.mae.es and http://www.mir.es.

For additional information on entry requirements to Andorra, travelers should also contact the Permanent Mission of the Principality of Andorra to the United Nations, Two United Nations Plaza, 25th Floor, New York, NY 10017, Tel: (212) 750-8064/8065; Fax: (212) 750 6630; E-mail: andorra@un.int; web site: http://www.andorra.ad

Americans living in or visiting Andorra are encouraged to register at the Consular Section of the U.S. Embassy in Madrid or at the U.S. Consulate General in Barcelona, where they may obtain updated information on travel and security within Andorra.

The U.S. Embassy in Madrid, Spain, is located at Serrano 75; Tel:

(34)(91) 587-2200 and Fax: (34)(91) 587-2303. U.S. citizens who register in the Consular Section at the U.S. Embassy, Consulate General, or one of the Consular Agency's listed below can obtain updated information on travel and security within Andorra. Additional information is available through the U.S. Embassy's web site: http://madrid. usembassy.gov/.

The U.S. Consulate in Barcelona is located at Paseo Reina Elisenda 23-25; Tel: (34)(93) 280-2227 and Fax: (34)(93) 205-5206. Visitors to Barcelona can access additional information from the Consulate General's web site: http://barcelona.usconsulate.gov/.

There are six Consular Agencies in Spain, which provide limited services to American Citizens, but are not authorized to issue passports. **Fuengirola** near Malaga, at Avenida Juan Gomez Juanito #8, Edificio Lucia 1C, 29640, Fuengirola, Tel: (34)(952) 474-891 and Fax: (34)(952) 465-189, Hours 10:00 a.m. to 1:00 p.m.; **La Coruna**, at Canton Grande 6, Tel: (34)(981) 213-233 and Fax: (34)(981 22 28 08), Hours 10:00 a.m. to 1:00 p.m.; **Las Palmas**, at Edificio Arca, Calle Los Martinez de Escobar 3, Oficina 7, Tel: (34)(928) 222-552 and Fax: (34)(928) 225-863, Hours 10:00 a.m. to 1:00 p.m; **Palma de Mallorca**, Edificio Reina Constanza, Porto Pi, 8, 9-D, 07015 Palma de Mallorca, Spain. Tel: (34)(971) 40-3707 or 40-3905 and Fax: (34)(971) 40-3971. Hours 10:30 a.m. to 1:30 p.m.; **Seville**, at Paseo de Las Delicias 7, Tel: (34)(954) 231-885 and Fax: (34)(954) 232-040, Hours 8:30 a.m. to 1:30 p.m.; **Valencia**, at Doctor Romagosa #1, 2-J, 46002, Valencia, Tel: (34)(96)-351-6973 and Fax: (34)(96) 352-9565, Hours 10:00 a.m. to 1:00 p.m.

United Kingdom: The British Honorary Consulate resides in Madrid and the Consul General resides in Barcelona. The Andorran British Honorary Consulate is located at Casa Jacint Pons, 3/2 La Massana, Principat d'Andorra; Tel: (34) (933) 666-200; Fax: (34) (933) 666-221; E-mail: britconand@mypic.ad. The British Consulate-General is located at Edificio Torre de Barcelona, Avineda Diagonal 477-13, 08036 Barcelona; Tel: (34) (933) 666-200; Fax: (34) (933) 666-221.

Republic of Austria

CAPITAL:	VIENNA
POPULATION:	8,188,207
LANGUAGE:	GERMAN, (ENGLISH UNDERSTOOD)
CURRENCY:	EURO (€)
AREA:	83,858 SQUARE KM
ETHNIC GROUPS:	GERMAN 88%, NON-NATIONALS 9.3% (INCLUDES CROATIANS, SLOVENES, HUNGARIANS, CZECHS, SLOVAKS, ROMA), NATURALIZED 2% (INCLUDES THOSE WHO HAVE LIVED IN AUSTRIA AT LEAST THREE GENERATIONS)
RELIGION:	ROMAN CATHOLIC 78%, PROTESTANT 5%, MUSLIM AND OTHER 17%

PASSPORT HIGHLIGHTS: Investors of at least US$2 million in approved projects in Austria may be considered for citizenship under a law seeking to attract extraordinary contributions to the nation. Otherwise, persons with a residence in Austria and at least US$25,000 in annual income are eligible for permanent residency, which confers eligibility to apply for naturalization in five years, in most cases.

Landlocked Austria is located in central Europe, north of Italy and Slovenia, with five other countries forming its national borders. It is largely mountainous, with 40% under forest cover. The Danube, central Europe's major river, flows through the nation, which celebrated the first millennium of its founding in 1996.

Vienna was once the seat of the Habsburg dynasty and of the powerful Austro-Hungarian Empire they ruled. The city retains much of the legendary elegance and charm it possessed as the capital of Central Europe and the magnet that drew in and harbored artists, composers, chefs, decorators, intellectuals, and literary geniuses for many centuries. Vienna will forever be associated with names of Mozart, Haydn, Beethoven, Schubert, Schnitzler, Freud, and dozens of other leaders in all creative fields. Outstanding museums and universities, splendid architecture, top-class orchestras and opera companies, beautiful parks around the former palaces, fine restaurants, and fabled pastry shops draw visitors and expatriates the banks of the "Beautiful Blue Danube." The rest of the country is not without its charm and attractions, with the annual Mozart festival in the composer's birth city of Salzburg, historic churches and monasteries in the countryside or in or near many of the major cities, and renowned winter sports Meccas in the mountains.

After Germany's defeat in World War I, Austria shrank to a minor republic. In 1938, it became a part of Nazi Germany in an ill-fated *Anschluss* (annexation). At the end of World War II, Austria was occupied by the four victorious Allied powers. In a 1955 state treaty, Austria was declared a "permanently neutral" country as a condition of Soviet military withdrawal from the occupied nation. The Soviet Union's subsequent collapse finally relieved pressure on Austria to remain unaligned, but by now, neutrality has become attractive to Austrians. In spite of recent international controversy, the official U.S. State Department bulletin on Austria, dated January 19, 2000, stated: "Austria is a highly developed stable democracy with a modern economy."

There has been an ongoing public debate over whether the nation can remain aloof from European security structures, but, in 1995, Austria joined the European Union after a large majority voted in favor of doing so. As a committed neutral, Austria has not joined the defensive military alliance of the North Atlantic Treaty Organization (NATO). There's evidence that outside pressure is counter productive at best. In local Austrian elections in 1996, the major issue raised by the right-wing Freedom Party was EU interference in Austria's internal affairs and threats to national sovereignty. EU attacks on the banking secrecy laws added to the resentment. Again, in early 1998, the Freedom Party increased its following in elections and, in early 2000, joined a new government coalition.

What makes Austria particularly interesting in the context of dual nationality and second passports is its post-war history as a major processing center for the resettlement of refugees, especially those who fled Communism's take-over of eastern Europe and, more recently, the Balkan Wars. The United Nations long has had a bureaucracy of "relocation experts" headquartered in Vienna providing temporary housing for stateless people. Austria offers its sympathy, life support, and even an "Austrian Refugee Passport." Austria also expects refugees to be temporary visitors, soon to move on to other destinations.

In recent years, the influx of refugees has been so great that curbing immigration has become a major issue in nation elections, leading to the fall of the long-time Socialist-Christian Democrat coalition government. This was a major issue that brought the Freedom Party, headed by Carinthian governor Jörg Haider, into power in coalition with the Christian Democrats, much to the discomfort of some in the EU.

Unique European Banking Secrecy

Strategically located on the eastern European border between former Cold War blocs, East and West, the Austrian Republic has long been a bastion of banking privacy. From 1945 to the Soviet collapse in 1992, Russia and the U.S. remained locked in confrontation, but both West and East Bloc governments used this convenient banking haven as a go-between.

When Austrian national banking laws were officially codified in 1979, the well-established tradition of bank secrecy was already two centuries old. During this time, Austrian bank secrecy and privacy produced two major types of so-called "anonymous accounts." These accounts usually required no account holder identification, no mailing address, and no personal references. Just deposit funds and use the account as you pleased, all anonymously.

Current Austrian bank secrecy laws forbid banks to "disclose or make use of secrets which have been entrusted or made accessible to them solely due to the business relationships with customers." This prohibition is waived only in criminal court proceedings involving "intentional fiscal violations [crimes], with the exception of fiscal petty offenses." The prohibition does not apply "if the customer expressly and in writing consents to the disclosure of the secret."

Austria ranks among the ten richest countries in the world on a per capita basis. Its capital gold reserves rank third in the Western World. Its political and economic stability is reflected in its currency's performance prior to the adoption of the euro. The Austrian schilling appreciated against the U.S. dollar by 150% in its last 20 years.

Immigration

Because of its diminutive size, Austria does not accept many new resident aliens. Indeed, limiting immigration has become a major political issue giving rise to the conservative Freedom Party that opposes further immigration.

Although Austria does not have an economic citizenship program per se, statutory law does allow the granting of citizenship to a foreign person if he or she is judged to contribute in some extraordinary way, including economic, to the interests of Austria. However, this is a very difficult way to acquire citizenship and may require a year at a minimum. Applicants are approved on a case-by-case basis and must be willing to invest at least US$2 million in an approved project in Austria. Investment proposals are submitted to the Office of Economic Development. Those that provide export stimulation or local employment, receive preference. Representation by a knowledgeable Austrian lawyer is essential, and is likely to cost considerably more than US$50,000. There are also citizenship opportunities for academics, such as university professors. Henley & Partner can provide details on these Austrian possibilities.

Special Residence Status

Austria offers non-Europeans the possibility of a quick path to official EU resident status. With Austrian residency, visa-free travel is possible throughout all Schengen countries. Persons of independent means with a proven minimum annual income of at least US$25,000, a home place in the country, and full health insurance coverage are eligible for Austrian residency. After five years, and in some cases less, residents may apply for citizenship.

In special circumstances, a person who can demonstrate that their proposed residence in Austria will make a unique scientific or technological contribution that benefits the public interest, will be admitted in a tax-free status. This special status is reviewed annually by the Ministry of Finance.

The following documentation is required for an Austrian residency application:

Document:	For:
Personal information form	Each person, including children
Birth certificate (certified copy)	Each person, including children
Marriage certificate (certified copy)	Married couples
Divorce certificate (certified copy)	Divorced persons
Certificate of no criminal record (original)	Each person (18 years and over)
Proof of apartment rental in Austria	Main applicant

Proof of health & accident insurance	Each person, including children
Copy of passport or ID document (photocopy)	Each person, including children
Four (4) color passport photos	Each person, including children
Power of attorney	Each person (18 years and over)

The main applicant must also submit an original bank reference proving assets of US$20,000 for each person. If documents are not in German, they must be accompanied with a certified translation in German.

Consider the foreigner who uses Austria as their second residence, but not as the "center of their vital interests," (a phrase from Austrian tax law). The person goes skiing for three or four weeks each year in Austria. Their legal domicile (the place where they live most of the time and to which they eventually intend to return) is in another country. In their case, any Austrian source income is taxable in Austria, but all other income not earned in Austria is taxable in the country where they live, their domicile. Their exact tax status and obligations will be determined under the terms of a double taxation treaty that may exist between Austria and their country of domicile.

It's definitely a good deal worth considering.

Is Austrian Residence Status for Sale?

To be frank, yes, if you are a wealthy foreigner who is a reputable person, there will be few obstacles to becoming a resident. Residency gives you the best of both worlds: life in an extremely desirable location, but without the high taxes that Austrian citizens must pay.

Once in residence, you could apply for citizenship, but that defeats the purpose. As an Austrian citizen, you'd be liable for full taxation. The only additional advantage would be having an Austrian passport and the right to purchase as much real property as you wish, which is otherwise very difficult for a foreigner merely residing in Austria.

Austrian citizenship provides one of the most desirable of all second passports and is comparatively easy to obtain.

Contacts

Henley & Partners Representative Office, Karntner Ring 3/Top 22, 1010 Vienna, Austria; Tel: +(43) 1 505 53 66; Fax: +(43) 1-815-92 23; Contact: Dr. Manfred Strasser Email:manfred.strasser@henleyglobal.com

Web site: http://www.henleyglobal.com/austria.htm

United States: A U.S. passport is required for entry into Austria. A visa is not required for business or tourist stays up to 90 days. For further information concerning entry requirements for Austria, travelers should contact the Embassy of Austria at 3524 International Court, NW, Washington, D.C. 20008, Tel: (202) 895-6767 or the nearest Austrian Consulate General in Chicago, Los Angeles, or New York. The Austrian Embassy to the United States maintains a web site in English that answers, in detail, questions concerning the laws and regulations of Austria, including residency, driver's license requirements, and permission to work: http://www.Austria.org/index.html

U.S. citizens are encouraged to register at the Consular Section of the U.S. Embassy in Vienna or at the Consular Agency in Salzburg and obtain updated information on travel and security within Austria. The U.S. Embassy in Vienna is located at Boltzmanngasse 16 in the 9th District. The Consular Section of the U.S. Embassy is located in the Marriott Building, on the fourth floor of Gartenbaupromenade 2, in the First District. The telephone number for both the Embassy and the Consular Section is (43)(1) 31-339. There is also a Consular Agency in Salzburg at Alter Markt 1, Tel: (43) (662) 84-87-76, open Monday, Wednesday and Thursday from 9:00 A.M. to 12:00 noon. U.S. citizens in Salzburg who require assistance outside of these hours may contact the U.S. Embassy in Vienna. Web site: http://www.usembassy-vienna.

United Kingdom: The British Embassy in Vienna is located at Jauresgasse 12, 1030 Vienna; Tel: (43) (1) 716130; Fax: (43) (1) 71613 2999 Chancery; E-mail: press@britishembassy.at visa-consular@britishembassy.at Web site: http://www.britishembassy.at The British Consulate is located at Jauresgasse 10, 1-1030 Vienna, Tel: (43) (1) 71613-5151, Fax: (43) (1) 71613-5900 (28120 AMBLUX G Telex). There are other British Consulates located in Bundesstrasse 110, A-6923 Lauterach/Bregenz; Tel: (43) (5574) 78586; Fax: (43) (5574) 70928; Graz: Schmiedgasse 8-12, A-8010 Graz, Tel: (43) (316) 82 161 621, Fax: (43) (316) 82 161 645; Innsbruck: Kaiserjaegerstrasse 1/Top B9, A-6020 Innsbruck, Tel: (43) (512) 588320, Fax: (43) (512) 579973-8 and Salzburg: Alter Markt 4, A-5020 Salzburg, Tel: (43) (662) 848133, Fax: (43) (662) 845563 (263 308 Telex).

Czech Republic

CAPITAL:	PRAHA (PRAGUE)
POPULATION:	10,249,216
LANGUAGE:	CZECH
CURRENCY:	CZECH KORUNA (CZK)
AREA:	78,866 SQUARE KM
ETHNIC GROUPS:	CZECH 81.2%, MORAVIAN 13.2%, SLOVAK 3.1%, POLISH 0.6%, GERMAN 0.5%, SILESIAN 0.4%, ROMA 0.3%, HUNGARIAN 0.2%, OTHER 0.5%
RELIGION:	ROMAN CATHOLIC 39.2%, PROTESTANT 4.6%, ORTHODOX 3%, OTHER 13.4%, ATHEIST 39.8%

PASSPORT HIGHLIGHTS: Entrepreneurs setting up businesses in the Czech Republic are eligible for permanent residency, which may lead to naturalization after five years.

The Czech Republic is a landlocked country in central Europe surrounded by Poland, Germany, and Slovakia. Once part of the Holy Roman Empire and, later, the Austro-Hungarian Empire, Czechoslovakia became an independent nation in 1918 at the end of World War I. Independence ended with the Nazi German military takeover in 1939. After World War II, Czechoslovakia fell under the Soviet sphere of influence. In 1968, an invasion by Warsaw Pact troops snuffed out anti-Communist demonstrations. With the collapse of the Soviet Union in 1991, Czechoslovakia regained its freedom. On January 1, 1993, the country peacefully split into its two traditional ethnic components, the Czech Republic, comprising Bohemia and Moravia, and Slovakia.

The medieval Kingdom of Bohemia was absorbed into the Habsburg Empire at the height of its splendor, and the country's nobility continued to lavish cultural and architectural marvels on it throughout the Austro-Hungarian period. Prague, the capital, is known as one of the most beautiful cities in Europe, with a vibrant and innovative cultural life. It is perhaps not a coincidence that the Czechs bestowed the country's presidency upon a playwright, Vaclav Havel, as soon as they threw off the Soviet yoke. The country offers palaces, churches, museums, orchestras, fine dining, world-famous beer and wine, and a relaxed but edgy lifestyle to the visitor or expatriate.

The Czech Republic, largely by aspiring to become a NATO and EU member, has moved toward integration in world markets. Nevertheless, the government has had a difficult time convincing the public that membership in NATO is crucial to Czech security. At the same time, support for eventual EU membership continues. Coupled with the country's economic difficulties, Prague's political scene, troubled for the past few years, looks to remain so for the near future.

With all its problems, of all the former Soviet bloc Communist countries, the Czech Republic is probably the most westernized. The transition to a free market economy seems to have progressed more smoothly than other countries. Privatization and restitution of Communist confiscated property is nearing completion.

Residence and Citizenship

The Czech Government will welcome any foreign national willing to establish a new business or is self-employed. Naturalization can be applied for after five years of formal residence. During that period, a permanent resident enjoys most rights of full Czech citizens, including the right to purchase real property. Czech passports are valid for five years, allow visa-free travel to most EU countries as well as Switzerland, but excluding France and the U.S.

Contacts

United States: A valid U.S. passport is required for entry into the Czech Republic. Visas are not required for U.S. citizens for tourist, short study or business visits of up to 90 days. Visas are required for longer stays and for any gainful activity. For more information, contact the Embassy of the Czech Republic at 3900 Spring of Freedom St. NW, Washington, D.C. 20008, Tel: (202) 274-9103 or visit the Embassy's web site at http://www.mzv.cz/washington

Americans living in or visiting the Czech Republic are encouraged to register at the Consular Section of the U.S. Embassy in the Czech Republic and obtain updated information on travel and security within the Czech Republic. The U.S. Embassy in Prague is located at Trziste 15, 118 01 Prague, Czech Republic, Tel: (420) 257 530 663; for after hours emergencies only – Tel: (420) 257 532 716; Web site: http://www.usembassy.cz

United Kingdom: The British Embassy, Chancery, Consular/Visa, Economic, Press and Public Affairs Section, Defence Section is located at Thunovska 14, 118 00 Prague 1, Tel: (420) 25740 2111; Fax: (420) 25740 2296, (420) 25740 2280 (Consular/Visa); E-mail: info@britain.cz, Consular/Visa.Prague@fco.gov.uk (Consular/Visa); Web site: http://www.britain.cz/

France

CAPITAL:	PARIS
POPULATION:	60,180,529
LANGUAGE:	FRENCH 100%, RAPIDLY DECLINING REGIONAL DIALECTS AND LANGUAGES (PROVENCAL, BRETON, ALSATIAN, CORSICAN, CATALAN, BASQUE, FLEMISH)
CURRENCY:	EURO (€)
AREA:	547,030 SQUARE KM
ETHNIC GROUPS:	CELTIC AND LATIN WITH TEUTONIC, SLAVIC, NORTH AFRICAN, INDOCHINESE, BASQUE MINORITIES
RELIGION:	ROMAN CATHOLIC 83%-88%, PROTESTANT 2%, JEWISH 1%, MUSLIM 5%-10%, UNAFFILIATED 4%

PASSPORT HIGHLIGHTS: Non-EU nationals may receive permanent residency, and eventually naturalization, in France. The criteria for residency status are stiff and the procedures time-consuming and often frustrating. Naturalization is available after five years residency.

Although ultimately a victor in World Wars I and II, France lost many citizens, much wealth, its extensive empire, and its rank as one of the world's dominant nation-states. The Vichy collaboration with the Nazi occupiers also tarnished national honor and history. Since then, the nation has struggled with success to construct a strong presidential democracy that avoids the parliamentary instability that characterized France in the earlier 20th Century. Its reconciliation and cooperation with Germany, now its largest trading partner, has been key to the economic integration of Europe.

The largest nation (in area) in western Europe, France borders the Bay of Biscay and the English Channel on the west, between Belgium and Spain, and, on the south, borders the Mediterranean Sea between Italy and Spain. France's reputation for style and elegance are well deserved, at least in Paris, and the rest of the country's regions retain many of the local culinary and cultural traditions that made traveling around the "Hexagon" so rewarding in years past. However, mass culture and consumerism have made visible inroads into France's former charms, while high prices (even without regard to foreign exchange fluctuations) and heavy taxation have eliminated most of the "bargains" once associated with travel and life in France.

Visas and Entry

Foreign nationals wishing to establish residence in France use different procedures depending on their national origin. The three general groups are: nationals from France's fellow EU countries; those from countries with which France has immigration or visa-free travel accords, such as the United States; and persons from all other countries.

The EU requires all member states to allow free international movement of EU persons, including the right to freely engage in commercial business. While the official French policy agrees with this EU principle, they argue that this cannot surmount the French right to live in safety. The French have set up a system of police, judicial and customs, which they say compensates for the removal of border controls between member states. Immigration has been a very touchy issue in France for two decades, mainly because of the large influx of Muslim, black, and other racial groups from the former French colonies in Africa and elsewhere.

France requires other EU nationals wishing to do business within its borders to apply to regional police headquarters (Préfecture de Police) for a residency card (carte de séjour). The applicant must show what business is intended and provide copies of contracts, leases, and corporate documents for a new French company or a business registration certificate for a foreign company opening a French branch.

In the second entry-seeking group are those from countries that have mutual agreements allowing up to three months of visa-free travel in France. These include the non-EU countries of Andorra, Canada, Iceland, Japan, Monaco, Norway, San Marino, South Korea, Switzerland, the Vatican, and the United States. These agreements also allow citizens of each nation to take up residence, temporary or permanent, within France, but they must go through immigration procedures for approval of their status and prove they have sufficient economic means for support.

Citizens from all other countries must first obtain a visa to enter

France, without regard to the purpose of the visit, even as a tourist. Proof of intent to return to the applicant's home nation is required. Strong ties to one's home country, such as presence there of close family members, income, assets, and professional status are examined.

Obtaining full citizenship is relatively easy after five years residency, but has drawbacks. Foreign citizens who are considered to have acquired French citizenship may be subject to compulsory military service and other aspects of French law while in France.

Employment

French immigration procedure is tedious, bureaucratic, prolonged, and, often, fruitless. The law views potential resident aliens in terms of "employment," "independent professions," or "commercial activities."

Except in cases of unique executive-level and management jobs, statistical unemployment in the geographic region or the type of job sought precludes approval. Professional positions, medical, legal, accounting, engineering, and architecture require French or equivalent academic and professional qualifications for admission. In less professional positions, such as writers, artists, composers, consultants, and teachers, a simplified, speedier examination process is used. The performing arts are unionized and considered to be employment.

In each case, the prospective employer must initiate the application process. Applications for specific events or for a limited number of engagements are approved quickly, but long-term contracts are less likely to be approved.

For foreign nationals seeking permission to buy and sell goods or render services, a special merchant's card is issued in addition to a residency card. That includes commercial agents and company executives. Anyone other than managers of major international companies are likely to have a difficult time obtaining residency and business permission in France. In each case, proof of financial means and a business plan are required.

Taxes

It was a French finance minister who gave the essential government view towards raising tax revenues. "The art of taxation," Jean-Baptiste Colbert (1619-83), the comptroller general of finances, told Louis XIV before that king's spending got really out of hand, "is to pluck from the goose the most feathers with the least hissing." In France, the hissing is getting very loud. According to Forbes magazine's annual "tax misery index" in 2004, the highest (worst) rating goes to France at 193%, up another 8% in the last year. A US$50,000-a-year manager costs a French company 143% of that amount pre-tax (and 89% on an after tax basis), after calculating the employer's share of social security and other taxes.

Unless one has a truly compelling reason to work or locate a business in France, the taxes alone should give major pause. The socialist French Government's share of gross domestic product now exceeds 45%, up from 35% just 30 years ago. In France, a successful US$200,000-a-year executive or entrepreneur gets to keep just US$97,050 after the state has taken its cut. That may explain why 500,000 French citizens now live in the U.K., and 60,000 French engineers call California's Silicon Valley home today.

Contacts

Henley & Partners AG, Kirchgasse 22 8001 Zurich Switzerland. Tel: +(41)-44-266-22-22; Fax: +(41)-44-266-22-23; E-mail: zurich@henley-global.com; Web site: http://www.henleyglobal.com

United States: A passport is required for entry to France. A visa is not required for tourist or business stays up to 90 days in France. For further information concerning entry requirements for France contact the Embassy of France at 4101 Reservoir Road, NW, Washington, D.C. 20007, Tel: (202) 944-6000 or the French Consulates General in Atlanta , Boston , Chicago , Houston , Los Angeles , Miami , New Orleans , New York , or San Francisco. Web site: http://www. consulfrance-washington.org.

Americans living in or visiting France are encouraged to register at the Consular Section of the U.S. Embassy in Paris or the nearest Consulate and to obtain updated information on travel and security within France. The Consular Section of the U.S. Embassy in Paris is located at 2 Rue St. Florentin, 75001 Paris (Place de La Concorde, Metro Stop Concorde), Tel: (011) (33) (143) 12-22-22 or (in France) (01) (43) 12-22-22; Fax: (011) (33) (142) 61-61-40. Web site: http://www.amb-usa.fr.

The Consulate General in Marseille is located at Place Varian Fry, 13086 Marseille, Tel: (011) (33) 4-91-54-92-00, ext. 304, or (in France) (04) (91) 54-92-00, ext. 304; Fax: (011) (33) (491) 55-09-47. The Consulate General in Strasbourg is located at 15 Avenue d'Alsace, 67082 Strasbourg, Tel: (011) (33) (388) 35-31-04 or (in France) (03) (88) 35-31-04; Fax: (011) (33) (388) 24-06-95. The Consulate General in Strasbourg does not produce passports on the premises. American citizens in this area whose passports are lost or stolen and who have urgent travel needs should contact the U.S. Embassy in Paris. The Consular Agency in Nice is located at 7, Avenue Gustave V, 3rd floor, 06000 Nice, Tel: (011) (33) (493) 88-89-55 or (in France) (04) (93) 88-89-55; fax 011-33-4-93-87-07-38. The U.S. Government also has consular representation in Bordeaux , Lille , Lyon , Rennes , and Toulouse that provide some emergency services to Americans. However, their primary focus is economic and commercial.

United Kingdom: The British Embassy is located at 35 rue du Faubourg St Honoré, 75383 Paris Cedex 08; Tel: (331) 44-51-31-00; Fax: (331) 44-51-32-88; Web site: http://www.amb-grandebretagne.fr/. The British Consulate-General has offices in:

Paris: 18 bis rue d'Anjou, 75008 Paris, Tel: (331) 44-51-31 00, Fax: (331) 44-51-31 27; E-mail: webmaster@amb-grandebretagne.fr; **Bordeaux:** 353 Boulevard du President Wilson, 33073 Bordeaux Cedex, Tel: (335) 57-22-21-10, Fax: (335) 56-08-33-12, E-mail: postmaster.bordeaux@fco.gov.uk.

Lille: 11 Square Dutilleul, 59000 Lille, Tel: (333) 20-12-82-72, Fax: (333) 20-54-88-16; E-mail: postmaster.lille@fco.gov.uk;

Lyon: 24 rue Childebert, 69002 Lyon, Tel: (334) 72-77-81-70, Fax: (334) 72-77-81-79, E-mail: }postmaster.lyon@fco.gov.uk and

Marseille: 24 Avenue de Prado, 13006 Marseilles, Tel: (334) 91-15-72-10, Fax: (334) 91-37-47-06, E-mail: postmaster.marseille@fco.gov.uk.

German Federal Republic

CAPITAL:	BERLIN
POPULATION:	82,398,326
LANGUAGE:	GERMAN, ENGLISH WIDELY SPOKEN
CURRENCY:	EURO (€)
AREA:	357,000 SQUARE KM
ETHNIC GROUPS:	GERMAN 91.5%, TURKISH 2.4%, OTHER 6.1% (MADE UP LARGELY OF SERBO-CROATIAN, ITALIAN, RUSSIAN, GREEK, POLISH, SPANISH)
RELIGION:	PROTESTANT 34%, ROMAN CATHOLIC 34%, MUSLIM 3.7%, UNAFFILIATED OR OTHER 28.3%

PASSPORT HIGHLIGHTS: Permanent residency may be obtained by immigrants able to contribute to the German economy, especially in the eastern states. Naturalization is available after ten years in residence.

Modern German history is characterized by the immigration of massive numbers of foreign nationals, many of them refugees, but many recruited workers. Germany easily has been the favorite destination of European immigrants, but also the target of those from Africa, Asia, and Eastern Europe. The nation took in over 4 million foreigners by the end of the decade in 1999. Along with Austria, Germany has served as a major refugee nation. Germany also has an established policy of admitting ethnic Germans from other countries. Many thousands of these German-speaking persons have immigrated from Russia, Poland, the Ukraine, and elsewhere.

One reason for the refugee influx was the former policy of supplying all needy arrivals with housing, medical attention, and relocation financial assistance as well as a temporary passport. However, with high unemployment in the 1990s, there came a wave of internal political protest against free immigration. Particular resentment has been directed against Turks and some other ethnic minorities.

Germany enjoys the world's third most powerful economy, but

artificially high wages, costly welfare, and unemployment benefits have dragged down its capitalist market system. Taxes, both on personal and corporate income, are extremely high. The German nation continues to wrestle with the economic and political integration of eastern Germany, an adjustment that may take decades to complete fully.

The astonishing rebuilding of war-ravaged western Germany in the Federal Republic's "Economic Miracle" of the 1950s and '60s was not paralleled in the eastern regions under Soviet domination. The contrast between the two sectors remains striking nearly a decade and a half after reunification. Continued drabness and an air of desperation in the former Democratic Republic can still shock those familiar only with the brash consumerism (with a touch of glitz) of the West.

Residence for Investment

Germany encourages entrepreneur or business immigration with offers of loans, tax concessions, and subsidies for new businesses that will provide jobs or stimulate the local economy. Particular preference is given to investors who create jobs in the former East Germany. Artists, creative persons, the self-employed, and those who will not compete for local jobs may be able to obtain residence permits and identity cards that have the added benefit of being valid for travel throughout the EU.

Naturalization for full citizenship may be applied for after ten years of residence. This time period can be reduced in special cases. These include descendants of refugees from Germany or other countries due to Nazi persecution or invasion, and ethnic Germans. The naturalization process may require as much as one year.

Contacts

United States: A passport is required for entry into Germany. A visa is not required for tourist/business stays up to 90 days within the Schengen Group of countries, which includes Germany. Further information on entry, visa and passport requirements may be obtained from the German Embassy at 4645 Reservoir Road NW, Washington, D.C. 20007, Tel: (202) 298-4000, or the German Consulates General in Atlanta, Boston, Chicago, Houston, Los Angeles, Miami, New York, or San Francisco. Information may also be obtained from their web site: http://www.germany-info.org/newcontent/index_consular.html

Inquiries from outside the United States may be made to the nearest German embassy or consulate. Americans living in Germany are encouraged to register at the consular section of the U.S. Embassy or any of the U.S. consulates and obtain updated information on travel and security within Germany. Individuals planning extended stays in Germany are encouraged to register in person at their local consular section. A new initiative of the American Embassy in Berlin allows all Americans in Germany to obtain automatic security updates and Public Announcements by e-mail. To subscribe to this service, simply send a blank e-mail to GermanyACS@state.gov and put the word "SUBSCRIBE" on the subject line. The U.S. Embassy in Berlin is located at: Neustaedtische Kirchstrasse 4-5; Tel: (49)(30) 238-5174 or 8305-0; the consular section is located at Clayallee 170; Tel: (49)(30) 832-9233; Fax: (49)(30) 8305-1215.

U.S. Consulates General are located at: **Duesseldorf:** Willi-Becker-Allee 10, Tel: (49)(211) 788-8927; Fax: (49)(211) 788-8938; **Frankfurt:** Siesmayerstrasse 21, Tel: (49)(69) 75350; Fax: (49)(69) 7535-2304; **Hamburg:** Alsterufer 27/28, Tel: (49)(40) 4117-1351; Fax: (49)(40) 44-30-04; **Leipzig:** Wilhelm-Seyfferth-Strasse 4, Tel: (49)(341) 213-8418; Fax: (49)(341) 21384-17 (emergency services only); **Munich:** Koeniginstrasse 5, Tel: (49)(89) 2888-0; Fax: (49)(89) 280-9998. There is also a U.S. consular agency in **Bremen** located at Bremen World Trade Center, Birkenstockstrasse 15, Tel: (49)(421) 301-5860; Fax: (49)(421) 301-5861. When calling another city from within Germany, dial a zero before the city code (for example, when calling Berlin from Munich, the city code for Berlin is 030).

United Kingdom: The British Embassy is located at Wilhelmstrasse 70 10117 Berlin, Tel: (49) (30) 20457-0; Fax: (49) (30) 20457-571 Ambassador, (49) (30) 20457 579 Consular; Web site: http://www. britischebotschaft.de/

British Consulates are located in **Düsseldorf:** Yorckstrasse 19, D-40476 Düsseldorf, Tel: (49) (211) 94480, Fax: (49) (211) 48 81 90 Passport and Consular E-mail: Consular.Section@duesseldorf.mail.fco. gov.uk, Web site:http://www.britischebotschaft.de; **Munich:** Bürkleinstrasse 10, D-80538 Munich, Mail from UK only should be addressed: British Consulate-General, Munich, PO Box 2010, BFPO 105, Tel: (49) (89) 211090, Fax: (49) (89) 21109 144; **Frankfurt:** Triton Haus, Bockenheimer Landstrasse 42, D-60323 Frankfurt-am-Main, Mail from UK only should be addressed: British Consulate General, Frankfurt, PO Box 2009, BFPO 10, Tel: (49) (69) 170-0020, Fax: (49) (69) 729553, Email: info@Frankfurt.mail.fco.gov.uk, consecfrankfurt.frankfurt@ fco.gov.uk. **Stuttgart:** Breite Strasse 2, D-70173 Stuttgart, Tel: (49) (711) 16-2690, Fax: (49) (711) 16-26930;

Hamburg: Harvestehuder Weg 8a, D-20148 Hamburg, Tel: (49) (40) 448-0320, Fax: (49) (40) 410-7259; **Bremen:** Herrlichkeiten 6, Postfach 10 38 60, D-28199 Bremen, Tel: (49) (421) 59090; **Hannover:** Karl-Wiechert-Allee 50, 30625 Hannover Germany, Tel: (511) 388 38 08, Fax: (511) 56 04 16 90; Kiel: United Baltic Corporation GmbH, Schleuse Maklerstrasse 1, D-24159 Kiel, Tel: (49) (431) 331-971, Fax: (49) (431) 35395 and Nuremberg: M Schmitt & Sohn Gmbh, Hadermuhle 9-15, D-90402 Nuremberg, Tel: (49) (911) 2404-303, Fax: (49) (911) 2404 111.

Greece (Hellenic Republic)

CAPITAL:	ATHENS
POPULATION:	10,665,989
LANGUAGE:	GREEK 99% (OFFICIAL), ENGLISH, FRENCH
CURRENCY:	EURO (€)
AREA:	131,940 SQUARE KM
ETHNIC GROUPS:	GREEK 98%, OTHER 2%, THE GREEK GOVERNMENT STATES THERE ARE NO ETHNIC DIVISIONS IN GREECE
RELIGION:	GREEK ORTHODOX 98%, MUSLIM 1.3%, OTHER 0.7%

PASSPORT HIGHLIGHTS: Persons born abroad of Greek parents are eligible for citizenship in Greece upon application. Children or grandchildren of Greek refugees from the country's civil war of the 1940s may also claim and receive Greek citizenship. Greek nationality is available to men five years after they marry a Greek citizen, and to women, ten years after marriage to a Greek. Those living and working in Greece for five years may become naturalized citizens if they can show that their employment will continue for at least three more years.

Greece occupies the southernmost area of the Balkan Peninsula in southeast Europe. It borders Albania, Macedonia, and Bulgaria on the north; and Turkey, its largest neighbor, to the east. Over 20% of the nation consists of islands in the Mediterranean, Aegean, and Ionian Seas. Visitors from all over Europe flock to the Aegean islands for their warm, Mediterranean climate, abundant sunshine on the beaches, and picturesque villages perched on craggy hillsides.

Greece was the seat of the earliest known European civilization, the Minoan, that flourished on the island of Crete from 2300 B.C. to 1400 B.C. By the 2nd Century A.D., Greece was part of the Roman Empire, later part of the Byzantine Empire with its capital in Constantinople. Architectural and archeological remnants of Greece's Classical and medieval past constitute another major drawing point for visitors from abroad. In ensuing centuries, Greece was controlled by the Turks of the Ottoman Empire. Despite ongoing hostility toward Turkey, vestiges of Turkish rule linger in Greece's cuisine and the thick, sweet coffee preferred throughout the country. The monarchy established in 1828 lasted intermittently, until 1973, when Greece was declared a republic. Today, Greece is a member of the European Union, thus its citizenship allows free access to all of Europe.

Greece has a mixed capitalist economy with the public sector accounting for about half of GDP, although the government plans to privatize some leading state enterprises. Tourism is a key industry, providing a large portion of GDP and foreign exchange earnings. Greece is a major beneficiary of EU aid, equal to about 4% of GDP. The economy has improved steadily over the last few years, as the government has tightened policy so that Greece could join the EU's single currency, the euro. In particular, Greece has cut its budget deficit to just over 2% of GDP and tightened monetary policy, with the result that inflation fell below 4% by the end of 1998, the lowest rate in 26 years. The current outlook is good with the budget deficit and inflation both expected to decline further, while GDP growth stays near 3%.

Citizenship

A foreign-born child of Greek citizen parents is automatically eligible for Greek citizenship. A foreign-born child with a Greek father and a foreign mother also qualifies. In order to claim Greek citizenship of a foreign-born child, a certified birth certificate must be registered with the Greek Embassy nearest the place of birth. This should be accompanied by the parents' marriage certificate and the father's birth certificate, if possible.

If the child's birth certificate does not state the Greek father's place of birth, the application must be made through the Ministry of Information, in Athens. Usually, providing the parents' marriage certificate and/or the father's birth certificate is sufficient.

A person who has, or had, Greek parents or grandparents who fled the nation during the Greek Civil War, in the late 1940s, is entitled to return to Greece and claim Greek nationality. This process requires from two to six months, but personal presence in Greece is needed only during the last two weeks before completion.

If a foreign national marries a Greek woman, he will be eligible for naturalization after five years of continuous residency in Greece. By comparison, a foreign woman who marries a Greek man receives a residence permit automatically and is eligible for citizenship after six months.

A male foreign national who lives in Greece for more than five years can apply for naturalization with proof of guaranteed employment for a further three years. A foreign wife is eligible for citizenship only after ten years continuous residence with her husband in Greece. During this period, she is allowed no more than three months a year away from the country.

In rare, special instances, it is possible for foreigners to be granted Greek citizenship on the recommendation of the Greek Ministry of the Interior. Greece recognizes dual nationality, but those holding a second citizenship may be subject to Greek laws, which impose special obligations such as compulsory Greek military service and other aspects of Greek law while in Greece. Many younger Greeks seek foreign citizenship in order to avoid obligatory military service.

Contacts

A passport is required, but no visa is needed for tourist or business stays of up to three months. An AIDS test is required for performing artists and students on Greek scholarships; U.S. test results are not accepted.

United States: TA passport is required, but no visa is needed for tourist or business stays of up to 90 days. For other entry requirements, travelers should contact the Embassy of Greece located at 2221 Massachusetts Avenue, NW, Washington, DC 20008, Tel: (202) 939-5800 or Greek consulates in Atlanta, Boston, Chicago, Houston, Los Angeles, New Orleans, New York, and San Francisco and Greek embassies and consulates around the world. For additional information visit the web site http://www.greekembassy.org.

Americans living in or visiting Greece are encouraged to register at the consular section of the U.S. Embassy/Consulate General and to obtain updated information on travel and security in Greece. The U.S. Embassy in Athens is located at 91 Vasilissis Sophias Boulevard, Tel: (30)(210) 721-2851. The U.S. Consulate General in Thessaloniki is located at Plateia Commercial Center, 43 Tsimiski Street, 7th floor, Tel: (30)(2310) 242-905. The Embassy's web site is http://www.usembassy. gr. The Embassy's web site has link to the Embassy's Olympics web site at http://www.usembassy.gr/olympics/index.html. The e-mail address for the Consular Section is athensconsul@state.gov. The U.S. Consulate's web site addresses are http://www.usconsulate.gr. The e-mail address for the U.S. Consulate General Thessaloniki is amcongen@compulink.gr.

United Kingdom: United Kingdom: The British Embassy is located at 1 Ploutarchou St, 106 75 Athens; Tel: (30) (210) 72-72-600, Fax: (30) 210 727 2720, E-mail: information.athens@fco.gov.uk, Web site: http://www.british-embassy.gr/; British Consulates are located at **Corfu:** British Vice Consulate, Menekratous 1, 491 00 Corfu, Tel: (30) 2661 030055, Fax: (30) (2661) 37995, E-mail: corfu@british-consulate.gr; **Heraklion (Crete):** 16 Papa Alexandrou Street, 712 02 Heraklion, Tel: (30) 281 0224012, Fax: (30) 281 0243935, E-mail: crete@british-consulate.gr; Kos: British Vice-Consulate, 8 Annetas Laoumtzi St, 853 00 Kos, Tel: (30) (242) 21549, Fax: (30) (242) 25948, E-mail: kos@british-consulate.gr; **Patras:** Votsi 2, 262 21 Patras, Tel: (30) 261 0277329, Fax: (30) 261 0225334; **Rhodes:** British Consulate Pavlou Mela 3, P.O. Box 47, 851 00 Rhodes, Tel: (30) (241) 27247 / 22005, Fax: (30) 2241 022615, E-mail: rhodes@british-consulate.gr; **Thessaloniki:** 21 Aristotelous Street, 546 24 Thessaloniki, Tel: (30) (2310) 278006, Fax: (30) (2310) 283868, E-mail: salonika@british-consulate.gr; **Syros:** 8 Akti Petrou Ralli,, Hermopolis, 841 00 Syros, Tel: (30) (281) 82232 / 88922, Fax: (30) 2281 083293 and **Zakynthos:** 5 Foskolos Street, 291 00 Zakynthos, Tel: (30) (2695) 22906 / 48030, Fax: (30) 26950 23769, E-mail: zakynthos@british-consulate.gr.

Republic of Ireland

CAPITAL:	DUBLIN
POPULATION:	3,924,140
LANGUAGE:	ENGLISH IS THE LANGUAGE GENERALLY USED, IRISH (GAELIC) SPOKEN MAINLY IN AREAS LOCATED ALONG THE WESTERN SEABOARD
CURRENCY:	EURO (€)
AREA:	70,282 SQUARE KM
ETHNIC GROUPS:	CELTIC, ENGLISH
RELIGION:	ROMAN CATHOLIC 91.6%, CHURCH OF IRELAND 2.5%, OTHER 5.9%

PASSPORT HIGHLIGHTS: Persons with one parent or grandparent born in Ireland are eligible for Irish nationality, conferring a passport valid for ten years. Permanent residents of Ireland are eligible for naturalization after five years in the country.

The Republic of Ireland lies in the Atlantic Ocean, separated from the United Kingdom by the Irish Sea to the east and bounded on the northeast by Northern Ireland.

Independent from the United Kingdom since 1922, Ireland is a member of the European Union. As a result, Irish citizens can live and work without visas or permits in all EU countries. Tens of thousands of well-educated Irish youths have fanned out all over Europe in technical and professional jobs and are a much sought after group of potential workers.

The vast numbers of Irish emigrants of the past two centuries scattered around the English-speaking world (and, indeed, many other regions as well, as the number of Irish names found among Latin Americans attests). They carried with them nostalgia for the "Emerald Isle" that translates into widespread observance of St. Patrick's Day and celebration of cultural figures from Yeats, Synge, and Joyce to U-2 and Sinead O'Connor. This has resulted in floods of tourists each year visiting the Republic. In Ireland one can still find rustic charm and picturesque relics of the Celtic and Anglo-Irish past in unspoiled natural settings, alongside a vibrant, cosmopolitan lifestyle and cultural scene in urban centers, especially Dublin.

The country is English-speaking, although Irish (Gaelic) is a second official language. Ireland is a common law nation with legal and commercial practices much like that of the U.K. It has excellent, modern telecommunications systems and the corporate tax breaks offered in the Dublin Free Zone have drawn multinational commercial operations from all over the world. The currency is the Irish pound, eventually to be replaced by the EU's euro.

Economic Citizenship Program Repealed

For a period of about ten years until the mid-1990s, Ireland offered one of the most popular economic citizenship programs, at least among people of great wealth. (It required a 5-year, unsecured investment of over US$1.7 million). Although this attractive instant citizenship program (approval required about 2-3 months) imposed some restrictions, its virtue was the unfettered access that an Irish passport gave to all other EU countries, plus visa-free travel to over 150 countries, including those of the British Commonwealth. The program required purchase of a home in Ireland, but only 60 days residence in the nation during the first two years after citizenship was granted – hardly a burden. Under the program, the Minister for Justice was given discretion to grant a certificate of naturalization, and about 20 applicants were approved annually.

In spite of the false claims of some commercial passport hucksters that the Irish economic investment program has only been "suspended," this program was abolished by law and there is little prospect of it being revived anytime soon. Avoid anyone who tells you anything different. It is clearly no longer possible to become a citizen of Ireland through investment.

Citizenship by Ancestry

Remarkably, with a population of only 3.6 million, Ireland has about 14 million current official passports in worldwide circulation! In part, this large number of passport holders stems from the principle of Irish nationality law that views blood lines as determining a birthright to citizenship – even without ever having lived in the country, the so-called doctrine of *jus sanguinis*.

Citizenship is governed by the Irish Nationality and Citizenship Acts of 1956 and 1986. These laws confer Irish nationality by reason of one's birth in Ireland (the only EU nation that does so), by Irish parentage or ancestry, and by marriage to an Irish citizen. Until 1986, a citizen of any nation who had at least one grandparent of Irish descent was entitled to receive full Irish citizen status and the coveted passport that goes with it. A 1986 amendment changed mere blood lines to a requirement that at least one parent or grandparent actually must have been born in Ireland. An applicant must prove this claim of Irish descent by submitting an ancestor's official marriage and birth certificates.

With three photographs, proper proof of Irish ancestry, and proof of legal residence in the country where you make application, a 10-year, renewable Irish passport will be issued in due course bearing the stamp of Ireland and the European Community. Obviously, Ireland permits dual citizenship. It does not require an oath of exclusive allegiance, nor does it notify the country of origin of its new passport holders. Contact the nearest Irish Consulate or Embassy for application forms and assistance.

Finding proof of Irish ancestry can be a problem since many church and court records were destroyed in "The Troubles," the long running, sometimes violent Irish independence struggle against the British. Irish Consulates and Embassies are adept at verifying affidavits and genealogical research. A company called "Inside Ireland" publishes the authoritative Genealogical Supplement. This book is available to subscribers of the Inside Ireland Quarterly Review available from Brenda Weir, Inside Ireland, P.O. Box 1886, Dublin 16, Ireland.

Even without Irish ancestry, it is also possible to obtain Irish citizenship and a passport after a five-year period of residence. Irish residence is not generally sought because of the nation's high income taxes. Perhaps, reflecting the poetic Irish soul, the one exception to confiscatory income taxes is made for royalty income paid to artists, writers, and composers.

Taxation

Irish residents domiciled in Ireland are subject to taxation on all their worldwide income. Non-resident Irish citizens who live abroad are exempted from taxation. Current official practice is to allow new citizens to declare formally that they don't intend to live in Ireland and are, therefore, non-domiciled. They then are obligated to pay income tax only on income actually remitted to Ireland. This practice makes Ireland an attractive tax venue for naturalized citizens.

A large number of Irish residents have abused these tax rules by obtaining offshore bank accounts, many in the Isle of Man. They then claimed non-residency while actually maintaining an Irish home. Irish revenue officials have cracked down on this practice, imposing fines and penalties.

A foreign-born person who marries a person of Irish birth or descent may become an Irish citizen after three years of marriage by formally declaring acceptance of Irish citizenship. The marriage must continue at the time of application and grant of citizenship. A married applicant must file a notarized form at an Irish Consulate or Embassy within 30 days of its execution. Once Irish citizenship is established, an application for an official passport can be filed.

Contacts

Henley & Partners AG, Kirchgasse 22 8001 Zurich Switzerland. Tel: +(41)-44-266-22-22; Fax: +(41)-44-266 22 23; E-mail: zurich@henley-global.com; Web site: http://www.henleyglobal.com

United States: A passport is necessary for travel into Ireland. A visa is not required for tourist or business stays of up to 90 days. For information concerning entry requirements for Ireland, travelers can contact the Embassy of Ireland at 2234 Massachusetts Avenue NW, Washington, DC 20008, Tel: (202) 462-3939 or the nearest Irish consulate in Boston, Chicago, New York, or San Francisco. The Irish Embassy web site is http://www.irelandemb.org

qAmericans living in or visiting Ireland are encouraged to register at the consular section of the U.S. Embassy in Ireland and obtain updated information on travel and security within Ireland. The Embassy in Ireland is located at 42 Elgin Road, Ballsbridge, Dublin 4, Tel: (353)-(1)-668-8777, after hours number: (353) (1) 668-9612, Fax: (353) (1) 668-8056. Travelers to Northern Ireland should also consult the Consular Information Sheet for the United Kingdom. Further information and answers to many frequently asked questions are available on the Embassy Dublin's web site at http://dublin.usembassy.gov.

United Kingdom: The British Embassy is located at 29 Merrion Road, Ballsbridge, Dublin 4, Tel: (353)(1) 205 3700 Main Switchboard, Fax: (353) (1) 205 3890, E-mail: consular.dubli@fco.gov.uk, Web site: http://www.britishembassy.ie.

Republic of Italy

CAPITAL:	ROME
POPULATION:	57,998,353
LANGUAGE:	ITALIAN (OFFICIAL), GERMAN (PARTS OF TRENTINO-ALTO ADIGE REGION ARE PREDOMINANTLY GERMAN SPEAKING), FRENCH (SMALL FRENCH-SPEAKING MINORITY IN VALLE D'AOSTA REGION), SLOVENE (SLOVENE-SPEAKING MINORITY IN THE TRIESTE-GORIZIA AREA)
CURRENCY:	EURO (€)
AREA:	301,230 SQUARE KM
ETHNIC GROUPS:	ITALIAN (INCLUDES SMALL CLUSTERS OF GERMAN-, FRENCH-, AND SLOVENE-ITALIANS IN THE NORTH AND ALBANIAN-ITALIANS AND GREEK-ITALIANS IN THE SOUTH)
RELIGION:	ROMAN CATHOLIC 98%, OTHER 2%

PASSPORT HIGHLIGHTS: Italian immigration laws favor the children of Italian nationals, who are accorded Italian citizenship automatically. Those whose grandfathers were Italian nationals also benefit from the 1992 nationality law. Persons with jobs in Italy generally have little difficulty obtaining work permits.

Before the birth of Christ, Italy was a major world influence under the Roman Empire. Rome-based influence continued during the spread of Christianity. Arab, German, and Viking influences in the Middle Ages contributed to rounding out the Italian national character. Modern Italy dates from its unification as a Kingdom in the 1860s. Adoption of the republican form of government on June 10, 1946 brought Italy to its present political state.

Long a favored and relatively inexpensive tourist destination, Italy still offers attractive cultural, gastronomic, and recreational experiences, although (as in much of Western Europe) bargain prices are few and far between. A large expatriate population continues to form substantial colonies in Rome, Milan, and Venice, on the Riviera, in the Alpine Lake District, along the Amalfi coast, and on the islands off of the Bay of Naples.

Retroactive Citizenship

In 1992, Italy radically changed its immigration and passport policies, recognizing the principle of dual nationality. Now, regardless of where they are (or were) born, offspring of Italian nationals automatically are recognized as Italian citizens. The change is retroactive, meaning Italian nationals who lost citizenship in the past by acquiring different nationality can be reinstated. These broad rules apply to Italian citizenship for children and grandchildren as well.

The 1992 law allowed a two-year grace period during which those eligible had only to file a declaration of intent to regain citizenship. Since 1994, one year of legal residency in Italy is required for reinstatement. Foreign citizens born in Italy, and those who hold Italian nationality, may be subject to compulsory military service and other laws imposing other obligations while they are within Italy.

The new program favors the family paternal line. The children and grandchildren of former Italian nationals can qualify for citizenship on the basis of any of the following: 1) a father who was an Italian citizen at the time of a child's birth; 2) a mother who was an Italian citizen at the time of a child's birth after January 1, 1948; 3) the father was not born in Italy, but the paternal grandfather was an Italian citizen at the time of birth; or 4) the mother was not born in Italy, but for those born after January 1, 1948, the maternal grandfather was an Italian citizen at the time of the mother's birth.

In addition, ethnic Italians who cannot qualify under ancestry rules can qualify for naturalization after only three years legal residence in Italy. Foreign nationals can gain citizenship through marriage to an Italian, but the spouse must be legally resident in Italy for at least six months before applying for marriage-based naturalization. Non-Italian foreign nationals wishing to be naturalized must live in Italy for at least ten years.

As a member of the 15-nation EU, the Italian passport is valid for visa-free travel within the EU. Italy, alone in the EU, requires an annual validation tax stamp to keep its passport current during its five-year life.

Tourist visas are easy to obtain and renewable indefinitely for those who can show adequate means of financial support. Despite high unemployment, a foreign national with a definite job offering should have little trouble getting a work permit with the employer's assistance. Foreigners intent upon opening a new business or investing are given red carpet treatment.

Once resident in Italy, registering as a resident or domiciliary means only a visit to the local, neighborhood police station. Registration is renewable at three-month intervals, but local police will give six and 12-month permits once a foreign person is established and known in the community.

Taxes

Italians themselves are heavily taxed, and it is no exaggeration to say that tax evasion has become a national way of life. In Italy, businesses are either over-regulated, highly taxed, or government-owned, in which case, they are often inefficient and corrupt. As a result, some estimates say that up to 40% of the gross domestic product of Italy is produced off-the-books in the black market. But Italy offers foreign nationals, as residents, many tax concessions, including no taxes imposed on their offshore income.

Campione d'Italia

We strongly recommend the Italian enclave of Campione, located within Switzerland, as a tax- free residency. See the Switzerland chapter for details.

Contacts

Henley & Partner, Inc., Kirchgasse 24, 8001 Zurich, Switzerland; Tel: +(41) 1-267-6090; Fax: +(41) 1-267-6091; E-mail: zurich@henley-global.com; Web site: http://www.henleyglobal.com.

United States: A valid passport is required for entry into Italy. Italian authorities may deny entry to travelers who attempt to enter without a valid passport. A visa is not required for tourist stays up to 90 days. However, for all other purposes, such as work, study, etc., a visa is required and must be obtained from the Italian Embassy or Consulates before entering Italy. For further information concerning visas and entry requirements, travelers may contact the Embassy of Italy at 1601 Fuller St. NW, Washington, D.C. 20009, Tel: 202-328-5500. Web site: http://www.italyemb.org. Travelers may also contact Italian Consulates General in Boston, Chicago, Detroit, Houston, Los Angeles, Miami, Newark, New Orleans, New York, Philadelphia, or San Francisco, accessible through the above web site.

Under Italian law, tourists are required to register with a local police station and obtain a "permesso Di soggiorno" (permit to stay) within eight working days of their arrival, regardless of the intended length of stay. Visitors may be required to show police that they have sufficient means of financial support. Credit cards, ATM cards, travelers' checks, prepaid hotel/vacation vouchers, etc. may be evidence of sufficient means. Americans residing, studying or working in Italy, and longer term tourists, are encouraged to register at the Consular Section of the U.S. Embassy in Rome or at one of the three U.S. Consulates General and obtain updated information on travel and security. The U.S. Embassy in Rome is located at Via V. Veneto 119/A, Tel: 39-06-46741, Fax: 39-06-4674-2217. Web site: http://www.usembassy.it.

The U.S. Consulates are located in **Florence:** Lungarno Amerigo Vespucci 38, Tel: 39-055-266-951, Fax: 399-055-215-550; **Milan:** Via Principe Amedeo 2/10, Tel: 39-02-290-351, Fax: 39-02-290-35-273; **Naples:** Piazza della Repubblica, Tel: 39-081-583-8111 and Fax: 39-081-583-8275. There are U.S. Consular Agents located in **Genoa:** Via Dante 2, Tel: 39-010-584-492, Fax: 39-010-553-3033; **Palermo:** Via Vaccarini 1, Tel: 39-091-305-857, Fax: 39-091-625-6026; **Trieste:** Via Roma 15, Tel: 39-040-660-177 and Fax: 39-040-631-240.

United Kingdom: The British Embassy is located at Via XX Settembre 80a, I-00187 Roma RM; Tel: (39) 06-4220-0001, Fax: (39) 06-487-3324, E-mail: InfoRome@fco.gov.uk, Web site: http://www.britain.it.

British Consulates are located in **Florence:** Lungarno Corsini 2, I-50123 Firenze FI, Tel: (39) 055-284133, (39) 055 289556 Commercial Office, Fax: (39) 055-219112, E-mail: Consular.Florence@fco.gov.uk; **Milan:** Via San Paolo 7, I-20121 Milano MI, Tel: (39) 02-723001, Fax: (39) 02 8692405 Information, Web site: http://www.britain.it/business; **Genoa:** c/o Coeclerici Armatori S.p.A., Via Di Francia 28, 16149 Genoa, Tel: (39) 010 416828, Fax: (39) 010 416958; **Turin:** Via Madame Cristina 99, 10126 Turin, Tel: (39) 011-6509202, Fax: (39) 011-669-5982, E-mail: bcturin@yahoo.com, Web site: http://www.britain.it; **Venice:** Piazzale Donatori Di Sangue 2/5, 30171 Venice-Mestre, Tel: (39) 041 505 5990, Fax: (39) 041 950254, E-mail: britconvenice@tin.it **Trieste:** Via Dante Alighieri 7, 34122 Trieste TS, Tel: (39) 040 347-8303, Fax: (39) 040 3478311, E-mail: jododds@tin.it; **Naples:** Via dei Mille 40, 80121 Naples, UK postal address: Consulate BFPO 8, London, Tel: (39) 081 4238911, Fax: (39) 081 422434, E-mail: information.Naples@fco.gov.uk; **Bari:** Via Dalmazia 127, I-70121 Bari BA, Tel: (39) 080 5543668, Fax: (39) 080 5542977, E-mail: gavan@tin.it; **Cagliari:** Viale Colombo 160, I-09045 Quartu SE CA,

Tel: (39) 070 828628, Fax: (39) 070 862293, E-mail: agraham@iol.it;
Catania: Via G Verdi 53, I-95129 Catania CT, Tel: (39) 095 7151864,
Fax: (39) 095 7151503 and **Palermo:** S Tagliavia & Co, Via Cavour
117, I-90133 Palermo PA, Tel: (39) 091 582533, Fax: (39) 091 584240,
E-mail: luigi@tagliavia.it.

Republic of Malta

CAPITAL:	VALLETTA
POPULATION:	400,420
LANGUAGE:	MALTESE AND ENGLISH (BOTH OFFICIAL)
CURRENCY:	MALTESE LIRA (MTL)
AREA:	316 SQUARE KM
ETHNIC GROUPS:	MALTESE (DESCENDANTS OF ANCIENT CARTHAGINIANS AND PHOENICIANS, WITH STRONG ELEMENTS OF ITALIAN AND OTHER MEDITERRANEAN STOCK)
RELIGION:	ROMAN CATHOLIC 98%

PASSPORT HIGHLIGHTS: Persons with assets located outside Malta of at least LM150,000 (US$360,000), or a worldwide income of at least LM10,000 (US$24,000) are eligible for permanent residency. Applicants must demonstrate ability to remit to Malta a minimum annual income of LM6,000 (US$14,400), plus LM1,000 (US$2,400) for each dependant. Malta does not grant citizenship to non-Maltese.

South of Europe is Malta, a group of islands in the central Mediterranean Sea, south of the Italian island of Sicily and well-positioned as a cultural and political stepping stone between Europe and north Africa. About 95% of the islanders are natives, descendants of the ancient Carthaginians and Phoenicians. The islands contain vestiges of millennia of human settlement, including some of the oldest Stone Age megalithic structures in the world. All of the subsequent cultures that flourished on the islands have left monuments, including Crusader castles and churches from the Middle Ages and ornate churches and public buildings of the Renaissance and Baroque periods. As a popular winter vacation destination, Malta has a large number of golf courses, horse ranches, and resort areas. Eco-tourists are drawn to the country's rugged landscapes and Mediterranean sea life.

In 1530, Malta was ceded to the governance of the Knights of Malta by the Holy Roman Emperor, Charles V. They built fortifications in the harbor of Valetta, the capital, so well that, in 1565, a Turkish siege was repelled largely due to excellent defenses, that still are in existence today. In 1798, Napoleon invaded Malta and expelled the Knights. At the Congress of Vienna, in 1815, Britain was given possession of Malta. With the 1869 opening of the Suez Canal, Malta became an important strategic British base. During World War II, Malta was bombed heavily by the German Air Force, since it was a valuable Allied convoy port. In 1947, Malta was granted self-government and, in 1964, it became independent.

Malta is an ancient nation, but one with a thoroughly modern outlook. In recent years, the Maltese Government has actively courted foreign capital with an attractive program of incentives aimed at investors and entrepreneurs. It includes generous tax incentives and inducements such as soft loans, training grants, and customized facilities at subsidized costs. This pro-business policy seeks to build on Malta's many existing strengths: favorable trade relations with countries around the world; a strategic location on world shipping lanes; a high quality, productive, English-speaking workforce; an excellent climate and quality of life; and modern health care and educational systems.

The Economy

In the last decade, Malta's economy has averaged an annual growth rate of over 7%. The nation has maintained a surplus balance of payments, stable currency, and low inflation (less than 1%) all impressive numbers. These reflect the overall strength and diversity of the Maltese economy. Traditionally, agriculture was important, but the economy has undergone significant change. Manufacturing, especially high-tech industries, now accounts for over a quarter of Malta's GDP. About 26% of the labor force works in services, 22% in manufacturing, 37% in government, and 2% in agriculture. Major industries now include textiles, machinery, food and beverages, and high-tech products, especially electronics. Tourism is also a growing and increasingly important sector. Key sectors that provide exceptional investment opportunities include trade, tourism, manufacturing, maintenance services, and international financial services.

The Maltese Government has enacted legislation to increase the islands' role as a leader in international finance services. These provide a variety of tax and financial incentives to banks, insurance companies, fund management firms, trading companies, trusts, and investment companies.

Residence But Not Citizenship

These sunny Mediterranean islands cater to expatriates looking for a second or retirement home. There are no property taxes and permanent residents pay a 15% income tax on offshore income remitted to the country. Malta has three types of taxes: income, corporate, and estate taxes, the latter applies only to property located on the island. Income tax rates for foreign residents range from 2-30%. A permanent resident is not taxed on capital gains paid from offshore unless the person also is domiciled in Malta.

Foreign nationals are not eligible for Maltese citizenship, but they are welcomed as residents. Maltese residency is of three types: 1) visitors staying less than three months are counted as non-residents; 2) those remaining more than three months are temporary residents; and 3) permanent residents are granted a permit entitling them to live on the islands.

Malta is one of the most attractive locations in Europe for tax-advantaged private residence. For non-Maltese persons there is the possibility of acquiring Permanent Residence status through an attractive and efficient program. Persons of all nationalities are eligible to apply for residence permits without discrimination.

A permanent residence permit entitles its holder to reside permanently in Malta with the freedom to come and go. Malta was admitted to the European Union in 2004 and is now part of the Schengen Area agreement allowing residents of Malta to travel within the that area without obtaining a visa. A permanent resident enjoys a privileged tax status while at the same time benefitting from Malta's wide network of double taxation treaties. A further advantage of this status is that as long as the resident abides by the rules, they need not spend any particular time actually residing in Malta.

Those in the latter category must own assets located outside Malta of at least LM150,000 (US$360,000), or have a worldwide income of at least LM10,000 (US$24,000). Applicants for permanent residence must demonstrate ability to remit to Malta a minimum annual income of LM6,000 (US$14,400), plus LM1,000 (US$2,400) for each dependant. A residence permit can be inherited by a surviving spouse, but not by other surviving descendants.

Contacts

Henley & Partners, 34 Cathedral St., Silema SLM06, Malta, Tel: (356) 2131 4257 Fax: (356) 2131 4253. E-mail: malta-office@henleyglobal. com Web site: http://www.henleyglobal.com/malta1.htm

United States: A passport is required for entry into Malta. A visa is not required for U.S. citizens for stays of up to 90 days. For more information concerning entry requirements for Malta, travelers should contact the Embassy of Malta at 2017 Connecticut Avenue, NW, Washington, D.C. 20008, Tel: (202) 462-3611. For additional information visit the web site: http://www.foreign.gov.mt/ORG/ministry/missions/washington2.htm or call the Maltese Consulate in New York City, Tel: (212) 725-2345.

Americans living in or visiting Malta are encouraged to register at the Consular Section of the U.S. Embassy in Malta and obtain updated information on travel and security within Malta. The U.S. Embassy in Malta is located on the third floor of Development House, St. Anne Street, Floriana, Valletta, Tel: (356) 2561 4000. The Consular Section's telephone number is (356) 2156-4115, Fax: (356) 21-243-229, Web site: http://usembassy.state.gov/malta/wwwhcons.html. The Consular Section is open to the public Monday, Wednesday, and Friday from 8:00 a.m. to 11:00 am.

United Kingdom: Whitehall Mansions, Ta'Xbiex Seafront, Ta'Xbiex MSD 11 Malta GC, Tel: (356) 2323 0000 (General), Fax: (356) 2323 2234 (Consular & Visa), E-mail: consular.visa.valletta@fco.gov.uk, Web site: http://www.britishhighcommission.gov.uk/malta.

Principality of Monaco

CAPITAL:	MONACO
POPULATION:	32,130
LANGUAGE:	FRENCH (OFFICIAL), ENGLISH, ITALIAN, MONEGASQUE
CURRENCY:	EURO (€)
AREA:	1.95 SQUARE KM
ETHNIC GROUPS:	FRENCH 47%, MONEGASQUE 16%, ITALIAN 16%, OTHER 21%
RELIGION:	ROMAN CATHOLIC 90%

PASSPORT HIGHLIGHTS: The main criteria for residency in Monaco are financial – high personal net worth and the ability to pay out up to US$20,000 in professional fees, plus the added cost of some of Europe's most expensive real estate.

This unique and ancient principality is not for everyone. If you want to make this your permanent home, it helps to have more than a modest amount of money and an assured income for life. Moreover, it doesn't hurt to know the Prince and his royal family. Monaco, in general, is for individuals who have already made their money — people who want to practice the art of living well while others mind the store for them — people who want to spend time on the Riviera. If tax avoidance is the only goal, there are other cheaper places.

Many residents are just upper-middle class people who have decided to retire in Monaco. They are drawn to the pleasant atmosphere, Mediterranean climate and leisure. Monaco has all the facilities that wealthy people consider necessary: country clubs, health clubs, golf and tennis clubs. Indeed, Monaco may have a population of only 32,000, and an area of only 1.08 square miles, but it has all the services and cultural activities of a city the size of San Francisco.

Monaco's prices are expensive, but no worse than London, Paris, or Geneva. These days, there are as many Italian restaurants as there are French ones. Most shops and supermarkets accept euros just as readily as Swiss francs. The European common currency, in this respect, has long been established in the principality.

Monaco is high-profile. The world remembers Grace Kelly, the Hollywood film star, who married Prince Rainier in 1956. The international spotlight followed her until she died in a tragic auto accident in 1982. During his long rule, Prince Rainier III has worked hard to expand the economic and professional scope of the country. Few recent monarchs can claim credit for extending their dominions by a fifth without conquest. But, by land filling the sea, the Prince has managed to expand his tiny principality by 23% in the 50 years since he succeeded his grandfather. This land expansion mirrors Prince Rainier's determination to make this a dynamic modern mini-state.

It has also been at the heart of a remarkable economic development based around trading, tourism, and financial services in a tax-friendly environment. On its small area and population, Monaco manages to generate, annually, over €11 billion worth of business. The state has an annual budget of €1 billion, carries no debts, and possesses unpublished liquid reserves of at least €2.5 billion.

The Principality is no longer just a frivolous playground for the rich, its government is funded primarily through casino gambling proceeds. It is now a modern economy participating at a global level in a diverse range of sectors. Recently, concerns about Monaco's future stability have been growing because of Prince Rainier's continued illnesses.

Undeniably, there are tax benefits to be gained from a move to Monaco. The authorities do not like the Principality to be known as the tax haven that it is. It's a low-tax area, rather than a no-tax area, but still a haven. Since 1869, there have been no income taxes for Monegasque nationals and resident foreigners, one of the main attractions for high net worth individuals. There are no direct, withholding, or capital gains taxes for foreign nationals, except for the French, who because of a bilateral tax treaty with Paris, cannot escape the clutches of the French tax system. There are first time residential registration taxes, but no real estate taxes.

There are corporate and banking advantages, too. Confidentiality is good, as far as business records go, and the same can be said for the banking services. The Bank of France is responsible for the Monegasque banking system and carries out regular inspections. Since 1993 there has been an anti-money laundering law. The banking services in Monaco are not as comprehensive as they could be and attempts are being made to loosen the banking secrecy rules. Prosecutors in Nice, France have expressed grave concerns about financial infiltration by the so-called "Red Mafia," the rich and ruthless

Russian crime syndicates.

Some people may find Monaco's police presence a little severe. The Principality has the lowest crime rate of any highly urbanized area in the world. This physical security is, of course, one of its great advantages.

Can we make any predictions about Monaco? It's not going to become a ghost town. It is stable and any major changes are unlikely to come from inside. In 1997, the Principality celebrated its 700th anniversary under the rule of the Grimaldi family. Prince Rainier III is now in his late 70s and in poor health. His children, of course, have wild reputations and the details of their private lives constantly appear in the gossip columns of the European press.

Residency and Citizenship

It is actually much easier to obtain a residency permit here than many might suppose. A clean record, solid bank references, and a net worth of US$500,000 should do it. Fees for establishing residency are likely to cost in the US$10,000 to US$20,000 range.

The Principality has offered financial and fiscal concessions to foreign nationals for a long time. These have been restricted by the Conventions with France in 1963 and, more recently, by agreements with France after pressure from the EU. And here lies the major concern. Monaco isn't likely to initiate changes. But the rest of Europe, especially France, who has always exhibited a jealous attitude towards the Principality, might pressure it into getting into line. This might be all the more valid if Monaco is unable to shake rumors associating it with the Mafia and money laundering activity.

If you're on the move already, stability may not be an important issue. However, you might be looking for a base and would do well to consider Monaco. The lifestyle is attractive, but is not everybody's cup of tea. If you are contemplating a move purely for financial or fiscal reasons, you might, depending on your specific requirements, do better elsewhere.

Once there, keep a low profile. Foreign nationals who are resident are afraid to make any public criticisms of the country. Why? If the authorities consider you a troublemaker, they can issue a 24-hour notice of expulsion. There's no one to appeal to and you'll be out the door.

Contacts

Henley & Partner, Inc., Kirchgasse 22, 8001 Zurich, Switzerland; Tel: +(41) 44-266-2222; Fax: +(41) 44-266-2223; E-mail: zurich@henley-global.com; Web site: http://www.henleyglobal.com/monaco.htm

United States: A passport is required for entry into Monaco. A visa is not required for tourist/business stays up to 90 days in Monaco. For further information on entry requirements to Monaco, travelers may contact the Consulate General of Monaco at 565 5th Avenue, New York, N.Y. 10017, Tel. (212) 759-5227. The Consulate General's web site is http://www.monaco-consulate.com.

Americans living in or visiting Monaco are encouraged to register at the Consular Section of the U.S. Embassy in Paris or the Consulate General of Monaco listed above to obtain updated information on travel and security within France and Monaco. The Consular Section of the U.S. Embassy in Paris is located at 2 Rue St. Florentin, 75001 Paris (Place de La Concorde, Metro Stop Concorde), Tel. 011-33-1-43-12-22-22 or (in France) 01-43-12-22-22, Fax: 011-33-1-42-61-61-40. Further information can be obtained at the U.S. Embassy's web site at http://www.amb-usa.fr.

United Kingdom: The British Consulate General is located at 33 Boulevard Princesse Charlotte, BP 265, MC 98005 Monaco, Tel: (377) 93 50 99 54, Fax: (377) 97 70 72 00.

The Netherlands

CAPITAL:	AMSTERDAM
POPULATION:	16,150,511
LANGUAGE:	DUTCH (OFFICIAL LANGUAGE), FRISIAN (OFFICIAL LANGUAGE)
CURRENCY:	EURO (€)
AREA:	41,526 SQUARE KM
ETHNIC GROUPS:	DUTCH 83%, OTHER 17% (OF WHICH 9% ARE NON-WESTERN ORIGIN MAINLY TURKS, MOROCCANS, ANTILLEANS, SURINAMESE AND INDONESIANS)
RELIGION:	ROMAN CATHOLIC 31%, PROTESTANT 21%, MUSLIM 4.4%, OTHER 3.6%, UNAFFILIATED 40%

PASSPORT HIGHLIGHTS: Five years' residency in the Netherlands renders a person eligible for Dutch citizenship. The stay may be decreased if certain prior contacts with Holland existed, including parents or grandparents born on Dutch soil; or if the person forms a domestic partnership, heterosexual or homosexual, of three years' duration with a Dutch national.

The Kingdom of the Netherlands, or Holland as it is also known, is the largest of the Low Countries in the northwest corner of Europe. Almost 30% of the land is below sea level, protected by a series of earthen dykes erected to prevent the reclaimed land from being flooded by the sea. There are also several Dutch overseas territories, including the Netherlands Antilles and Aruba in the Caribbean, an autonomous region.

The prosperous and open Dutch economy is based on private enterprise with a large measure of government involvement. Industrial activity features food processing, petroleum refining, and metalworking. The highly mechanized agricultural sector employs only 4% of the labor force, but provides large surpluses for export and the domestic food processing industry. As a result, the Netherlands ranks third worldwide in value of agricultural exports, behind the U.S. and France. Sharp cuts in subsidy and social security spending since the 1980s helped the Dutch achieve sustained economic growth combined with falling unemployment and moderate inflation.

Citizenship and Residence

Any foreign national who lives in the Netherlands for five years, even illegally, and who masters some ability with the Dutch language, is a likely candidate for citizenship. Five years continuous residence or "factual abode" in the Netherlands and/or the Dutch Antilles, immediately before applying, is usually required. Factual abode is broadly interpreted to include those who have lived there illegally without residence permits.

Various demonstrable personal ties with the Dutch can lower or even waive residence requirements. The requirement is reduced to two additional years for those who, earlier in life, lived in the Netherlands and/or the Dutch Antilles for at least eight years and then return. For persons formally adopted by a Dutch national, or for the foreign spouse of a Dutch national, residency is waived. The Dutch Nationality Act requires that spouses be screened for criminal records, but a foreign spouse of either sex is entitled to a "specially privileged naturalization procedure," meaning waiver of any residence requirement after three years of marriage. Dutch law recognizes homosexual relationships, so after a three-year non-heterosexual relationship, a non-Dutch partner can apply for naturalization.

The Netherlands, always in the vanguard of social policy change, requires only a three-year residency before naturalization for foreign persons who have an extra-marital relationship of at least three years duration with a Dutch national. The affair is evidence that the foreigner is "socially integrated" into Dutch society.

In all Dutch naturalization cases, past "good conduct" is necessary or citizenship can and will be denied. Good conduct is measured by whether there is a "serious suspicion that the alien in question constitutes a danger to public order, good morals, public health or the security of the Kingdom." Included in prohibited categories are convicted drug dealers, those convicted of serious felonies, and spies on behalf of foreign countries. Those who espouse extreme political views are not necessarily excluded.

Dutch nationality also can be derived from a Dutch parent. Article 3, paragraph 1 of the Netherlands Nationality Act states, "Any person whose father or mother is a Netherlands national at the time of his/her birth, as well as the person whose Netherlands parent was deceased at the time of his/her birth, is a Netherlands national."

While birth in the Netherlands to foreign citizen parents does not confer Dutch citizenship, a unique "third generation" rule is contained in Article 3, paragraph 3, "Any person born in The Netherlands or in The Netherlands Antilles whose father or mother was resident there at the time of birth, while the relevant parent's mother [the child's grandmother] was resident there at the time of that parent's birth, is a Netherlands national."

Dutch law also allows a limited version of the *jus soli* rule. A person who is born in the Netherlands of foreign citizen parents and lives there continuously thereafter may elect to acquire Dutch citizenship prior to reaching the age of 25.

Contacts

United States: A passport is required for entry into the Netherlands. Visas are not required for U.S. citizens for tourist visits of up to 90 days. To be admitted into the Netherlands, travelers must have a passport with a validity that exceeds the intended stay by at least three months, a return airline ticket and enough money to finance the planned stay. For further information on entry requirements, contact the Embassy of the Netherlands at 4200 Linnean Ave. NW, Washington, D.C. 20008, Tel: (202) 244-5300. Additional information is available at web site: http://www.netherlands-embassy.org/homepage.asp or one of the Dutch consulates in Chicago, Houston, Los Angeles, New York or Miami. You may also visit the National Bureau for Tourism's web site at http://www.goholland.com.

Americans living in or visiting the Netherlands are encouraged to register at the Consulate General in Amsterdam and obtain updated information on travel and security within the Netherlands. The U.S. Embassy is located in Hague at Lange Voorhout 102, Tel: (31)(70) 310-9209. However, all requests for consular assistance should be directed to the Consulate General in Amsterdam at Museumplein 19, Tel: (31)(20) 664-5661, (31)(20) 679-0321 or (31)(20) 575-5309. The after-hours emergency telephone number is (31)(70) 310-9499. The U.S. Embassy and Consulate General web site at http://thehague.usembassy.gov/main.htm answers many questions of interest to Americans visiting or residing in the Netherlands.

United Kingdom: The British Embassy is located at Lange Voorhout 10, 2514 ED, The Hague; Tel: (31) (70) 427-0427, Fax: (31) (70) 427 0345, E-mail: library@fco.gov.uk, Web site:

http://www.britain.nl. British Consulates are located in **Amsterdam:** Koningslaan 44, 1075 AE Amsterdam, (PO Box 75488, 1070 AL Amsterdam), Tel: (31) (20) 676 43 43, Fax: (31) (20) 676 10 69, E-mail: PassportEnquiries.amsterdam@fco.gov.uk, OtherConsularEnquiries@fco.gov.uk, Web site: http://www.britain.nl/; **Willemstad, Curaçao:** Jan Sofat 38, PO Box 3803, Curacao, Netherlands Antilles, Tel: (599) (9) 747-3322, Fax: +(599) (9) 747-3330, E-mail: britconcur@attglobal.net.

Republic of Portugal

CAPITAL:	LISBON
POPULATION:	10,102,022
LANGUAGE:	PORTUGUESE (OFFICIAL), MIRANDESE (OFFICIAL - BUT LOCALLY USED)
CURRENCY:	EURO (€)
AREA:	92,391 SQUARE KM
ETHNIC GROUPS:	MEDITERRANEAN STOCK, BLACK AFRICANS FROM EX-COLONIES
RELIGION:	ROMAN CATHOLIC 94%, PROTESTANT 6%

PASSPORT HIGHLIGHTS: Citizenship in Portugal is available to individuals six years after being granted permanent residency upon making an approved investment of US$100,000. Spouses of Portuguese nationals who live in the country for three years continuously are eligible for naturalization. Permanent residents must own or rent a home in Portugal.

Portugal is on the Atlantic coast of the Iberian Peninsula in southwestern Europe, surrounded by Spain. Its territory includes the Azores and Madeira, island groups a few hundred kilometers offshore in the Atlantic.

Portugal became part of the Roman Empire in the 2nd Century B.C. and embraced Christianity by the 5th Century. The Moorish conquest of the Peninsula in 716 resulted in Muslim rule until the 9th Century. By the early 16th Century, Portuguese explorers had extended its international empire to Africa, Asia, and Brazil. For a time, Portugal was controlled by Spain. The early 17th Century saw an absolute monarchy that remained for 200 years. The Napoleonic Wars unsuccessful invasion of the Iberian Peninsula, by France, caused the royal family to flee to Brazil. The abolition of slavery, in 1869, further weakened Portugal's overseas colonies. In 1910, Portugal officially became a republic, but the first three-quarters of the 20th century saw a succession of dictatorships. In 1949, Portugal became a founding member of NATO and, in 1955, a member of the U.N. It has been a member of the EU since 1986.

Exchange controls are in effect, but they do not impact on foreign income or assets held abroad. Annual property taxes are around one month's rental value, or 1% of total real estate value. Residents of Portugal are taxed on their worldwide income at rates varying from 16 to 40%, but, in fact, taxes are collected only on income generated within Portugal. In 1992, the government embarked on a massive privatization program and now offers major incentives to foreign investors.

Portugal has been the poor relation of Western Europe with the lowest EU living and labor costs. Tourism in the southern coast Algarve region, and in Lisbon, has brought foreign wealth into the country over the last two decades. English is widely spoken and there are large British expatriate communities. Wealthy foreigners are a major source of income and the government protects the expatriate community and its property. This trend was somewhat weakened with new real estate taxes aimed at expatriate land ownership.

Beaches and golf courses are amongst the best in the world. The finest merchandise, wines, and foods are available at typically very low prices. In undiscovered areas, adequate condominium apartments start at US$25,000, while good farm houses with land sell for under US$50,000. Mansions with grounds, a pool, and a sea view sell in the US$1 million range. Competent, cheap household help is available everywhere.

Travel from Portugal to most European destinations, particularly to London, is low cost. The government subsidizes air routes to the autonomous Azores and Madeira Islands in the Atlantic Ocean.

Citizenship and Immigration

Citizenship rules are quite liberal and marriage is one avenue available. Portugal is under pressure to conform to EU standards that allow a foreign spouse to apply for citizenship only after three years of continuous residence with no more than six months' absence from the country. Other avenues towards citizenship include family reunification.

For an approved investment in Portugal of US$100,000, one can obtain permanent residence leading to citizenship in six years. Anyone with verifiable offshore income sufficient to support themselves will qualify. Investment may be in an existing business, or by establishing a new enterprise, as long as the income generated is adequate to support the foreign applicant and dependants.

A permanent resident applicant must purchase or rent a home place prior to final approval. Problems have occurred with real estate agents who promise, and fail to secure, residence status for buyers as part of a purchase arrangement.

An applicant for a residence visa must submit: 1) a written declaration stating reasons for applying and evidence of financial support; 2) a local certificate that adequate housing has been obtained; 3) documentation showing establishment of a Portuguese bank account denominated in escudos, and a sufficient deposit, averaging a minimum of US$5,000 per applicant; 4) a certificate of good character; 5) a medical certificate of good health; 6) copies of a current passport; 7) three passport-size photos; 8) three copies of the executed official visa application Form V-3; and 9) testimonials from acquaintances in Portugal (optional).

Application processing through a Portuguese Consulate can require from six to 24 months with an average of 12 months. A successful applicant receives a residence visa and an official residence card is issued once the person arrives in Portugal. Initially, a one-year, type "A" residence card is issued, renewable annually. After five years residence, a type "B" card valid for five years is issued. After 20 years, foreign residents may apply for a type "C" card, valid for life. Although these residence cards are not valid for travel within the EU, they assure that visas can be obtained easily from EU countries.

After six years of residence, a resident qualifies for naturalization and a passport. Continuous presence in Portugal is not a requirement, but some proof of actual residence during the period may be required when applying for citizenship.

The government also issues to some legal residents what is called a "Portuguese Aliens Passport." This allows for visa-free travel throughout the EU, but is only issued "under exceptional circumstances," usually, to stateless refugees. A foreigner with good, local legal representation who is also willing to make an investment in Portugal may qualify.

After a three-year residency period, reciprocal Brazilian citizenship is allowed with visa-free movement to and from this former colony. Brazilians are allowed to vote in Portuguese elections after registration as a resident.

A new Portuguese citizen must swear allegiance and give a pro forma renunciation of prior nationality. After obtaining Portuguese nationality, dual nationality is permitted, in theory, by the rule "once Portuguese, always Portuguese." Foreign citizens who acquire

Portuguese citizenship may be subject to certain aspects of Portuguese law, such as mandatory voting and military service. This should be checked beforehand.

Portugal's immigration bureaucracy, the *Servi de Estrangeiros*, is notoriously slow moving. A residence permit can require a year's time and 18 months is not unusual. A well-connected local lawyer can usually speed the process. Even without a permit, foreign residents who cause no problems are not officially bothered. Local police have a reputation for being among the friendliest in Europe. The Portuguese are non-racist and have provided a home for 100,000 African and Asian stateless people, mostly former colonials, who now call this their home.

Contacts

United States: A passport is required for entry into Portugal. A visa is not required for tourist or business stays of up to 90 days. Portuguese law requires some non-European Union foreign nationals to register with immigration officials within three days of entering Portugal. The law affects those who transit Austria, Belgium, Denmark, Finland, France, Germany, Greece, Italy, Luxembourg, Spain, Sweden and the Netherlands by air en route to Portugal and stay at noncommercial accommodations. For further information concerning entry requirements for Portugal, travelers may contact the Embassy of Portugal at 2310 Tracy Place, NW, Washington, D.C. 20008, Tel: (202) 332-3007 or the Portuguese consulates in Boston, MA; New Bedford, MA; Providence, RI; New York, NY; Newark, NJ; San Francisco, CA; or Los Angeles, CA. Web site: http://www.portugalemb.org.

Americans living in or visiting Portugal are encouraged to register at the Consular Section of the U.S. Embassy in Lisbon and obtain updated information on travel and security. The Embassy in Portugal is located on Avenida das Forças Armadas, Sete Rios, Tel: (351)(21) 727-3300, Fax: (351)(21) 726-9109, Web site: http://www.american-embassy.pt. The U.S. Consulate is located in Ponta Delgada on the island of San Miguel in the Azores. The address is Av. Principe do Monaco, 6-2o, Ponta Delgada, Tel: (351) (296) 282-216, Fax: (351) (296) 28-72-16. There is also a Consular Agency located in Funchal, Madeira, on Rua Alfendega, no 10-2, Room A-B, Funchal, Tel: (351) (91) 235-636, Fax: (351) (291) 229-630, open Monday through Friday from 10:00 a.m. to 12:00 noon.

United Kingdom: The British Embassy is located at Rua de São Bernardo 33, 1249-082 Lisboa, Tel: (351) (21) 392 40 00, Fax: (351) (21) 392 41 85, E-mail: PPA.lisbon@fco.gov.uk Web site: http://

www.uk-embassy.pt British Consulates are located in **Funchal:**
Avenida de Zarco 2, CP 417, 9000-956 Funchal, Madeira, Tel: (351)
(291) 212 860 – 867, Fax: (351) (291) 212 869, E-mail: brit.
confunchal@mail.eunet.pt; **Portimão:** Largo Francisco A Mauricio 7,
8500-535 Portimão, Tel: (351) (282) 490 750, Fax: (351) (282) 490 758,
E-mail: portimao.lisbon@fco.gov.uk and **Oporto:** Av da Boavista,
3072, 4100-120 Oporto, Tel: (351) (22) 618 4789, Fax: (351) (22) 610
0438, E-mail: All.oporto@fco.gov.uk.

Spain

CAPITAL:	MADRID
POPULATION:	40,217,413
LANGUAGE:	CASTILIAN SPANISH 74%, CATALAN 17%, GALICIAN 7%, BASQUE 2%, NOTE: CASTILIAN IS THE OFFICIAL LANGUAGE NATIONWIDE, THE OTHER LANGUAGES ARE OFFICIAL REGIONALLY
CURRENCY:	EURO (€)
AREA:	504,782 SQUARE KM
ETHNIC GROUPS:	MEDITERRANEAN AND NORDIC
RELIGION:	ROMAN CATHOLIC 94%, OTHER 6%

PASSPORT HIGHLIGHTS: Ordinary immigrants to Spain must maintain permanent residency there ten years before becoming eligible for naturalization. Nationals of former Spanish colonies may have the waiting period reduced to two years if they "originate" from their country of citizenship. Persons living in Spain for six years become eligible to work there.

With its smaller neighbor, Portugal, to the west, Spain occupies the Iberian Peninsula in southwest Europe. It's the third largest European country, a few miles from North Africa, just across the Straits of Gibraltar. External Spanish territories include the Balearic Islands off the southeast coast in the Mediterranean Sea, as well as the enclaves of Ceuta and Melilla in North Africa. In spite of Spanish claims of sovereignty over Gibraltar, it remains under U.K. control, although active discussions about the future of The Rock continue with the stated British guarantee that any change must be with the approval of Gibraltar's residents.

Spain's long history dates back before 1000 B.C. In 27 B.C., Iberia came under Roman dominance until the 4th Century. From then until 1212, Christians and Muslim Moors vied for control. In the latter year, Moorish influence was confined to a small area of Granada. Led by Spanish-sponsored explorers, such as Christopher Columbus, in the Middle Ages, colonial interests grew rapidly. Columbus' 1492 voyage reached the Americas and made Spain a New World power. However, by the Spanish-American War, in 1899, Spain had lost most of its colonial possessions and the war added Cuba and the Philippines to that list.

After 40 years of control, the death of the dictator Francisco Franco, in 1975, brought the restoration of the Spanish monarchy. At the same time, Spain joined the United Nations, remaining outside NATO until 1982.

Reminders of its past inhabitants and rulers abound on Spain's soil. Throughout the countryside, local customs and cuisine reflect the heritage of Iberians, Romans, Arabs, Jews, Crusaders, and Moors. The great wealth brought from the New World by Habsburg and Bourbon monarchs adorns Madrid and its environs in the form of palaces and museums, while a resurgent Catalan culture, suppressed under the Franco regime, undergoes a vibrant cultural renaissance in Barcelona. Growing affluence since Spain joined the European Union is producing a boom of glittering new construction throughout the country, including world-class museums and public structures as well as housing and offices.

World Favorite

Spain is one of the most popular tourist destinations in the world and has much to offer as a location for investment, vacation or residence. There are more than 50 million visitors each year, a number greater than its total population. Developers and speculators reap fortunes in real estate, property, and building developments. Restaurants, transportation companies, brewers, hotel operators, golf and tennis clubs, and the tourist industry are all prospering.

Prime Spanish attractions include year-round sunshine, low prices, and low rents. Spain is not as inexpensive as Portugal, but prices are below the European average. Domestic help is inexpensive, but strict Spanish employment laws provide that after a year service, employees have a right to 30 paid days of vacation annually.

While home ownership is not required to become a permanent resident, owning may be more economically desirable than renting because real estate here is an excellent long-term investment. For the rich, country club communities and private villas are protected from burglars by dogs, guards, and high walls.

Residence and Citizenship

The integration of Spain into the European Union has created an attractive gateway to Europe. Gain citizen status in any one of the 25 European Union countries and you have free run of the continent.

It used to be that marriage provided the easiest means to citizenship in Spain. Under the old law, foreign-ers were able to apply as a spouse or ex-spouse of a Spaniard, even if the marriage had been dissolved. Now, tighter rules -require a foreigner to be married to a Spaniard at the time of application and for at least one year prior.

One can still acquire Spanish citizenship by birth in Spain or in certain Spanish territories. If one parent was born in Spain, citizenship can also be claimed. A Spanish Embassy or Consulate can explain the needed qualifications.

In the ordinary course of events, a foreign person must first be a resident in Spain for a staggering ten years before naturalization. Certain refugees are granted citizenship after only five years residence. Citizens of some of Spain's former colonies can apply for a Spanish passport after only two years residence in Spain, but must prove that they are "of origin" in the former colony. That shorter route is available through citizenship in some former Spanish colonies. This can prove an easy path into the EU. Persons of Spanish-Jewish descent are also eligible for Spanish citizenship after two years of residence.

Purchasing a home is not a requirement for obtaining citizenship. And with or without citizenship, you'll likely have the legal right to work, though six months of residence is usually required first. Prerequisites include the ability to speak passable Spanish and maintenance of a real presence in the country. During resi-dency (between two and ten years depending on your catego-ry), international travel is unrestricted. However, "token" residence is not acceptable.

Spanish police keep close tabs on foreigners and actually visit homes and interview neighbors to confirm residence and good reputation. Authorities will expel a resident alien considered undesirable. It's relatively easy to prove residence in the country by obtaining a *renta*, a permanent residence income tax form. All permanent residents also have an ID card (called an NIF) that identifies them as Spanish resident taxpayers.

Spanish authorities require naturalization applicants to renounce their existing citizenship and to swear an oath of allegiance to Spain. Dual nationality is recognized only if the applicant's home nation has a dual nationality treaty with Spain. Currently, such treaties exist with Chile, Peru, Paraguay, Nicaragua, Guatemala, Bolivia, Ecuador, Costa Rica, Honduras, the Dominican Republic, Argentina, Colombia, and

Venezuela. Those of Spanish-Jewish descent are also allowed to hold dual nationality.

In 2004, it was estimated that about 2% of Spain's population are immigrants from other countries, but a large number of these are from Spain's North African enclaves that work as low paid agricultural workers in the southwest coastal area.

Taxation in Spain

If you're a permanent resident of Spain, you'll be taxed on your world-wide income at rates from 20% to in excess of 50%. Income is established by authorities based upon your home, car, and lifestyle. It's not surprising that many wealthy Spanish -passport holders establish legal residence in a tax haven nation for tax avoidance purposes. Unlike the U.S., Spain does not tax its non-resident citizens.

Tax laws consider an indi-vidual to be a resident if they stay in the country for longer than 183 days annually, or if their main professional, business, or economic activity is located in Spain. If a spouse or dependants remain resident in Spain, a head of household is also considered a resident unless you can prove residence for more than 183 days in another country. Temporary absences are included in the tax collector's calculations.

Spain has double taxation tax treaties with many non-EU countries, including the U.S. and Switzerland. Wealthy foreigners should consider Spain a fine place for leisure, but not a place to live tax-free after acquiring a passport.

Despite these discouraging tax implications, a Spanish passport is an excellent guarantee of visa--free travel to many more places than a U.S. passport allows. In addition, Spain has a good relationship with its former colonies, much as the U.K. does with Commonwealth members.

EU nationals can remain in Spain for up to six months without a residency permit, non-EU nationals for three months. Requirements for obtaining a permit are: payment of a small fee; four passport photos; a residency visa from the Spanish Consulate in your home nation; proof of income or pension; the Form E111 endorsed by Spanish health authorities, or proof of medical insurance; a certificate that you have registered with your nation's consulate in Spain; and an *escritura* (rental contract).

Contacts

Henley & Partner, Inc., Kirchgasse 22, 8001 Zurich, Switzerland; Tel: +(41) 44-266-2222; Fax: +(41) 44-266-2223; E-mail: zurich@henleyglobal.com; Web site: http://www.henleyglobal.com.

United States: A passport is required for entry into Spain. A visa is not required for tourist or business stays up to 90 days. Individuals who enter Spain without a visa are not authorized to work. American citizens planning to study in Spain should be aware that Spanish immigration regulations require applications for student visas to be submitted 60 days before anticipated travel to Spain. For further information concerning entry requirements for Spain, travelers should contact the Embassy of Spain at 2375 Pennsylvania Avenue NW, Washington, D.C. 20037, Tel: (202) 728-2330, or the nearest Spanish consulate in Boston, Chicago, Houston, Los Angeles, Miami, New Orleans, New York, San Francisco, or San Juan. The web site of the Spanish Embassy in the United States is http://www.spainemb.org. Additional Spanish government web sites with information about entry requirements (in Spanish) can be found at http://www.mae.es and http://www.mir.es

Americans living in or visiting Spain are encouraged to register at the Consular Section of the U.S. Embassy in Madrid or at the U.S. Consulate General in Barcelona, where they may obtain updated information on travel and security within Spain. The U.S. Embassy in Madrid, Spain is located at Serrano 75, Tel: (34)(91) 587-2200 and Fax: (34)(91) 587-2303. U.S. citizens who register in the Consular Section at the U.S. Embassy, Consulate General or one of the Consular Agency listed below can obtain updated information on travel and security within Spain. Additional information is available through the U.S. Embassy's web site at http://madrid.usembassy.gov/.

The U.S. Consulate in Barcelona is located at Paseo Reina Elisenda 23-25; Tel: (34)(93) 280-2227 and Fax: (34)(93) 205-5206. Visitors to Barcelona can access additional information from the Consulate General's web site: http://barcelona.usconsulate.gov/. There are six Consular Agencies in Spain, which provide limited services to American Citizens, but are not authorized to issue passports. **Fuengirola** near Malaga, at Avenida Juan Gomez Juanito #8, Edificio Lucia 1C, 29640, Fuengirola, Tel: (34)(952) 474-891 and Fax: (34)(952) 465-189, Hours 10:00 a.m. to 1:00 p.m.; **La Coruna**, at Canton Grande 6, Tel: (34)(981) 213-233 and Fax: (34)(981 22 28 08), Hours 10:00 a.m. to 1:00 p.m.; **Las Palmas**, at Edificio Arca, Calle Los Martinez de Escobar 3, Oficina 7, Tel: (34)(928) 222-552 and Fax: (34)(928) 225-863, Hours 10:00 a.m. to 1:00 p.m.; **Palma de Mallorca**, Edificio Reina Constanza, Porto Pi, 8, 9-D, 07015 Palma de Mallorca, Spain. Tel: (34)(971) 40-3707 or 40-3905 and Fax: (34)(971) 40-3971. Hours 10:30 a.m. to 1:30 p.m.; Seville, at **Paseo de Las**

Delicias 7, Tel: (34)(954) 231-885 and Fax: (34)(954) 232-040, Hours 8:30 a.m. to 1:30 p.m.; **Valencia**, at Doctor Romagosa #1, 2-J, 46002, Valencia, Tel: (34)(96)-351-6973 and Fax: (34)(96) 352-9565, Hours 10:00 a.m. to 1:00 p.m.

United Kingdom: The British Embassy is located at Calle de Fernando el Santo 16, 28010 Madrid, Tel: (34) (91) 700 8200, Fax: (34) (91) 700 8210, E-mail: presslibrary@ukinspain.com, Web site: http://www.ukinspain.com British Consulates are located in: **Alicante:** Plaza Calvo Sotelo 1-2, Apartado De Correos 564, 03001 Alicante, Tel: (34) 96 521 6022, Fax: (34) 96 514 0528, E-mail: enquiries.alicante@fco.gov.uk; **Las Palmas de Gran Canaria**, (Canary Islands): Edificio Cataluña, C/Luis Morote 6-3º, 35007 Las Palmas, Tel: (34) (928) 262-508, Fax: (34) (928) 267-774, E-mail: LAPAL-Consular@fco.gov.uk Web site: http://www.ukinspain.com/; **Malaga:** Edificio Eurocom, Bloque Sur, Calle Mauricio Moro Pareto 2-2°, 29006 Málaga, Spain; Postal Address: Apartado de Correos 360, 29080 Málaga, Spain, Tel: (34) 95 235 23 00, Fax: (34) 95 235 92 11, E-mail: malaga@fco.gov.uk; **Santa Cruz de Tenerife** (Canary Islands): Plaza Weyler 8-1, Santa Cruz de Tenerife 38003, Tel: (34) (922) 286-863, Fax: (34) (922) 289-903; **Vigo:** Plaza de Compostela 23-6º (Aptdo 49) 36201 Vigo, Tel: +(34) (986) 437-133, Fax: (34) (986) 437-133, E-mail: tenerife.enquiries@fco.gov.uk; **Barcelona:** Edificio Torre de Barcelona, Avenida Diagonal 477-13, 08036 Barcelona, Tel: (34) 933 666 200, Fax: (34) 933 666 221, E-mail: barcelonaconsulate@ ukinspain.com/; **Bilbao:** Alameda de Urquijo 2-8, 48008 Bilbao, Tel: (34) (94) 415-7600, Fax: (34) (94) 416-7632.

The Latin American Route to EU Citizenship

Everyone wants a passport from one of the European Union member countries. With that document in hand, you're free to roam, live, and do business in any of the EU countries, few questions asked. However, EU member states don't grant citizenship easily, but some of their former colonies do. Few know it, but for those who qualify, the quickest backdoor route to EU citizenship is through several South American countries, long ago colonies of Spain and Portugal. A similar arrangement exists between Spain and another of its former colonies, the Philippines. In recent years, Spain has been much stricter on applicants using the "colonial route," who now must prove their personal origins in the country from which they move to Spain.

One can apply directly for residence in one of the various EU countries, but unless you qualify for either immediate citizenship or a reduced period of residence due to marriage or your ancestry, you won't become eligible to be an EU citizen for from five to ten years.

Spain will grant citizenship within two years after application to persons of "Spanish blood" or descendants of Sephardic Jews. Spanish blood is normally taken for granted whenever an applicant is already a citizen of a former Spanish colony or has a Spanish surname and speaks Spanish. Latin American passport in hand, the next step is acquisition of a house or apartment in Spain and a Spanish residence permit. After the special reduced period of residence based on your Latin American second citizenship, you can apply for a Spanish passport.

An Argentine passport allows visa-free travel to 133 countries, including most of Europe and nearly all of South and Central America. It's also the first passport in South America that entitles its holder to visa-free entry into the U.S., although some post 9-11 restrictions now may apply. Argentineans also qualify for a reduced, two-year residence period in Spain when seeking Spanish nationality.

A Guatemalan passport is good for travel to most countries in Europe without a visa, and dual citizenship is common in the nation. Most upper class Guatemalans hold U.S. and Spanish passports. Spain gives special consideration to Guatemalans, who, by treaty, need only two years of residence in Spain to acquire Spanish citizenship or vice-versa. Both a Honduran and a Uruguayan passport entitle holders to Spanish citizenship after two years of residency in Spain.

Portugal also offers special considerations to members of its former colonies. Brazilian citizens qualify for Portuguese nationality after only three years of official residence; no visa is required to enter or take up residence in Portugal. Citizens of former Portuguese colonial enclaves in India (Goa, Daman, and Diu); and parts of Asia, Timor (a former Indonesian province), Macao in China, and Africa (Cape Verde, Guinea-Bissau, Angola, Mozambique, and São Tome-Principe) may also qualify for Portuguese citizenship. The same goes for Brazil, the biggest Portuguese ex-colony on the world map. However, Brazilian citizenship is not cheap. Any one of these former colonies could be your short cut into the EU.

Switzerland

CAPITAL:	BERN
POPULATION:	7,318,638
LANGUAGE:	GERMAN (OFFICIAL) 63.7%, FRENCH (OFFICIAL) 19.2%, ITALIAN (OFFICIAL) 7.6%, ROMANSCH (OFFICIAL) 0.6%, OTHER 8.9%
CURRENCY:	SWISS FRANC (CHF)
AREA:	41,290 SQUARE KM
ETHNIC GROUPS:	GERMAN 65%, FRENCH 18%, ITALIAN 10%, ROMANSCH 1%, OTHER 6%
RELIGION:	ROMAN CATHOLIC 46%, PROTESTANT 40%, OTHER 5%, UNAFFILIATED 9%

PASSPORT HIGHLIGHTS: Obtaining residency in Switzerland has never been easy, and has become increasingly difficult as the Swiss, like most Western Europeans, have begun to resist the migration of workers from the Mediterranean basin and Africa. Once accepted for residency, however, Swiss citizenship is available after twelve years.

For many centuries the Swiss have maintained more or less strict neutrality towards other countries, including those with which it shares a common border — France, Germany, Liechtenstein, Austria, and Italy. Isolated in the valleys of their Alpine redoubt, the various Burgundian, Germanic, and Italianate people who formed the Swiss Confederation found common cause in rebuffing imperial efforts from all sides: rejecting French, Habsburg, Lombard, and Piedmontese over-lordship. The Swiss talents for precision machinery from cuckoo clocks to hydropower generators, chemicals from explosives to pharmaceuticals, and culinary delights from fondue to chocolate, all driven by a genius for industrial organization and distribution, continue to bring the country customers from all over the world.

In 1945, after the second "war to end all wars" in the 20th Century, the Swiss people overwhelmingly rejected membership in the United Nations. Not until a narrow national vote in 2003 did they join the UN. In national polls, Swiss voters also rejected membership in the European Union, rightly fearing EU bureaucratic interference with Swiss privacy and banking laws. In 2004 Switzerland signed several bilateral accords with the EU. A few years ago a national ballot soundly rejected a specific proposal to ease Swiss bank secrecy laws. Since 1992, Switzerland has been a member of both the World Bank and the International Monetary Fund.

After each of these national plebiscites, even greater amounts of foreign cash flowed into Swiss banks, confirming the widespread notion that Switzerland is the place to safeguard cash and other personal assets. It is currently estimated that Swiss banks manage at least one-third of all assets held offshore by the world's wealthy, an estimated three to four trillion U.S. dollars. As a safe haven for cash, Switzerland has become something of a modern cliché.

Difficult, Not Impossible

For a foreign national, Switzerland is not the easiest place in the world to obtain either permanent residence or full citizenship, but neither is an impossible goal.

Birth in Switzerland does not guarantee citizenship unless at least one parent is Swiss. A foreign national who marries a Swiss can obtain citizenship after a five-year residency. If it's later discovered to be a marriage of convenience, citizenship or residence is instantly revocable.

Residence permits are difficult to arrange, but not impossible. Swiss cantonal, not federal, authorities issue what can be described as a combination residence-work permit allowing work in that canton for a specific employer. (A "canton" is the local term for a state or province).

Swiss Residence

Switzerland has one of Europe's highest percentages of foreigners living within its borders. Of seven millions residents, about 1.4 million, or 20%, are from other countries, especially workers from Spain, Portugal, Italy, and the former Yugoslavia. In recent years, there has been a growing resistance to immigration and granting citizenship. Many areas now require a public referendum on admitting specific lists of applicants and many have been rejected.

For financially independent individuals, business investors, and entrepreneurs, it may be possible to obtain residence in Switzerland. There are generally two ways to establish official Swiss resident status:

1)) Business Investment: Each canton makes its own rules, but all

offer some form of tax breaks and/or subsidies for foreign nationals who agree to relocate a business or start a new one in Switzerland. It must create new employment and help economic development. If the business is substantial, residence permits for the foreign director/owner and his or her family are normally granted without delay. In some cantons, it is permissible to simply open your office and work on your own.

2) Retirement: Wealthy, financially independent foreign applicants over 55 years of age who can show close ties to Switzerland may also be eligible for residence. Although done on an individual basis and at the discretion of the cantonal authorities, such persons may negotiate a one-time agreement on an annual lump sum income tax payment on their worldwide income, far below usual Swiss tax rates.

Residency Permits

1) Annual Residence Permit: The standard one-year residence permit issued to foreigners during their first years of residence in Switzerland is known as the "B" permit. After 5 or 10 years, depending on existing bilateral conventions, the "B" permit holder will become eligible for a permanent resident or "C" permit. The "B" permit allows specific employment and is renewable annually.

2) Permanent Residence Permit: This "C" permit gives its holder full residence status with most of the same rights as Swiss citizens enjoy, except such political rights as voting or holding office.

3) Seasonal Work Permit: This "A" permit is limited to nine consecutive months within a 12-month period, usually for seasonal employment in the building, hotel, and tourism industries. Entry and exit dates are strictly enforced.

4) Border Commuter Work Permit: The "L" permit is issued only to foreign nationals who are residents near the Swiss national border and work in Switzerland.

Swiss Citizenship

After 12 years residence in Switzerland, a foreign national with permanent resident status may apply for naturalization as a Swiss citizen. For foreign national children, any years spent in the country between the ages of ten and 20 years count double for application purposes. Conditions for granting citizenship depend on laws and rules of the canton and community where the foreign person lives. Generally, the applicant must be acquainted with national customs, be well-integrated in society, and, usually, be fluent in one of the national languages.

The application process may involve an in-depth investigation, plus detailed personal questioning of Swiss neighbors. Swiss rules allow instant citizenship for "Persons of International Stature," including noted poets, authors, deposed royalty, movie stars, scientists, ex-heads of state, and religious leaders, but very rarely is citizenship granted on this unique basis.

Switzerland accepts the principle of dual nationality, but foreign citizens who also have Swiss citizenship may be subject to compulsory military service and other requirements while in Switzerland. Switzerland has a liberal attitude toward foreign tourists, allowing visits twice a year for up to three months each time, so long as visits are separated by an adequate time period.

Swiss Taxes

Switzerland certainly is not an automatic no-tax haven nation. However, non-Swiss foreign investors can avoid many local taxes by choosing certain types of investments that escape taxes.

By law, Swiss banks collect a withholding tax of 35% on all interest and dividends paid by Swiss companies, banks, the government, or other sources. Foreign investors to whom this tax applies may be eligible for refunds of all or part of the tax under the terms of bilateral tax treaties between Switzerland and the person's home nation. Making application for this refund to your home nation government, of course, compromises your financial privacy, and this factor should be weighed against the possible refund.

In 2004 Switzerland signed an agreement with the European Union to enforce withholding taxes on EU nationals with Swiss interest income. Although names will not be revealed, taxes will be collected and remitted to the foreign nationals home governments.

Under the terms of Article 23 of the 1996 Swiss-U.S. Tax Treaty, Switzerland now taxes U.S. citizens resident within the nation on all their worldwide income, but the taxpayer is eligible for a U.S. tax credit for payment of these taxes in order to avoid double taxation.

Although it is not generally known, for those who wish to retire in Switzerland, it is possible to negotiate a lump sum annual income tax payment (known as a *forfait*) with cantonal tax authorities. The more populous and popular cantons are likely to charge more, but the smaller ones, such as Appenzell, will settle for less per year, regardless of your actual total income. The difficulty is in obtaining a Swiss residency permit, an extremely scarce commodity. Nevertheless, if you are wealthy, and offer proof of sufficient future income, you may qualify.

There is no Swiss withholding on payments to foreigners arising from Swiss life insurance or annuities. Nor is there tax on dividends or interest from securities that originate outside Switzerland. For this reason, many Swiss banks offer investment funds with at least 80% of earnings in foreign investments or, even better, investments in money market funds based in Luxembourg or Ireland. As we go to press, the U.S. Internal Revenue Service is pressing Swiss banks to reveal the names of all U.S. persons who invest through each bank.

Personal income taxes in Switzerland vary depending on the canton and local community in which an individual resides, works, or has his/her investments. While a Swiss federal tax applies throughout Switzerland, each of the 26 cantons has its own tax system and sets its own tax rates. As a rule, individuals who are deemed resident for tax purposes in Switzerland are subject to income tax on their worldwide income regardless of source.

Trying to figure out total Swiss taxes is not easy. Federal, cantonal, and communal taxes all have complex tax rates and deductions. Federal income tax rates range from 0-11.5%. Cantonal and communal tax rates vary, but are generally twice as high as federal rates. Switzerland has a network of over 40 bilateral international tax treaties.

Swiss nationals domiciled in Switzerland and foreign nationals holding "C" permanent residence permits are assessed income and net wealth taxes based on their filing periodic tax returns. The individual taxpayer then is responsible for tax compliance and payment of income taxes when billed by the state.

Border commuters and foreign nationals living in Switzerland who do not hold a "C" permit, usually, are subject to withholding taxes levied employers on gross taxable earned income. Progressive withholding tax rates depend on gross taxable income, marital status, and the number of dependants.

Campione d'Italia — Little known Swiss Back Door

Switzerland may be the world's most famous haven country, but there's another residential haven that's not only more exotic, but is itself an enclave inside of Switzerland. And it's Italian!

Campione d'Italia, on the shores of beautiful Lake Lugano, is distinguished by its very uniqueness; a little plot of Italian soil, completely surrounded by Swiss territory. There are no border controls and complete freedom of travel. Home to about 2,000 people, it's located in the southern Swiss canton of Ticino, about 16 miles north of the Italian border and five miles by road from Lugano, Switzerland, a beautiful scenic drive.

With no border controls, there is complete freedom of transit. The village uses Swiss banks, currency, postal service, and telephone system. Even automobile license plates are Swiss. Strangely enough, because of ancient history and treaties, the enclave legally is considered part of the territory of Italy.

Foreigners find Campione a useful back door to Switzerland. A local permanent residence permit is comparatively easy to obtain, allowing the holder free movement throughoutSwitzerland and Liechtenstein as well. Campione has no income taxes and no local taxes. Almost all local revenue is derived from the local municipal casino. Not surprisingly, a large number of foreign tax exiles call it home.

Campione is also a very pleasant place to live, located in the heart of one of the best Swiss tourist areas. The region boasts lakes, winter sports, and the cultural activities of Milan, Italy, only one hour away by auto. All that's needed to become an official resident is to rent or buy property here, although formal registration is required. However, living here is very expensive; US$750,000 for a very small townhouse. Foreigners may buy real estate without restrictions, unlike Switzerland. But real estate prices are well above surrounding Ticino. Condominiums range from US$5,500 to $6,500 per square meter, and broker fees add a 3% commission.

Corporations registered in Campione have distinct advantages over Swiss companies. They use Swiss banking facilities and have a mailing address that appears to be Swiss, while escaping Switzerland's relatively high income and withholding taxes. Corporations are governed by Italian corporate law and can be formed with a minimum capitalization of about US$1,000. Corporations can be owned and directed entirely by foreigners, a status Swiss law denies. Corporate registrations are usually handled by Italian lawyers in Milan, and fees are modest. As part of Italy, EU business regulations do apply to Campione businesses, as do Italian corporate taxes. Campione's tax breaks apply only to natural persons.

Obtaining facts about Campione is much more difficult than for other tax havens because the enclave does not promote itself. There is no central office of information. Outsiders are not unwelcome, but no one readily volunteers news about this secret haven. A personal visit is mandatory for anyone seriously interested in making this their home. If you want to know more about Campione, visit: www.escapeartist.com/ditalia/ditalia.htm.

Contacts

Henley & Partner, Inc., Kirchgasse 22, 8001 Zurich, Switzerland; Tel: +(41) 44-266-2222; Fax: +(41) 44-266-2223; E-mail: zurich@henley-global.com; Web sites: http://www.henleyglobal.com/switzerland.htm http://www.henleyglobal.com/campione.htm

United States: A passport is required for entry into Switzerland. A visa is not required for U.S. citizens for stays of up to 90 days. For more information on entry requirements travelers may contact the Embassy of Switzerland at 2900 Cathedral Avenue, NW, Washington, D.C. 20008, Tel: (202) 745-7900 or the nearest Swiss Consulate General in Atlanta, Chicago, Houston, Los Angeles, New York, or San Francisco. Additional information is available at http://www.swissemb.or.

U.S. citizens are encouraged to register and obtain updated information on travel and security within Switzerland at the U.S. Embassy in Bern or at the two U.S. Consular Agencies, which offer limited consular services to U.S. citizens, in Zurich and Geneva. The U.S. Embassy in Bern is located at Jubilaeumstrasse 93, 3005 Bern, Tel: (41)(31) 357-7011, Fax: (41)(31) 357-7280. The Embassy's 24 hour emergency telephone number is (41)(31) 357-7777. The Embassy's e-mail address is bernacs@state.gov. Web site: http://www.usembassy.ch/ answers many questions of interest to Americans visiting and residing in Switzerland.

The U.S. Consular Agency in **Zurich** is located at the American Center of Zurich, Dufourstrasse 101, 8008 Zurich, Tel: (41)(1) 422-2566, Fax: (41) (1) 383-9814. The U.S. Consular Agency in **Geneva** is located at the American Center Geneva, 7 Rue Versonnex, 1207 Geneva, Tel: (41)(22) 840-5160, Fax: (41)(22) 840-5162, E-mail: consulate.us@ties.itu.int

United Kingdom: The British Embassy is located at Thunstrasse 50, 3005 Berne, Tel: (41) (31) 359-7700, Fax: (41) (31) 359-7701; E-mail: info@britain-in-switzerland.ch; Web site: http://www.britain-in-switzerland.ch/. British Consulates are located in: **Geneva:** 37-39 Rue de Vermont (6th Fl), 1211 Geneva 20, Tel: (41)(22) 918-2400, Fax: (41) (22) 918-2322; **Montreux/Vevey:** 13 chemin de l'Aubousset, 1806 St Légier, Vaud, Tel: (41)(21) 943-3263, Fax: (41)(21) 943-3263;

Valais: Rue des Fontaines, 3974 Mollens-Valais, Tel: (41)(27) 480-3210, Fax: (41)(27) 480-3211; **Zurich:** Hegibachstrasse 47, 8032 Zurich, Tel: (01) 383-6560, Fax: (01) 383-6561 and Lugano: Via Sorengo 22, CH-6903 Lugano, Tel: (0041) 91-950-0606, Fax: (0041) 91-950-0609.

United Kingdom

CAPITAL:	LONDON
POPULATION:	60,094,648
LANGUAGE:	ENGLISH, WELSH, SCOTTISH FORM OF GAELIC
CURRENCY:	BRITISH POUND (£)
AREA:	244,820 SQUARE KM
ETHNIC GROUPS:	ENGLISH 81.5%, SCOTTISH 9.6%, IRISH 2.4%, WELSH 1.9%, ULSTER 1.8%, WEST INDIAN, INDIAN, PAKISTANI, AND OTHER 2.8%
RELIGION:	ANGLICAN AND ROMAN CATHOLIC 40 MILLION, MUSLIM 1.5 MILLION, PRESBYTERIAN 800,000, METHODIST 760,000, SIKH 500,000, HINDU 500,000, JEWISH 350,000

PASSPORT HIGHLIGHTS: Full UK citizenship is attainable after only five years' residence. Retirees over 59 years of age with £25,000 in annual income are eligible to settle in the UK. Residency is granted to investors bringing in at least £200,000 to run a business employing UK residents or £750,000 in passive investment in a UK company not primarily a property holding concern. Work permits are available in several categories, also leading to permanent residency and naturalization.

Located off Western Europe, between the Atlantic Ocean and the North Sea and northwest of France, Great Britain, now known as the United Kingdom, is a highly developed constitutional monarchy comprising England, Scotland, Wales, and Northern Ireland.

Great Britain was the dominant industrial and maritime power of the 19th Century. It played a leading role in developing parliamentary democracy and in advancing trade, industry, literature, and science. At its zenith, the British Empire covered approximately one-fourth of the Earth's surface, with African possessions stretching "from the Cape to

Cairo" and others encompassing virtually every region in the rest of the world. Its keystone was India (including what are now Pakistan, Bangladesh, and Burma). In the first half of the 20th Century, its strength was seriously depleted by two world wars. Since the end of World War II, the British Empire has been dismantled and Britain has rebuilt itself into a prosperous, modern European nation with significant international political, cultural, and economic influence. As the 21st Century begins, Britain is debating its degree of integration with continental Europe. While a member of the European Union, for the time being, it is staying out of the euro currency area in favor of retention of the pound sterling.

In many ways, the United Kingdom is one of the more attractive places in the world both to live and do business. Among the many U.K. advantages are: 1) complex immigration laws offering many useful options; 2) full citizenship after only five years' residence; 3) a tax system favorable to resident foreigners; 4) competitive tax rates; 5) an attractive lifestyle; and 6) excellent transport, communications, and financial services.

Immigration, Residence and Citizenship

The British immigration law is one of the world's most complex. However, the law offers foreign nationals numerous possibilities for low-tax residence, plus the option to acquire British citizenship after only five years of legal residence. Some of these possibilities are:

1) **Business-Investor:** Immediate entry is granted to business persons who invest at least £200,000 in the U.K., creating at least two new jobs for the resident labor market. If the venture is new, then a comprehensive business plan is required. When buying into an existing U.K. business, audited accounts must be provided. The larger the amount invested, the more likely and quickly approval can be had. The amount invested can be, in part, the value of plant and equipment, and can be spread over more than one enterprise. These applications are usually filed abroad at a U.K. Embassy or Consulate and require about three months to process, with final approval and visa issuance taking up to twelve months.

2) **Investor:** This requires a commitment to invest at least £750,000 in U.K. Government bonds or a U.K. registered company, but not a company principally engaged in property holding. A minimum initial deposit of £250,000 is required. The applicant must maintain his/her main residence in the U.K. and have sufficient means of support without having local employment. The main attraction of

this category of U.K. residency admission is that the requirements are straightforward and applications are quickly approved once qualifications are met.

3) **Retirement:** A person at least 60 years old with investment or rental income of not less than £25,000 per year may be granted residence if they can demonstrate close U.K. ties. These ties may be U.K. close relatives, previous residence, business connections, or even a strong sense of identity with the United Kingdom. While an applicant must show an income that they receive "without working," they can manage their investments, including U.K. real property investments, and they can hold non-executive directorships. While a retiree is not allowed to work in the U.K., after four years residence, they may apply for permanent residence and once granted, there are no restrictions on working.

4) **Ancestry:** Ancestry: Commonwealth citizens with a grandparent born in the U.K. are admitted for a four-year period of employment, after which permanent residence is usually granted. For those not Commonwealth citizens who do meet the ancestry requirement, it may be possible to acquire Commonwealth status through an economic citizenship program offered by a nation such as Dominica or Grenada.

5) **Work Permit:** The U.K. employer, and not the prospective employee, may apply to obtain a work permit for an overseas employee. Stringent requirements include a minimum pay level and the employer's certification that the employee's talents are unique and unattainable locally. There are special provisions for entertainers, sports stars, and models. Work permit applications are considered by the U.K. Department for Education and Employment and processing generally takes between one and two months, resulting in a permit for between six months and four years. The full work permit is usually granted to high-level executives, managers, and those with technical skills not readily available in the U.K. and the European Union.

6) **Key workers:** So-called "key worker" permits are often granted to those who, while not high-level executives, have language, cultural, or culinary knowledge rare in the U.K. This category of permit is often used for hotel/restaurant managers, head chefs, highly skilled waiting staff, and senior hotel receptionists. Key worker permits will not generally be granted or extended for more than a total of three years. Thus, they do not lead to permanent residence.

7) **Sole Company Representative:** YRepresentative: You may apply as the representative of an overseas company whose major business is offshore and has no U.K. branch, subsidiary, or other agent. To qualify, one must be a present employee of an established, legitimate foreign firm, and not the majority owner of that firm. No significant investment is required and applications are usually processed quickly. Residence is granted for one year, renewable based on the continued success of the business.

8) **Permanent Residence and Citizenship:** In the above investor, business-related, or work permit categories, U.K. permanent residence is usually granted after four years. The person may then apply for U.K. citizenship after one additional year's residence.

9) **Special Status:** Under special provisions, nationals of Bulgaria, the Czech Republic, Hungary, Poland, Romania, and Slovakia, as well as foreign lawyers, writers, and artists of any nationality are exempt from the investment or employment creation requirements. Thus, they can more easily start a U.K. business and obtain immediate residence.

Foreign lawyers and legal professionals may enter the U.K. to establish self-employment or to join other lawyers in partnership. They can only practice non-U.K. law, and must have accreditation from their local foreign Bar Association. Those establishing a new office must prove sufficient funding. Performing artists and authors (whether of words or music), may enter the U.K. to pursue their career if they can demonstrate a successful record elsewhere during the preceding year. Such persons must present a realistic business plan and show adequate finances. Upon first arrival, they must have a valid entry visa issued by a British Embassy or Consulate abroad.

There are numerous other categories allowing entry into the U.K. that work for extended periods of time; among them clergy and religious, students, young adult children of Commonwealth residents, and work trainees. A person who is a recognized dual national is entitled to a special "Right of Abode" stamp in their foreign passport to enable travel into the U.K. without any hindrances should they wish to use their second passport.

Naturalization

A person who has been physically present in the U.K. for a year as a permanent resident may apply to become a naturalized British citizen. The processing of an application is likely to require from 12 to 18 months. Other than those seeking naturalization after marriage, the following requirements must be met:

The applicant must be aged 18 or over and of sound mind and good character. They should have a sufficient knowledge of the English language. They should intend to live in the U.K. or work directly for the U.K. Government, an international organization of which the U.K. is a member, or be employed by a company or association established in the United Kingdom.

The five-year residency period is the period ending with the date the application is received by the Home Office. The requirements are as follows: the candidate must have been in the U.K. at the beginning of the five-year period and, during that period, must not have been outside the U.K. for more than 450 days; and in the last 12 months of the period must not have been outside the U.K. for more than 90 days; and in the last 12 months of the five-year period, the candidate's U.K. stay must not have been subject to any time limit under the immigration laws; and at no time, must the candidate have been in the U.K. in breach of the immigration laws.

Marriage

In order to prevent abuse of this category, the government imposes a number of conditions: 1) a visa is granted for only one year, at the end of which, if the marriage is still intact, permanent residence will be granted. After a three-year period, the spouse may apply for U.K. nationality; 2) to prevent arranged marriages, the U.K. citizen must have actually met the non-U.K. spouse; 3) the couple must intend to live together permanently; 4) the couple must possess sufficient funds for themselves and their dependants without recourse to public funds; 5) housing for the couple and any dependants must be available; and 6) spouses seeking U.K. entry on the basis of marriage should apply for entry clearance before entering the U.K. Children of the marriage under 18 years old are allowed entry and can apply at the same time as the main applicant.

In recent years there has been considerable debate in the U.K. about adoption and enforcement of stricter political asylum laws. This has been prompted by the influx of many thousands of refugees from former British colonial areas and from Eastern Europe.

Contacts

Henley & Partner, Inc., H&P Trust Company Ltd, Salisbury House, 1 - 9 Union Street, St. Helier, Jersey JE4 8RH, Channel Islands, Tel: +44 1534 514 888 Fax: +44 1534 514 999 E-mail: jersey-office@

henleyglobal.com

United States: A passport is required for entry into the United Kingdom. Tourists are not obliged to obtain a visa for stays of up to 90 days. Those planning to stay in the United Kingdom for any purpose longer than six months must obtain a visa prior to entering. Further information on entry requirements may be obtained from the British Embassy at 3100 Massachusetts Avenue NW, Washington, DC 20008, Tel: (202) 588-7800. Inquiries may also be directed to British consulates in Atlanta, Boston, Chicago, Houston, Los Angeles, New York, and San Francisco. The web site of the British Embassy in the United States is http://www.britainusa.com/embassy and information on visas can be found at http://www.britainusa.com/visas/visas.asp.

Americans living in or visiting the United Kingdom are encouraged to register at the Consular Section of the U.S. Embassy in London or at the U.S. Consulates General in Edinburgh or Belfast and obtain updated information on travel and security within the U.K. The U.S. Embassy is located at 24 Grosvenor Square, London W1A 1AE, Tel: 020-7499-900 (in country), 011-44-20-7499-9000 (from the U.S. 24 hours) Consular Section fax: 020-7495-5012 (in country) 011-44-20-7495-5012 (from the U.S.). The Embassy web site is http://www.usembassy.org.uk.

The U.S. Consulate General in Edinburgh, Scotland is located at 3 Regent Terrace, Edinburgh EH7 5BW, Tel: 0131-556-8315 (in country), 011-44-131-556-8315 (from the U.S.). After hours: 01224-857097 (in country), 011-44-1224-857097 (from the U.S.). Fax: 0131-557-6023 (in country), 011-44-131-557-6023 (from the U.S.). Information on the Consulate General is included on the Embassy's web site at http://www.usembassy.org.uk/scotland.

The U.S. Consulate General in Belfast, Northern Ireland, is located at Danesfort House, 228 Stranmillis Road, Belfast BT9 5GR, Tel: 028-9038-6100 (in country), 001-44-28-9038-6100 (from the U.S.). Fax: 028-9068-1301 (in country), 011-44-28-9068-1301 (from the U.S.). Information on the Consulate General is included on the Embassy's web site at http://www.usembassy.org.uk.

Section 5.
Middle East and Africa

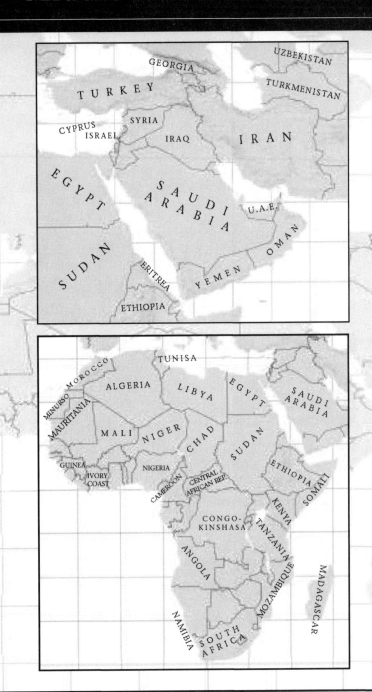

Republic of Cyprus

CAPITAL:	NICOSIA
POPULATION:	771,657
LANGUAGE:	GREEK, TURKISH, AND ENGLISH
CURRENCY:	CYPRIOT POUND (£C), TURKISH LIRA (TL)
AREA:	9,250 SQUARE KM
ETHNIC GROUPS:	GREEK 85.2%, TURKISH 11.6%, OTHER 3.2%
RELIGION:	GREEK ORTHODOX 78%, MUSLIM 18%, MARONITE, ARMENIAN APOSTOLIC, AND OTHER 4%

PASSPORT HIGHLIGHTS: Persons with modest annual income may become residents of Cyprus, but naturalization is generally not available. Certain classes of individuals with royalties or passive income are entitled to Cypriot residency if they are not domiciled there. This may be attractive to citizens of other countries whose tax relations with Cyprus provide a flat 5% tax in the country on investment income from abroad. Unfortunately, the United States and UK treaties with Cyprus do not make this benefit available.

Cyprus is a developed Mediterranean Island nation, south of Turkey. Archeologists have found remains of some of the oldest Neolithic settlements on the island, which was famous in Antiquity for the copper mined there. Indeed, its name is synonymous with the metal in Greek. Ruins from virtually every period of recorded history abound on Cyprus, which is also justly famous for excellent wines and local variants on Greek and Turkish cuisine, especially seafood.

It is politically divided into two distinct geographic areas. The Government of the Republic of Cyprus is the internationally recognized authority, but it controls only the Greek Cypriot southern part of the island. The northern area operates under an autonomous Turkish Cypriot administration that governs about 37% of the land area. Another United Nations effort at reunification failed in 2004 when the Greek Cypriots rejected the plan.

Cyprus, a former British colony, independent since 1960, is a member of the United Nations, the Council of Europe, and the British Commonwealth. It became a member of the EU in 2004. It maintains politically and economically viable relations with the Arab countries, and has considerable trade with eastern European countries. Its ties to Britain and Greece are close.

After a 1974 invasion by Turkish forces, the northern portion of the island declared independence as the "Turkish Republic of Northern Cyprus." This divisive move actually bolstered the Greek, southern portion's role as an international tax haven.

The majority of the Cypriot population is Greek, with a minority of Turks and other nationalities. Languages are Greek and Turkish, but English is widely used, especially in the legal and business communities. Technical communications are excellent, and it is a popular tourist destination. As a result of its relationship with Great Britain, Cyprus is a common law country.

Retirement Tax Benefits

Cyprus usually does not offer citizenship to foreign nationals, but it may be a good place to settle as residents for some people. Residence is fairly straightforward if you can demonstrate an annual income of as little as US$7,500 for one, to US$19,000 for a family of four. Cyprus offers interesting tax benefits for a retired investor, author, musician, or inventor — from the right nation. To obtain these tax benefits, one must become resident, but not domiciled in Cyprus. There are also certain residency programs for foreign nationals willing to make substantial investment in the island's economy.

Cyprus is an attractive destination for a retired investor or anyone who receives substantial royalty income. It is relatively easy to obtain a residence permit with proof of adequate means of support. Foreigners who become residents are not allowed to carry on any local business on Cyprus unless granted permission. Nevertheless, they can conduct business from Cyprus anywhere in the world. U.S. citizens whom the Cypriot government considers to be Cypriot citizens may be subject to compulsory military service and other aspects of Cypriot law while in Cyprus.

Cyprus may suit your needs if: 1) you are a retired investor who receives dividends or interest from countries with which Cyprus has favorable income tax treaties; 2) you are an author, musician, or inventor who receives royalty income; 3) you already have a satisfactory citizenship and passport; or 4) you have a suitable legal domicile and have no problem retaining it.

Low Tax for Non-Domiciled Residents

A non-domiciled resident pays a flat tax of 5% on investment income received from abroad and remitted to Cyprus. The first £C2,000 (about US$4,000) of remitted investment income, and all investment income that is not remitted to Cyprus, is tax-free. Royalties are treated as investment income. Foreign earned income can be remitted to Cyprus in order to reduce foreign withholding taxes under one of Cyprus' many tax treaties. When that is done, any foreign withholding tax can be credited against any Cyprus tax owed. That may well wipe out the 5% Cyprus tax obligation.

Unfortunately, these benefits are not available under the terms of either the Cyprus-U.K. or Cyprus-U.S. tax treaties, but nationals covered by most other Cyprus tax treaties can benefit. Cyprus has tax treaties with the United Kingdom, Denmark, Sweden, Ireland, Norway, Greece, Germany, Hungary, Italy, France, Russia, Romania, the United States, Canada, and Bulgaria.

To qualify for local residency, an applicant must provide evidence of good character, show independent financial means, and document income. The Cypriot Immigration Control Board also imposes minimum amounts of income that must be received by residents during a tax year, as follows: 1) single applicant £C4,425/US$7,040; 2) with one dependant £C6,610/ US$10,500; 3) with two dependants £C8,790/ US$13,990; or 4) with three dependants, £C10,980/US$17,450. For information on residence applications, contact: Chief Immigration Officer, Migration Department, Ministry of Interior Affairs, Nicosia 1457, Cyprus; Tel: +(357) 2-302485; Fax: +(357) 2-449221

Foreigners allowed residency may purchase property in Cyprus, but only after obtaining a permit. For more information, contact the Cyprus Real Estate Agents Association (CREAA), P.O. Box 1455, Nicosia, Cyprus; Tel: +(357) 2-449500; Fax: +(357) 2-449048. Approval to buy real property is usually a formality for a house or apartment in which you plan to live.

Cyprus still has currency exchange controls, but a new foreign resident can remain as a non-resident for exchange control purposes. This allows keeping funds in foreign currencies both in Cyprus and abroad, but approval is needed to invest in Cyprus or to borrow money there. Cyprus imposes death taxes, but the estates of non-domiciled residents are liable for taxes only on assets located in Cyprus at the time of death.

Contacts

Cyprus maintains Embassies/High Commissions in the following countries: Australia, Austria, Belgium, Bulgaria, China, Czech Republic, Egypt, France, Germany, Greece, Hungary, India, Kenya, Libya, Mexico, the Netherlands, Russian Federation, Spain, Sweden, Syria, United Kingdom, the United States, and Yugoslavia.

A passport is required for travel to Cyprus. Tourist and business visas are issued at the port of entry for a stay of up to three months.

Henley & Partner, Inc., Kirchgasse 22, 8001 Zurich, Switzerland; Tel: +(41) 44-266-2222; Fax: +(41) 44-266-2223; E-mail: zurich@henley-global.com; Web site: http://henleyglobal.com

United States: A passport is required for entry into to Cyprus. Tourist and business visas are issued at the port of entry for a stay of up to 90 days. For further information on entry requirements for Cyprus, travelers can contact the Embassy of the Republic of Cyprus at 2211 R Street NW, Washington, D.C. 20008-4082, Tel: (202) 462-5772 or the Cypriot Consulate in New York at 13 East 40th St., 5th Floor, New York, N.Y. 10016, Tel: (212) 686-6016/17. The Embassy's web site is http://www.cyprusembassy.net.

Americans living in or visiting Cyprus are encouraged to register at the Consular Section of the U.S. Embassy in Cyprus and obtain updated information on travel and security within Cyprus. The U.S. Embassy is located at Metochiou and Ploutarchou Streets, Engomi, Nicosia. The telephone number within Cyprus is (22) 776-400, when calling from the U.S., dial 011 (357) (22) 776-400. The Consular Section's fax number within Cyprus is (22) 776 841. The fax number from the U.S. is 011 – (357) – (22) 776 841. The Embassy of the Republic of Cyprus web site is http://www.americanembassy.org.cy. The U.S. Government also maintains an office in north Cyprus at 6 Serif Arzik Street, Koskluciftlik, Nicosia. When calling from the U.S., dial 011 (357) (22) 669-965 or fax to 011 (357) (22) 679 014. When calling within north Cyprus dial (22) 73 930 or fax to (22) 78 514.

United Kingdom: The British High Commission is located at Alexander Pallis St, Nicosia; Tel: (357) (2) 861-100, Fax: (357) (2) 861-125, E-mail: infobhc@cylink.com.cy, Web site: http://www.britain. org.cy

Israel

CAPITAL:	JERUSALEM (PROCLAIMED AS CAPITAL IN 1950, BUT NEARLY ALL COUNTRIES MAINTAIN EMBASSIES IN TEL AVIV)
POPULATION:	6,116,533
LANGUAGE:	HEBREW (OFFICIAL), ARABIC (UNOFFICIAL), ENGLISH COMMONLY USED.
CURRENCY:	NEW ISRAELI SHEKEL (NIS)
AREA:	20,770 SQUARE KM
ETHNIC GROUPS:	JEWISH 80.1% (EUROPE/AMERICA-BORN 32.1%, ISRAEL-BORN 20.8%, AFRICA-BORN 14.6%, ASIA-BORN 12.6%), NON-JEWISH 19.9% (MOSTLY ARAB)
RELIGION:	JEWISH 80.1%, MUSLIM 14.6% (MOSTLY SUNNI MUSLIM), CHRISTIAN 2.1%, OTHER 3.2%

PASSPORT HIGHLIGHTS: Under the Law of Return, Jews are granted Israeli citizenship 90 days after immigrating there. Non-Jews who reside in Israel for three years of a five-year period, intending to settle there also may apply for Israeli citizenship, but they must renounce their former nationality.

The State of Israel is located at the eastern end of the Mediterranean Sea, which forms its western border. It also has common, but highly disputed, northern borders with Lebanon and Syria. Israel occupied the West Bank, Gaza Strip, Golan Heights, and East Jerusalem as a result of the 1967 War. By agreement with Israel, an elected Palestinian authority now exercises jurisdiction in most of Gaza and the major cities of the West Bank. Palestinian Authority police have responsibility for keeping order in those areas, and the Palestinian Authority exercises a range of civil functions in other areas of the West Bank.

The Israeli nation occupies an area in which history dates back to Biblical times, at least 4000 B.C. The ancestors of most modern Jews emigrated from the area later called Palestine in waves beginning in the 6th century B.C. and ending in the 2nd-6th centuries A.D., leaving a small remnant behind. Modern Israel is a parliamentary democracy with a modern economy. The first international Zionist conference, in 1899, called for an eventual Jewish state. By 1909, Jews had founded the new city of Tel Aviv in what was then Palestine. By 1914, over 60,000 Jewish immigrants had moved into an area with 450,00 Arab residents. To enlist the inhabitants' and foreign Zionists' aid in ousting the Ottoman Turks from the region (and probably to thwart French colonial aims as well), the British government promised land in Palestine for a "Jewish national home" via the Balfour Declaration which the Foreign Secretary signed in 1917. After Palestine came under a British mandate in 1929, restrictions on Jewish land purchases and immigration were imposed. By 1937, it was proposed, but the Arabs later rejected, that Palestine be partitioned into Arab and Jewish states. The British attempted controls on Jewish immigration but, by then, Jews in Palestine numbered 200,000, about 30% of the total population.

After World War II, the British abandoned their Palestine mandate, and a new partition plan emerged, culminating on May 14, 1948, when the United Nations proclaimed the existence of the State of Israel. Since then, the Middle East has been wracked with wars between Arabs and Israelis, and, only in the last few years, did negotiation replace violence, but not for long. The goal of stability for these lands remains elusive, as new cycles of violence have erupted.

Israel has become a leading center of high-technology development and manufacturing, and is the only democratic society in the Middle East area.

Residence and Citizenship

An Israeli passport is highly desirable because it is widely accepted throughout the world. It is the only non-European Union passport that gains entry to all EU countries without need for a visa. The Israeli passport can gain its holder reduced residence periods when applying for foreign citizenship in Spain and Germany. Many other countries, including the U.S., permit generous quotas for immigrants from Israel.

New immigrants with substantial income from foreign source investments are given a 30-year holiday from most exchange controls. The new citizen can keep assets wherever he/she wishes and in any currency. During the first seven years of residence, a new immigrant may even be exempt from income and capital gains taxes on foreign source income. At this writing, Israel has no money laundering laws or controls.

One drawback to citizenship is that all males, ages 18 to 48, are liable to serve in the military. Women between 18 and 25 also must serve.

The Law of Return

Israel's official policy has been to welcome the scattered Jews of the world ("the Diaspora") to the Jewish homeland. Adopted in 1950, the "Law of Return" decrees that anyone with one Jewish grandparent has an automatic right to Israeli citizenship, even if they are not observant religious Jews. The law has long provided an automatic second passport and dual citizenship for all who qualified.

Periodic outcries of dissatisfaction with the Law of Return are heard, usually from ultra-Orthodox jews or disgruntled taxpayers, but the tense state of Israeli-Palestinian relations has a tendency to sweep these movements aside. Those interested in exploring their rights under the law should check the current status of the Law of Return.

The Law of Return defines a "Jew" as anyone who is at least one-quarter Jewish (having one Jewish grandparent), or any convert to Judaism who does not embrace another faith. Documentary certification of a male's circumcision ceremony (*briss*) or other important Jewish ceremonies (e.g., bar mitzvah, Jewish wedding, synagogue membership) can serve as supporting evidence.

It is an Israeli custom for new immigrants to choose a Hebrew name. This involves a legal change of name using a simple procedure at the local office of the Ministry of Interior. Once the Hebrew name has been recorded, it is used in all official documents, including the Israeli passport.

Under the Law of Return, an accepted immigrant automatically becomes an Israeli citizen 90 days after entering Israel. It is government practice to grant a document known as a "laisser-passer," rather than an official passport during the first year of citizenship. This requires visas for most travel. Israel permits dual citizenship and does not report acquisition of citizenship to an immigrant's home country. Passports are renewable every five years.

A gentile (non-Jew) also can become a citizen at the discretion of the Ministry of Interior. The applicant must satisfy five conditions: 1) be present in Israel to apply; 2) have been in Israel three years out of the five-year period immediately preceding application; 3) be entitled to permanent resident status; 4) have settled in Israel or intend to do so; and 5) surrender former citizenship, or prove that foreign citizenship will end upon becoming an Israeli. Jews who become citizens through the Law of Return are not restricted in this way.

Israeli citizens naturalized in the United States retain their Israeli citizenship, and their children are considered Israeli citizens also. Children born in the U.S. to Israeli parents acquire both U.S. and Israeli nationality at birth. Israeli citizens, including dual nationals, are subject to serve in the armed forces. U.S.-Israeli dual nationals of military age who do not wish to serve in the military may contact the Israeli Embassy in Washington, D.C. to obtain proof of exemption or deferment before going to Israel. Otherwise, they may not be conscripted into military service or subject to criminal penalties for failure to serve. Israeli citizens, including dual nationals, must enter and depart Israel on their Israeli passports. All U.S. citizens with dual nationality must enter and depart the U.S. on their U.S. passports.

Contacts

United States: A valid passport, an onward or return ticket and proof of sufficient funds are required for entry into Israel. A no-charge, three-month visa may be issued upon arrival and may be renewed. Travelers carrying official or diplomatic U.S. passports must obtain visas from an Israeli embassy or consulate prior to arrival in Israel. Anyone who has been refused entry or experienced difficulties with his/her visa status during a previous visit or who has overstayed a visa, should consult the Israeli Embassy or nearest Israeli Consulate before attempting to return to Israel. For further information on entry requirements, travelers may contact the Embassy of Israel at 3514 International Drive NW, Washington, D.C. 20008, Tel: (202) 364-5500 or the Israeli Consulates General in Atlanta, Boston, Chicago, Houston, Miami, New York, Philadelphia or San Francisco.

Americans living in or visiting Israel, the West Bank or Gaza are encouraged to register at the Consular Section of the U.S. Embassy in Tel Aviv or the U.S. Consulate General in Jerusalem. E-mail registration for the U.S. Embassy is possible at amctelaviv@state.gov and for the U.S. Consulate General at jerusalemacs@state.gov. When registering, U.S. citizens can obtain updated information on travel and security in the area. The U.S. Embassy in Tel Aviv, Israel, is located at 71 Hayarkon Street. The U.S. mailing address is PSC 98, Box 0001, APO AE 09830, Tel: (972)(3) 519-7575. The number after 4:30 p.m. and before 8:00 a.m. local time is (972)(3) 519-7551, Fax: (972)(3) 516-4390, E-mail: amctelaviv@state.gov Web site: http://consular.usembassy-israel.org.il.

The Consular Section of the U.S. Embassy should be contacted for information and help in the following areas: Israel, the Gaza Strip, the Golan Heights and ports of entry at Ben Gurion Airport, Gaza International Airport, Haifa Port, and the northern (Jordan River) and southern (Arava) border crossings connecting Israel and Jordan. The Consular Section of the U.S. Consulate General in Jerusalem is located at 27 Nablus Road. The U.S. mailing address is Unit 7228, Box 0039, APO AE 09830. The telephone number is (972)(2) 622-7200. The number after 4:30 p.m. and before 8:00 a.m. local time is (972)(2) 622-7250. The fax number is (972)(2) 627-2233. The Consulate's e-mail address is jerusalemacs@state.gov and its web site is http://jerusalem.usconsulate.gov.

The U.S. Consulate General should be contacted for information and help in the following areas: West and East Jerusalem, the West Bank, and the Allenby Bridge border crossing connecting Jordan with the West Bank. There is a U.S. Consular Agent in Haifa at 26 Ben Gurion Boulevard, Tel: (972)(4) 853-1470, who reports to the Embassy in Tel Aviv. The Consular Agent can provide routine and emergency services in the north.

United Kingdom: The British Embassy is located at 192 Hayarkon Street, Tel Aviv 63405; Tel: (972)(3) 725-1222; Fax: (972)(3) 524-3313, E-mail: webmaster.telaviv@fco.gov.uk Web site: http://www.britemb.org.il/. The British Consulates are located in **Tel Aviv:** Migdalor Building (6th Floor) 1 Ben Yehuda Street, Tel Aviv 63801, Tel: (972)(3) 510-0166, Fax: (972)(03) 510-1167, E-mail: bricontv@netvision.net.il, web site: http://www.britemb.org.il/and **Eilat:** c/o Aqua Sport, Coral Beach, PO Box 300, Eilat 88102, Tel: (972)(8) 634-0810, Fax: (972)(8) 634-0810.

Republic of South Africa

CAPITAL:	PRETORIA (EXECUTIVE), CAPE TOWN (LEGISLATIVE), BLOEMFONTEIN (JUDICIAL)
POPULATION:	42,768,678
LANGUAGE:	AFRIKAANS, ENGLISH, NDEBELE, PEDI, SOTHO, SWAZI, TSONGA, TSWANA, VENDA, XHOSA, AND ZULU (ALL OFFICIAL)
CURRENCY:	RAND (R)
AREA:	1,219,912 SQUARE KM
ETHNIC GROUPS:	BLACK 75.2%, WHITE 13.6%, COLORED 8.6%, INDIAN 2.6%
RELIGION:	CHRISTIAN 68%, MUSLIM 2%, HINDU 1.5%, TRADITIONAL & ANIMISTIC 28.5%

PASSPORT HIGHLIGHTS: Persons investing approximately US$12,000-US$17,000 can apply for a twelve-month residence visa, renewable annually. This can lead to a permanent resident visa after three years. A three-year visa is offered to investors who bring R1,500,000 (US$240,000) into South African investments and live there off of the income. After five years, one can apply for South African citizenship and a passport.

The Republic of South Africa occupies the large landmass that forms the southern tip of the African continent. It surrounds one independent state, Lesotho. Namibia, Botswana, and Zimbabwe are on the north, while Mozambique and Swaziland are to the east.

At the dawn of South Africa's recorded history, about 8000 B.C., two major groups, the Bushmen (Khoi) and the Hottentots (San), roamed the land as hunter-gatherers and herders. In 1488, Portuguese explorers sailed around and landed at what is now the Cape of Good Hope. In 1652, the Dutch East India Company established a fort that grew into modern Cape Town. The Cape Dutch white settlers, known as Boers (farmers), and, in more recent times, as Afrikaners, were joined, in 1688, by French Protestant Huguenot refugees. Germans and other Europeans were also assimilated into the colony. Movement by whites into the interior resulted in fierce battles with black tribesmen, then known as Bantus.

The British consolidated their control over the area in the early 1800s, using it as an important staging post on the ocean route to Hong Kong, Australia, New Zealand, and the Pacific. In 1820, with the government in London encouraging settlers from Britain, clashes between the Bantu and European settlers increased dramatically, as did friction between the Afrikaners and the English. In 1830, an Afrikaner group from the Cape started what is now known as the "Great Trek," heading north and inland. Seeking to escape British domination, in 1843, they proclaimed a new state of the Transvaal, followed by the Orange Free State in 1854. The British were victorious over the Afrikaners in the Boer War (1899-1902) and on May 31, 1910, the Union of South Africa was formed as a self-governing British dominion.

In 1948, the National Party, dominated by white Afrikaners, came to power and imposed strict racial segregation ("apartheid"). That lasted until the whites, led by Willem de Klerk, voluntarily relinquished power in 1994. With the election of Nelson Mandela representing the African National Congress (ANC), the apartheid regime was dismantled and the new South Africa became a free and democratic nation. In 1999, Thabo Mbeki was elected to succeed Mandela as president and was re-elected in 2004 by an even larger margin.

South Africa first came into international economic prominence with the discovery of diamonds (1867) at Kimberly and other mineral wealth, including gold (1886), in the Johannesburg area. Mines and mining came to dominate the national economy, with cheap black labor as a major component of its success. The country is rich in natural resources such as coal. It has the largest deposits of chromium, manganese, vanadium, and platinum in the world and has long been the world's largest producer and exporter of diamonds and gold.

Great Possibilities

In South Africa, a person of relatively modest financial means, judged by U.S. or European standards, can live like a person of great wealth. This is especially true for foreign currency holders because of a highly favorable exchange rate. At this writing, the South African rand stands at about five to US$1 and eight to £1.

With the right currency in your offshore bank account, you can live in South Africa just like the proverbial king. Local prices in rands for real estate are extremely low and bargains abound. Many homes traditionally have accommodation for live-in servants whose monthly wages average about US$50. Wages, in general, are about a tenth of those paid in the U.K. or U.S. for comparable service jobs.

A magnificent ten-room mansion on the Indian Ocean near Cape Town can be bought for under US$200,000. Something similar in the U.K. would cost a million dollars. A luxury flat at cosmopolitan Sea Point on the Atlantic Ocean, in Cape Town, goes for around US$20,000. For retirees, having a flat in South Africa is a perfect way to enjoy the glorious summers (December to April), while the Northern Hemisphere is locked in winter. Summer in subtropical Durban lasts all year round.

South Africa is a great place to do business. The common language is English, there is a strong international community, good infrastructure and telecommunications, reliable electricity, and you can drink the local water without fear! The real need is for low-tech, labor-intensive businesses that will generate local employment. The tourism and services sectors are booming, especially in the Cape Town area. Now it is "politically correct" to visit and air fares have dropped dramatically, half of what they were only a few years ago.

The black middle class is growing quickly and has need for services and consumer goods which were for so long denied. A study released in early 2000 claimed that while the black share of wages, salaries, and other income rose dramatically over the five years to 1996, almost all of this increase occurred among the top 10% of black earners, while poorer blacks actually experienced a decline in income. While the report confirmed that racial inequalities of income persist — white per capita income was almost nine times higher than Africans' — it shows that there has been a "significant redistribution of income towards previously disadvantaged groups."

South Africa is a middle income, developing country with an abundant supply of resources, well-developed financial, legal, communications, energy, and transport sectors. It has a stock exchange that ranks among the ten largest in the world; and a modern infrastructure supporting an efficient distribution of goods to major urban centers throughout the region. However, growth has not been strong enough to cut into the 40% unemployment, and daunting economic problems remain from the apartheid era, especially the problems of poverty and lack of economic empowerment among the disadvantaged groups. Other major problems are rampant crime and government corruption.

The ANC Government has demonstrated its commitment to open markets, privatization, and a favorable investment climate with tax incentives to stimulate new investment in labor intensive projects. This is especially the case in expansion of basic infrastructure services, the slow restructuring and partial privatization of state assets, continued reduction of tariffs, subsidies to promote economic efficiency, improved services to the disadvantaged, and integration into the global economy. Serious structural rigidities remain, including a complicated and relatively protectionist trade regime, some currency controls, highly restrictive labor union rules, and the concentration of wealth and economic control in the hands of a few.

Some argue that eventual economic success is guaranteed because labor is plentiful and cheap. However, standing in the way, are restrictive labor rules and the lack of any real work ethic, a major drag on individual worker productivity. Continuing white-black wage differentials are a sore point, but a low-skilled white worker will work here for the equivalent of US$2 an hour. Highly skilled workers willing to remain are paid wages comparable to other countries to forestall their migration. The white "brain drain" has been significant. Nevertheless, there is strong optimism in the business community, and the transition to majority black rule occurred much more smoothly than anticipated.

The major unknown is how long the patience of the 75% black majority will endure. After six years of ANC majority rule, most citizens still await their share so long denied by poverty and deprivation. The ANC still has not made good on Mandela's pledge to build the houses and schools needed to accommodate this impatient majority, and the ANC bureaucracy is just as corrupt and incompetent as the former white National Party rulers.

Crime

Anyone seriously considering investing in South Africa must consider the question of the country's internal stability.

Crime is a significant threat to the country's overall stability and to the welfare of its citizens. There is still much violence, some of it tribal, and political conflicts among black factions. Political violence has significantly decreased in most areas of South Africa since the establishment of a democratically-elected government in May 1994. Some public gatherings, however, have provoked violent clashes between political factions, resulting in casualties. The highest incidence of such political violence occurs in the province of KwaZulu/Natal.

Crime is rampant and is the major cause of the continuing white exodus. Criminal activity, sometimes violent, is reported on a routine basis. Assault and armed robbery are particularly high in areas surrounding many tourist hotels and public transportation centers, especially in major cities. Notwithstanding government anti-crime efforts, crimes such as car jacking, mugging, "smash and grab" attacks on vehicles, and other incidents are regularly reported. Crimes against property, such as car jacking, are often accompanied by violent acts, including murder.

In the western Cape, police resources have been strained by continuing gang conflicts and vigilante violence in the townships near Cape Town. Some townships near major cities, most notably Durban, Johannesburg, and Cape Town have been scenes of violent demonstrations and factional conflict. Increasing complaints that foreigners were taking jobs away from South Africans resulted in the mob killing of three foreigners from other African countries in September 1998. In August 1998 and January 1999, American franchise restaurants in Cape Town were bombed and threats against American interests continue. In addition, a car bomb exploded in late January 1999 near a police station in Cape Town. There were over 200 bombings in the Cape Town area in the last few years, but only one related conviction. Credit card fraud, counterfeit U.S. currency, and various check-cashing scams are frequently reported.

Immigration

Since 1995, immigration requirements have tightened in an effort to stem migrations from poorer African countries to the north. South Africa admits only immigrants with special skills unavailable locally. Wages are low and real unemployment hovers around an astronomical 40%. Survival dictates that a huge part of the national economy operates in a gray market totally off-the-books.

Foreign investors and entrepreneurs receive special treatment. If you are willing to invest approximately US$12,000-US$17,000, you can apply for a twelve-month residence visa, renewable annually. This can lead to a permanent resident visa after three years. A three-year visa is offered to investors who bring R1,500,000 (US$240,000) into South African investments and live there off of the income. After five years, one can apply for South African citizenship and a passport. A South African passport is not one of the best, and visas are required for travel to most European countries.

A major roadblock to foreign investments are strict currency exchange controls that avoid what the government fears would be major capital flight. These rules allow single adults who leave the country for tourist travel to take only R23,000 (<US$5,000). Business

travelers are allowed a little more. Those leaving permanently are restricted to a paltry R100,000, under US$50,000. The emigration allowance for a whole family is only R200,000. Obviously, foreign nationals should only import as much cash as they need for their immediate purposes, lest they get caught in exchange controls.

A South African fortunate enough to have dual citizenship (and many white, English South Africans do hold U.K. passports) can arrange to transfer assets elsewhere. South Africans who do emigrate are allowed to receive only income earned from capital, but most of that capital must remain in South Africa. These self-defeating controls definitely discourage foreign investors, who might otherwise invest in a developing country with such great potential.

Permanent Residence and Citizenship

South African citizenship is granted in three primary ways: by birth, by descent, and by naturalization. Under existing statutes, citizenship by birth is limited to a child of a South African citizen, or to a child whose parents are both permanent residents. As implemented by the Department of Home Affairs, however, this rule is relaxed to a significant degree; if only one of the parents is a permanent resident, then the citizenship by birth may be claimed by the child of that parent. Children born in South Africa to temporary residents and to undocumented persons do not acquire citizenship at birth.

Citizenship by descent is granted to children born outside the republic who have at least one parent with South African citizenship, where notice of the birth is given to South African authorities. There is no cutoff to this transmission; thus, citizens born outside of South Africa may apparently transmit citizenship to their children born outside South Africa.

The citizenship system, therefore, is a mix of *jus soli* and *jus sanguinis* principles. Although most South Africans become citizens under *jus soli* rules, large numbers of persons born in South Africa do not acquire citizenship at birth. Nonetheless, it seems clear that there is comparatively greater weight placed on the *jus soli* principle in South Africa than in many other countries.

The bar against citizenship for a large class of people born in South Africa makes the conditions for obtaining naturalization of particular importance. For people born in South Africa to parents without permanent residence, it is only through naturalization that there is an opportunity of becoming a citizen. In order to be naturalized, a person must be: over 21; must be admitted for permanent residence; must have been continuously resident for one year before applying for naturalization; must have been ordinarily resident for at least four of the eight years preceding the application; must be of good character; must intend to continue to reside in the republic; must be able to communicate in one of the official languages; and must have knowledge of the responsibilities and privileges of South African citizenship.

Minors admitted to permanent residence may be granted citizenship without satisfying these conditions upon application by a parent. In the case of permanent resident aliens married to South African citizens, the only requirement for citizenship is residence with the citizen spouse in South Africa for two years. Citizenship by naturalization depends upon prior admission for permanent residence.

Permanent residence is governed by the Aliens Control Act. From December 1996, a permit for permanent residence (called an "immigration permit") is available to an applicant who is of good character; who will be a desirable inhabitant of the republic; who is not likely to harm the welfare of the republic; and who does not, and is not likely to, pursue an occupation in which there are already sufficient numbers of people available in the republic. Other provisions allow for (but do not mandate) immediate permanent residence without conditions for destitute, aged, or infirm family members, and for spouses or dependent children of permanent residents and citizens. Normally, applicants for permanent residence apply from outside South Africa. There are exceptions for persons in possession of a temporary residence work permit, persons who are destitute, aged, or infirm and a member of the family of a permanent resident or citizen who is able and willing to support that person, and persons who are married to or dependent children of permanent residents or citizens.

The Bill of Rights of the 1996 Constitution provides that almost all rights benefit all persons within South Africa, whether they are citizens or aliens. South Africa also recognizes the principle of dual nationality, but with some restrictions.

Visa Requirements

South Africa has tightened visa requirements for certain categories of visitors. Only visitors on tourism, short business consultations, or in-transit do not require visas; others need visas or will be refused admission and returned to their point of origin.

Citizens of the U.S., Canada, Australia, and New Zealand need only a valid passport to stay for up to three months in South Africa. EU nationals with a valid passport can stay for up to six months. All visitors need a valid return ticket; if you try to enter South Africa without one, you may be required to deposit the equivalent of your fare home with customs (the money will be refunded to you after you have left the country). Visitors must also be able to prove that they have sufficient funds to cover their stay.

Citizens of African and most eastern European countries require a visa to enter South Africa, and this must be obtained before arrival. Visas are not issued at the border. If you come under this category and plan on traveling to Lesotho and Swaziland, you'll need a multi-entry visa to get back into South Africa. If you don't have one, it will be issued free of charge on return, although this can be time consuming.

Contacts

United States: South Africa has tightened its visa requirements. Only visitors for tourism or short business meetings or in-transit do not require visas. All others visitors, including academics, students on educational trips, and volunteers, may need visas; otherwise they take the chance that they will be refused admission and returned to their point of origin. Travelers' passports must contain at least two clean (unstamped) pages whenever they enter South Africa. Otherwise, they run the risk of being turned back, even when in possession of a valid South African visa. All travelers are advised to carry a photocopy of the photo/bio information page of their passport and keep it in a location separate from their passport. It is strongly suggested that travelers check the requirements with the nearest embassy or consulate of South Africa before traveling. Visitors who intend to work in South Africa must apply for work permits abroad at the appropriate South African embassy or consulate. Travelers may obtain further information from the Embassy of South Africa, 3051 Massachusetts Avenue, NW, Washington, D.C. 20008, Tel: (202) 232-4400, web site at http://usaembassy.southafrica.net or the South African consulates in Los Angeles, Chicago, or New York. Overseas, inquiries should be made at the nearest South African embassy or consulate.

Americans living in or visiting South Africa are encouraged to register at the Consular Section of the nearest U.S. consulate and obtain updated information on travel and security within South Africa. The U.S. Embassy is located at 877 Pretorius Street, Arcadia in Pretoria, Tel: (27-12)342-4000 (from South Africa 012-342-4000), Fax: (27-12) 342-5504 (from South Africa 012-342-5504). The U.S. Embassy web site is http://usembassy.state.gov/pretoria/. The U.S. Consulate General in Johannesburg provides most consular services for Americans in the Pretoria area. The Consulate General in Johannesburg is located at No.

1 River Street (corner of River and Riviera Road), Killarney, Johannesburg, Tel: (27-11) 644-8000 (from South Africa 011-644-8000), fax (27-11) 646-6916 (from South Africa (011-646-6916). Its consular jurisdiction includes Gaiting, Mpumalanga, Limpopo, North West, and Free State provinces. The Consulate General in Cape Town is located at Broadway Industries Center, Heerengracht, Foreshore, Tel: (27-21) 421-4280 (from South Africa 021-421-4280), Fax: (27-21) 425-3014 (from South Africa 021-425-3014). Its consular jurisdiction includes Western Cape, Eastern Cape, and Northern Cape provinces. The Consulate General in Durban is located at the Old Mutual Building, 31st floor, 303 West Street, Tel: (27-31) 305-7600 (from South Africa 031-305-7600), Fax: (27-31) 305-7691 (from South Africa 031-305-7691). Its consular jurisdiction includes KwaZulu-Natal Province.

United Kingdom: The British High Commissions is located in **Pretoria:** 255 Hill St, Arcadia 0002, Tel: (27) (12) 421 7800, Fax: (27) (12) 421 7555, E-mail: media.pretoria@fco.gov.uk, Web site: http://www.britain.org.za/. British Consulate offices are located in **Cape Town:** British Consulate General 15th floor, Southern Life Centre, 8 Riebeek Street, Cape Town 8001. Postal Address: British Consulate GeneralPO Box 500, Cape Town 8000, Tel: (021) 405 2400 Consular/Passport Enquiries, Fax: (021) 405 2447, E-mail: Consular.SectionCT@fco.gov.uk; **Port Elizabeth:** PO Box 35098, Newton Park, Port Elizabeth 6055, Tel: (27)(41) 3638841, Fax: (27)(41) 3638842, E-mail: britconspe@eastcape.net and **Durban:** Suite 1901, 19th Floor, The Marine, 22 Gardiner Street, Durban 4001, Tel: (27) (31) 305 2920/2929, Fax: (27)(31) 3074661.

Section 6.
Asia and Oceania

Commonwealth of Australia

CAPITAL: CANBERRA

POPULATION: 19,731,984

LANGUAGE: ENGLISH

CURRENCY: AUSTRALIAN DOLLAR (A$)

AREA: 7,686,850 SQ KM

ETHNIC GROUPS: CAUCASIAN 92%, ASIAN 7%, ABORIGINAL AND OTHER 1%

RELIGION: ANGLICAN 26.1%, ROMAN CATHOLIC 26%, OTHER CHRISTIAN 24.3%, NON-CHRISTIAN 11%, OTHER 12.6%

PASSPORT HIGHLIGHTS: Australia grants residency to immigrants according to a "points" system based on job skills, age, and family ties in the country, among other criteria. Citizenship is available some two to three years after residency is obtained. Individuals with personal net worth greater than A$2.5 million who invest from A$1.5 million and A$2 million are granted a four-year provisional Investor's visa, leading to permanent residency and naturalization. If the investment is in a state-sponsored project, the probationary period is decreased to two years. Young travelers in Australia may benefit from the "working holiday" visa program as they tour the country.

Australia is the sixth-largest continent in the world, lying between the Pacific Ocean to the east and the Indian Ocean to its west. The country derives its name from the Latin word *australes*, meaning "southern," the word once was used to describe the Southern Hemisphere below the Equator.

Almost half of the Australian continent lies in the tropics, with much of the north coast consisting of rain forests and marshy lowlands. Off the northeastern coast, the Great Barrier Reef extends for nearly 1,300 miles southward from the tip of the Cape York Peninsula, covering an area of more than 135,000 square miles. Its 2,800 individual reefs harbor 1,500 species of fish amid 400 types of coral. Eco-tourism in Australia does not stop there, however. The continent contains a vast range of land forms and habitats, home to populations of animals and plants of types that are rare or non-existent in the rest of the world. Against that backdrop, Most of Australia's major cities, Sydney, Melbourne, and Perth, among others, lie in the Temperate Zone and are recognized as among the world's most vibrant and attractive places to visit and live.

There is strong evidence that the Aborigine people were living in Australia at least 40,000 years ago. The Dutch charted the coast of Tasmania in 1642 and, two years later, the British explored the west and southwest Australian coast. In 1770, Captain Cook chartered the east coast and claimed the land for Britain. In 1788, the first settlement was a British penal colony in the area around present-day Sydney. Self-government was introduced in 1850, and, in 1901, the Commonwealth of Australia was formed. Also in 1901, Parliament passed the Immigration Restriction Act, which in effect enshrined a "White Australia" policy that persisted for most of the 20th Century. In 1986, Australia gained full legal independence from Britain.

Australia has a prosperous Western-style capitalist economy with a per capita GDP at the level of the dominant west European economies. Rich in natural resources, Australia is a major exporter of agricultural products, minerals, metals, and fossil fuels. Commodities account for 57% of the value of total exports, so that a downturn in world commodity prices could have a big impact on the economy. Exports go largely to Europe, North America, and Latin America. The government is pushing for increased exports of manufactured goods, but competition in international markets continues to be severe. Australia suffered from the low growth and high unemployment characterizing European countries in the early 1990s, but the economy has expanded at reasonably steady rates in recent years. Canberra's emphasis on reforms is a key factor behind the economy's resilience to the Asian regional crisis and its stronger than expected growth rate that reached 4.5% in 1999.

Residence and Citizenship

Australia was founded as a nation of immigrants — a penal colony for those who languished in 19th Century British Imperial jails. After it became a commonwealth in 1901, it actively courted new immigrants. Population has more than doubled since World War II, and the former "all white, all English" flavor has been replaced by a cosmopolitan mix of six million immigrants, including Italians, Greeks, Slavs, and Russian Jews. Since 1990, a growing movement to curb new immigration has taken hold, largely because of the influx of southeast Asians seeking citizenship.

Australia is currently looking for skilled immigrants and investors. There are numerous immigration categories, and it pays to verify which is most appropriate for you, as it often happens that immigration is possible under two or more categories. This is also true for investors and business immigrants. Australia is also an ideal place to retire, and, to this end, Australia offers a special visa for retirees (minimum age: 55 years).

After only two years of residence in Australia, it is possible to become an Australian citizen and to obtain an Australian passport, which is an added attraction to some immigrants from countries whose passports restrict their traveling (such as India, China, and Vietnam). Many international businessmen from Asia settle in Australia to obtain this very attractive passport.

If you want to immigrate to Australia, depending on the category you choose, your age, education, professional occupation and experience, and other factors are assessed against a points system. A temporary business visa is available with a business investment of as little as A$250,000.

The Points System

Like neighboring New Zealand, Australia awards "points" towards residency based on education, work experience, age, and language skills. Points are added for family members or a sponsor in Australia. With certain job skills in demand by the government (lists available at any consulate), an immigration application can be speeded up. The process takes several months, but some applications have taken much longer. Australia no longer pays new residents for transportation, housing, or gives free English language training as they once did.

Formerly, citizenship and a passport were granted to desired new immigrants only one year after arrival. Now, it takes 2-3 years for full citizenship and a passport. That is still one of the world's shortest residence periods, with no fees or investments required by job-qualified immigrants.

Marriage and Relations

If you have family in Australia, or marry an Australian, you can more easily gain residence, but full citizenship still requires two years residence. Australia, along with Denmark, the Netherlands, and New Zealand, now officially recognizes same-sex relationships. Couples must prove they have lived together for six months in order for the non-Australian partner to qualify for residence.

The following may qualify if their sponsor has been an Australian citizen or a permanent resident for at least two years and has the following relationship to the sponsor: spouses, fiances, adopted children, parents, orphan relatives, special needs relatives, aged dependent relatives, remaining "isolated" relatives, and interdependent partners.

Business and Investor Program

In July 1991, the government made radical changes to its business migration program. Prior applicants only had to show assets of A$500,000 (US$350,000), and an intent to transfer the money into an Australian investment or bank account. They were initially granted permanent residency and the unlimited right to enter and leave Australia, and then, after two years of residence, Australian citizenship. This program was a bonanza for private "immigration consultants" who were paid by the government to do screening. This program was attacked because of the ability of would-be immigrants to circumvent currency controls.

The latest scheme concentrates more on business experience than wealth. A system similar to those used in Canada and New Zealand requires applicants to score a minimum number of points, with awards based on age, existing business type and size, assets, and English language skills.

Applications are reviewed by Department of Immigration officials, as well as by private sector consultants. Stricter monitoring procedures are in place, and a business skills visa can be canceled if its holder does not attempt to start a business within three years. Australia's immigration policy now favors people who establish permanent ties to the country rather than those who merely own capital.

The 1991 changes dramatically reduced applicants for the business migration program. During ten years of the former program, about 10,000 immigrants and 30,000 dependants were admitted to Australia. In the first six months of the new program, only about 150 applications were received.

As a result, the business migration program underwent substantial revision, in 1995, making new "investor" category citizenship more accessible. This new category requires individuals to invest between A$750,000 and A$2 million in designated government securities for a minimum of three years. Successful applicants must show satisfactory business or investment skills. Recent business and management experience is essential. Present parameters for the program require individuals to have a personal net worth greater than A$2.5 million. They must invest from A$1.5 million and A$2 million to be granted a four-year provisional Investor's visa, leading to permanent residency and naturalization. If the investment is in a state-sponsored project, the probationary period is decreased to two years.

In the past, applications were only accepted from people situated in their home country. Now, business people can have applications processed while they are in Australia on a temporary stay. The government is actively promoting the business migration program abroad and has simplified travel arrangements for this class of immigrant.

Business migration applicants do get a background check, which is intended to screen for major criminals. A conviction for something not considered a major crime in Australia will not necessarily be held against the applicant.

Preferred industries include non-polluting, high-tech, and export-oriented enterprises. Real estate "investors" are unwelcome, since Australians think "speculators" have already pushed land prices too high. Agriculture, Australia's major industry, has suffered from historically low commodity rates caused by the erosion of traditional European markets. Any product or service that would help local farmers compete more effectively will get fast consideration and approval.

Once residency is obtained, there is a simple straightforward path towards citizenship. Permanent residents are free to leave and return to Australia, and after two years of residence can apply for citizenship. The two-year residency need not be continuous, but it must either be cumulative in the previous five years or constitute one full year out of the two years before applying. There is also a brief interview and submission of required proofs, including testimony to good character.

This expansion of the business migration program has definitely opened things up and the number of applicants has risen dramatically.

Working Holiday Visa

This is an excellent way for young people to establish at least temporary residence, then explore various other options available for permanent residence and then citizenship. To qualify under this program, an applicant must: 1) be 18 to 25 years old; 2) desire to travel extensively in Australia, while working to supplement holiday funds; 3) hold a valid U.K., Irish, Canadian, Dutch, or Japanese passport; 4) have a return air ticket, or money for a return fare, plus "normal maintenance" finances for your planned holiday, about US$3,000; and

5) be childless.

The "Holiday Visa" is for young traveling types who want to supplement their funds with part-time casual work. In actual practice, the type of work or length of stay is limited only by the jobs available. The money requirement can be met with proof of a bank account balance. Once the visa is granted, no further checks are made. This visa does not qualify the holder for a passport, but it can lead to permanent residence based on in-country contacts.

Taxes

Individuals whose annual stay in Australia exceeds 183 days are considered residents for tax purposes, unless they prove Australia is not their home and they have no intention of establishing permanent residence in the country.

Resident taxpayers are taxed on their worldwide income. Migrants and visitors who are subject to Australian taxes must pay taxes on income derived from business activities in their country of origin or elsewhere offshore. Tax returns must be filed annually. Non-resident taxpayers are also liable for taxes on ordinary income earned in Australia, and interest and dividends from Australian bank accounts or shares in an Australian company. Offshore business activities of non-resident taxpayers are not generally subject to taxation.

When a foreign national becomes a resident for tax purposes, his or her assets (other than taxable Australian assets and those acquired before September 20, 1985) are assigned a cost basis of the current fair market value. At the disposal of assets, a capital gains tax is imposed. Land, buildings, and other assets situated in Australia as well as shares in Australian private companies and interests of 10% or more in public companies are all taxable. These stiff rules prompt some to sell certain assets before taking up residency.

There is a temporary loophole for some approved business migrants who initially may escape designation as a resident for tax purposes. They must show an intent to establish a permanent business in Australia but they need not immediately settle there. They can return to their country of origin, or travel elsewhere to honor existing business commitments. Absences from Australia are restricted only by the requirement that the migrant makes genuine efforts to establish a business in Australia. However, if they are in Australia for less than 183 days annually, they are not subject to Australian taxation. If they eventually wish to apply for citizenship, sooner or later, they cannot avoid becoming a resident for tax purposes. Tax authorities freely allow the use of offshore trusts that were established before immigration.

Unlike the U.S., Australians who evade taxes are not sent to jail, but an offender faces a civil fine plus penalties and interest on the amount owed. Tax fraud and other tax-related crimes that violate Australian law are punished harshly; with offenders prosecuted, jailed, and even extradited from other countries. Failure to report accurate income from interest, dividends, or profits on a personal tax return may be tax evasion, but in Australia it is not a crime. For a crime, there must be proof of active fraud, such as submission of false and forged bills and receipts seeking to justify false deductions and losses.

Switzerland has similar tax rules, but in the U.S. and Canada, failure to file a tax return or non-reporting of foreign bank accounts are criminal offenses for which prosecutors seek jail terms. American prosecutors have even claimed that any action to reduce your taxes may be, at the discretion of the U.S. Internal Revenue Service, considered an indictable criminal offense.

An Australian passport can be obtained without paying any legal fees, gratuities, or under-the-table money. A visit to your nearest Australian Consulate is the best plan. Pick up their brochures and job preference list. This has a do-it-yourself rating scale to figure out if you score enough points to qualify. And remember, after just two years of residence, you can qualify for a passport.

The Australian Citizenship Act does allow the government discretionary power to waive residency requirements for certain people in exceptional cases.

Contacts

United States: American citizens are required to have a valid U.S. passport to enter Australia. Americans may enter with an Australian visa or, if eligible, through Electronic Travel Authority (ETA). The ETA, which replaces a visa and allows a stay of up to 90 days, is free of charge and is available from airlines and many travel agents in the United States. Please note that American citizen's who overstay their ETA or visa, even for short periods, may be subject to detention and removal. More information about the ETA and entry requirements may be obtained from the Embassy of Australia at 1601 Massachusetts Avenue, NW, Washington, D.C. 20036, Tel: (202) 797-3000, Web site: http://www.austemb.org. All visa inquiries and applications except ETA should be directed to the Australian Embassy in Washington, DC.

Americans living in or visiting Australia are encouraged to register at the nearest U.S. Consulate to obtain updated information on travel and security within the country. In the Australian Capital Territory (ACT) or **Queanbeyan:** For emergency services (i.e. the arrest, death or serious injury of American citizens) please contact the U.S. Embassy in Canberra. The Embassy is located on Moonah Place, Yarralumla, A.C.T. 2600, Tel: (61)(2) 6214-5600, Fax: (61)(2) 6273-3191, Web site: http://canberra.usembassy.gov. NOTE: Passports and other routine citizen services for Canberra and the rest of the ACT are provided by the U.S. Consulate in Sydney. In **New South Wales**, **Norfolk Island**, **Lord Howe Island** and **Queensland:** For registration, passport, and other consular services for American citizens, please contact the U.S. Consulate General in Sydney located on Level 59, MLC Centre, 19-29 Martin Place, Sydney NSW 2000, Tel: (61)(2) 9373-9200, Fax: (61)(2) 9373-9184, Web site: http://sydney.usconsulate.gov/sydney. Hours open to the public: 8:00 a.m. to noon Monday to Friday (except American and Australian holidays). For emergency services (i.e. the arrest, death or serious injury of American citizens) after 4:30 p.m. weekdays or on holidays and weekends please call (61)(2) 4422-2201.

In **Victoria**, **Tasmania**, **South Australia** and the **Northern Territory**: For registration, passport and other consular services for American citizens, please contact the U.S. Consulate General in **Melbourne** located at 553 St. Kilda Road, Melbourne, VIC 3004, Tel: (61)(3) 9526-5900, Fax: (61)(3) 9525-0769, Web site: http://melbourne.usconsulate.gov/melbourne. Hours open to the public: 8:30 a.m. to 12:30 p.m. Monday to Friday (except American and Australian holidays and the last Wednesday of each month). For emergency services (i.e. the arrest, death or serious injury of American citizens) after 4:30 p.m. or on holidays and weekends, please call (61)(3) 9389-3601.

In **Western Australia**: For registration, passport, and other consular services for American citizens, please contact the U.S. Consulate General in **Perth** located on Level 13, 16 St. Georges Terrace, Perth WA 6000, Tel: (61)(8) 9202-1224, Fax: (61)(8) 9231-9444; Web site: http://perth.usconsulate.gov/perth. Hours open to the public for American Citizen Services: 8:30-11:30 a.m. daily. For emergency services (e.g., the arrest, death, or serious injury of American citizens), please call: (61)(8) 9476-0081.

United Kingdom: The British High Commission is located in Canberra: Commonwealth Avenue Yarralumla, Canberra, Tel: (61) (2) 6270 6666, Fax: (61) (2) 6273 3236, E-mail: bhc.canberra@mail.uk. emb.gov.au, Web site: http://www.britaus.net. British Consulates are located in **Adelaid:** Level 22, 25 Grenfell Street, Adelaide, Tel: (61) (8)

8212 7280, Fax: (61) (8) 8212 7282, E-mail: bc.adelaide@mail.uk.
emb.gov.au; **Melbourne:** 17th Floor, 90 Collins Street, Melbourne,
Victoria, Tel: (61) (3) 9652 1600, Fax: (61) (3) 9650 2990, E-mail:
bcgmelb1@mail.uk.emb.gov.au; **Brisbane:** Level 26, Waterfront Place,
1 Eagle Street, Brisbane Queensland, Tel: (61) (7) 3223 3200, Fax: (61)
(7) 3236 2576, E-mail: bcgbris2@mail.uk.emb.gov.au and **Perth:** Level
26 Allendale Square, 77 St George's Terrace Perth, Western Australia,
Tel: (61) (8) 9224 4700, Fax: (61) (8) 9224 4720, E-mail: bcgperth@
mail.uk.emb.gov.au.

New Zealand

CAPITAL:	AUCKLAND
POPULATION:	3,951,307
LANGUAGE:	ENGLISH (OFFICIAL), MAORI (OFFICIAL)
CURRENCY:	NEW ZEALAND DOLLAR (NZ$)
AREA:	269,000 SQUARE KM
ETHNIC GROUPS:	EUROPEAN 74.5%, MAORI 9.7%, OTHER EUROPEAN 4.6%, PACIFIC ISLANDER 3.8%, ASIAN AND OTHERS 7.4%
RELIGION:	ANGLICAN 24%, PRESBYTERIAN 18%, ROMAN CATHOLIC 15%, METHODIST 5%, BAPTIST 2%, OTHER PROTESTANT 3%, OTHER OR UNAFFILIATED 33%

PASSPORT HIGHLIGHTS: Applicants for entry under New Zealand's "Business Investor's Policy" must show that their capital was lawfully earned and resulted from personal business or professional skills. In addition to qualifying under a points system, a minimum investment of NZ$1 million is required. After three years of residence, a person is eligible for naturalization. A points system is applied to potential immigrants in all other categories.

New Zealand is a group of islands in Oceania in the Pacific Ocean, southeast of Australia. The nation also includes affiliated jurisdictions of the Cook Islands and Niue, both autonomous countries and several other small island groups. New Zealand's two main islands are mountainous, with several dormant volcanoes on and around the North Island. The craggy South Island draws adventure tourists from all over the globe for climbing, skiing, and white-water rafting, as well as admirers of the land's breathtaking beauty, recently made familiar to moviegoers globally in the highly successful "Lord of the Rings" films. Eco-tourists, too, congregate in New Zealand, where millions of years of isolation from other land masses have allowed a remnant population of animal and plant species with unique characteristics to develop from earlier forms, many extinct elsewhere.

Historically, the islands received migrants from the Polynesian Pacific as early as 800 A.D., the ancestors of the present day native Maori. Dutch East Indian Company explorers sighted South Island in 1642 and, in 1769, Captain John Cook became the first European to land and survey the area. European settlers began arriving in 1790. In 1840, Britain claimed rights to the area, and, in 1907, New Zealand became a Dominion under the British Crown.

Since 1984, the government has accomplished major economic restructuring, moving an agrarian economy dependent on British market access toward a more industrialized, free market economy that can compete globally. This dynamic growth has boosted real incomes, broadened the capabilities of the industrial sector and reduced inflationary pressures. Inflation remains among the lowest in the industrial world. Per capita GDP has moved to levels of major European economies. New Zealand's heavy dependence on trade leaves its growth prospects vulnerable to economic performance in Asia, Europe, and the U.S.

New Zealand has not always been so prosperous. After years of having the highest tax rates in the world, the government verged on bankruptcy. Massive overspending on welfare state schemes, plus low world commodity prices brought on a fiscal crisis. No one starved, but inflation, unemployment, and large-scale emigration were common.

As a result, major changes were implemented, labor unions curbed, inflation was reduced to less than 1%, and property prices leveled off. The government tried to attract new foreign investments, entrepreneurs, and talent by reducing confiscatory income taxes, making them lower than any European country and roughly equal to those in the U.S.

Immigration

Since 1988, there has been a dramatic turnaround in immigration policy. Whereas New Zealand once strictly limited immigration, it now welcomes and actively courts immigrants. The government issues annual statements of immigration intentions, setting quotas for "global immigration targets." The goal for 1999 was over 35,000 persons including refugees.

It is worth noting that a New Zealand passport is one of the most accepted worldwide with visa-free access to most countries. In addition, New Zealand passport holders have free entry into Australia, as would Australia citizens.

New Zealand has a points system, much like that used in Canada and Australia, except that persons 60 years and older generally are not admitted. The four categories used are general, family, humanitarian, and business investment.

1) **General category:** aimed at young persons and awards points for employability; education; work experience; age, with ages 25-29 scoring highest; and settlement factors, including assets, sponsorship, or an offer of skilled employment. Processing requires only six to eight weeks.

2) **Family category:** a) family reunion: this includes parents, children, brothers, and sisters; or b) partnership with a New Zealand citizen or resident is recognized and includes a legally married husband or wife, or a de facto or homosexual partner.

3) Residency is also granted for "humanitarian" reasons involving serious physical or emotional harm to the applicant or a resident of New Zealand.

4) New Zealand's "Business Investor's Policy" aims to increase the nation's human capital, enterprise, and innovation in foreign trade. The applicant must show his/her capital was lawfully earned and resulted from personal business or professional skills. In addition to qualifying under a points system, a minimum investment of NZ$1 million is required, conferring one point upon the potential immigrant. Additional points are awarded for larger investments, up to eleven points for an investment of NZ$6 million. After three years of residence, a person is eligible for naturalization. Foreign travel during these three years is unrestricted. Annually, about 500 approved applications are in this category.

Taxes

New Zealand law makes illegal intentional income tax avoidance without other proper justification. Worldwide income is taxed and various events within the nation, such as owning a second home there, may bring a person within the tax laws. There are no capital gains or estate taxes.

Contacts

United States: U.S. citizens eligible for a visa waiver do not need a visa for tourist stays of 90 days or less. For more information about visa waivers and entry requirements, contact the Embassy of New Zealand, 37 Observatory Circle, NW, Washington, D.C. 20008, Tel: (202) 328-4800, the Embassy's web site is http://www.nzemb.org or the Consulate General of New Zealand in Los Angeles, Tel: (310) 207-1605.

Americans living in or visiting New Zealand are encouraged to register at the Consular Section of the U.S. Consulate General in Auckland by mail, phone, fax or in person, where they can obtain updated information on travel and security. The U.S. Consulate General in Auckland is located on the third floor of the Citibank Centre, 23 Customs Street East, between Commerce and Queen Streets. The telephone number is (64)(9) 303-2724. The fax number is (64) (9) 366-0870. Web site: http://www.usembassy.org.nz. The U.S. Embassy is located at 29 Fitzherbert Terrace, Thorndon Wellington, Tel: (64)(4) 462-6000, Fax: (64)(4) 471-2380. For after-hours emergencies anywhere in New Zealand, a duty officer can be contacted by telephone. Persons seeking after-hours assistance may call (64)(4) 462-6000; after listening to a brief recording, the caller may leave a message on the voice mail system, describing the nature of the emergency and giving a point of contact. The phone system will automatically call the duty officer in Wellington or in Auckland, who will listen to the message and take the appropriate action.

United Kingdom: The British High Commission is located in Wellington: 44 Hill Street, Wellington 1, NZ, Tel: (64) (4) 924 2888, Fax: (64) (4) 924 2810, E-mail: PPA.Mailbox@fco.gov.uk, Web site: http://www.britain.org.nz. The British Consulate General is located on the Level 17 IAG House 151 Queen Street, Auckland 1. Mailing Address: Private Bag 92014 Auckland 1 NZ, Tel: (64) (9) 303 2973, Fax: (64) (9) 303 1836, E-mail: trade_enquiries.auckland@fco.gov.uk, Web site: http://www.brittrade.org.nz.

Republic of Singapore

CAPITAL:	SINGAPORE CITY
POPULATION:	4,608,595
LANGUAGE:	CHINESE, MALAY, TAMIL, ENGLISH (ALL OFFICIAL)
CURRENCY:	SINGAPORE DOLLAR (SG$)
AREA:	692.7 SQUARE KM
ETHNIC GROUPS:	CHINESE 76.7%, MALAY 14%, INDIAN 7.9%, OTHER 1.4%
RELIGION:	BUDDHIST (CHINESE), MUSLIM (MALAYS), CHRISTIAN, HINDU, SIKH, TAOIST, CONFUCIANIST

PASSPORT HIGHLIGHTS: Under the "Scheme for Entrepreneurs," potential immigrants pledge to invest a minimum of S$1 million, about US$600,000, half of which must be in approved industrial, commercial, or residential property, for a minimum period of five years. Foreign nationals with investment residence status are eligible to apply for naturalization after two years. Singapore does not recognize dual nationality.

The Republic of Singapore has the distinction of being a small island, a state, and a city all in one. Located just a few miles north of the Equator, it has Malaysia and Indonesia as close neighbors. The climate is equatorial, hot and very humid with rainfall of over two meters annually.

Singapore was a British colony until independence in 1965. Lee Kuan Yew became its autocratic leader and served until 1990. He built a one-party state that still does not tolerate dissent or opposition of any kind. There are no jury trials and civil matters, such as alleged libel or slander, can escalate into criminal issues with serious consequences. Draconian laws keep crime (and freedom) to a minimum, but the stability attracts foreign investment. Moreover, the streets are very clean.

Singapore has an open economy with strong service and manufacturing sectors as well as excellent international trading links.

Singapore weathered the effects of the Asian financial crisis better than its neighbors, but the crisis did pull GDP growth down to 1.3% in 1998 from 6% in 1997. Rising labor costs and appreciation of the Singapore dollar against its neighbors' currencies continue to be a threat to competitiveness. The government's strategy includes cutting costs, increasing productivity, improving infrastructure, and encouraging higher value-added industries. In applied technology, per capita output, investment, and labor discipline, Singapore has key attributes of a developed country.

The common language is English. Most Singaporeans are Asian, with commerce dominated by ethnic Chinese. Malays make up 15%, with Indians, Thais, Vietnamese, Laotians and a very small number of Europeans. Europeans tend to hold most management positions and are generally well regarded. In Singapore, state regulation has created a paradise if you like high-rise buildings, crass materialism, and minimal personal freedom.

Singapore is not a tax haven. It supports welfare state programs of free schools, low-fee universities, childcare, socialized medicine, and subsidized housing. Tax rates are slightly below those of the U.S. Income over S$400,000 is taxed at 33%. New exporters can usually get a 15-year tax holiday. Real estate is taxed at 15% of the annual rental value. The maximum estate tax is 10% with an exemption of S$500,000 to S$1 million, depending upon the nature of the assets. Import duties are very low, except on motor vehicles, which bear a 125% duty. Generally, Singapore is a shopper's paradise.

Restaurants and hotel services are of very high standard and charge about half of European prices. Prices in nearby Thailand are half of the Singapore rates. Some rate Singapore along with cities like San Francisco and Sydney for quality of life and economic opportunity.

Residence and Citizenship

Entrepreneurs

Singapore offers a foreign investors' citizenship program called the "Scheme for Entrepreneurs." It was designed mainly for wealthy residents of Hong Kong who wished to secure a place for themselves and their families in a similar bustling economic environment before Communist China's takeover in 1997.

The program begins with a commitment to invest a minimum of S$1 million, about US$600,000. At least 50% of the amount must be in industrial, commercial, or residential property. Prior government approval before a purchase of property is advised. These funds can be deposited with the Government Treasury at interest, but must be invested within two years, for a minimum period of five years. An acceptable condo can be had for S$300,000 and an equal amount might be invested in a local business, then capitalized with a loan.

Foreign nationals with investment residence status are eligible to apply for naturalization after two years. There is no requirement that the entire time be spent in Singapore, but a home must be maintained. Singapore does not recognize dual nationality. This means that there is an oath of allegiance and a requirement to surrender any passport from another nation before receiving the Singapore passport. The surrendered passport can be reissued with no notice to Singapore.

Dual nationality also means that the government strictly enforces universal national service for all male citizens and permanent residents until the age of 21. Travel abroad of males may require Singapore Government approval as they approach national service age and may be restricted. The Ministry of Defense can advise about national service obligations.

Those with desired skills or in certain professions need not make an investment to gain permanent resident status. After five years as a resident, they can apply for citizenship. Children born in Singapore are automatically citizens.

Contacts

Application forms: Immigration Unit, Singapore Economic Development Board, 250 North Bridge Road, Raffles City Tower #24-00, Singapore 0617; Tel: +(65) 330 6686; Fax: +(65) 330 6077.

An illustrated brochure called "Making Singapore Your Home" is available from the Immigration Department, Ministry of Home Affairs, 95 South Bridge Road #08-26, South Bridge Center, Singapore 0105, or at the nearest Singapore Embassy or Consulate.

United States: A valid passport is required for entry into Singapore. U.S. citizens do not need a visa if their visit is for business or pleasure and their stay is for 90 days or less. Travelers to the region should note that some neighboring countries, particularly Indonesia, do not allow Americans to enter with fewer than six months of validity remaining on their passport under any circumstances. Specific information about entry requirements for Singapore may be sought from the Embassy of the Republic of Singapore at 3501 International Place, NW, Washington, D.C. 20008, Tel: (202) 537-3100. Web site: http://www.mfa.gov.sg/washington/.

Americans living in or visiting Singapore are encouraged to register at the Consular Sections of the U.S. Embassy in Singapore or online via the Department of State Travel Registration web site. The Embassy is located at 27 Napier Road, Singapore 258508, Tel: (65) 6476-9100, Fax: (65) 6476-9340, Web site: http://singapore.usembassy.gov. In case of emergencies after working hours, the duty officer at the Embassy may be contacted by calling Tel: (65) 6476-9100.

United Kingdom: The British High Commission is located on Tanglin Road, Singapore 247919100 Tanglin Road Singapore 247919, Commercial Section: Tanglin PO Box 19, Singapore 247919, Tel: (65) 6424 4200, Fax: (65) 6424 4264, E-mail: commercial.singapore@ fco.gov.uk, Web site: http://www.britain.org.sg/.

Kingdom of Thailand

CAPITAL:	BANGKOK
POPULATION:	64,265,276
LANGUAGE:	THAI, ENGLISH (SECOND LANGUAGE OF THE ELITE)
CURRENCY:	BAHT (B)
AREA:	514,000 SQUARE KM
ETHNIC GROUPS:	THAI 75%, CHINESE 14%, OTHER 11%
RELIGION:	BUDDHIST 95%, MUSLIM 3.8%, CHRISTIAN 0.5%, HINDU 0.1%, OTHER 0.6%

PASSPORT HIGHLIGHTS: Thailand restricts immigration to 100 new permanent residents for each country of origin. For investors, a B10 million (US$250,000) investment for at least three years ensures permanent residency. Applicants are charged B7,600 each for processing and B191,400 for issuance of a residency permit book. A fee of B95,700 is required for a spouse and each dependant under 20. Entrepreneurs may obtain residency on a case-by-case basis, and retirees also are granted visas.

The Kingdom of Thailand, formerly known as Siam, is part of the Indochinese Peninsula in southeast Asia. The nation borders the Andaman Sea and the Gulf of Thailand, southeast of Burma. The Mekong River forms the border with Laos. The only country in Southeast Asia to maintain its independence during the European colonial expansion of the 17th-19th centuries, Thailand is richly endowed with architectural and artistic monuments of its Buddhist heritage. Terrain ranging from idyllic beaches to mountain rain forests and a warm, tropical climate provide recreational and adventure opportunities. A wide variety of tribal lifestyles may be observed among Thailand's many ethnic groups.

Thais think differently from Occidentals. Their culture, religion, and morality are quintessentially Oriental. Thais are proud and patriotic and revere their King. Thailand is the only Asian nation never colonized by European powers. In foreign relations, they go with the logical "winner" and, thus, have remained free. The government is a constitutional monarchy, but the army wields major power. The Buddhist religion is a major influence on national life and on individuals.

In 1997, Thailand got caught in international speculative pressure on the Thai baht. The government decided to float the currency, the symbolic beginning of the country's economic crisis, and the general Asian economic recession that followed. After rapid economic growth averaging 9% earlier in that decade, the Thai economy contracted 0.4% in 1997 and shrunk another 8.5% in 1998. In the years before the crisis, Thailand ran persistent current account deficits. With the depreciation of the Thai baht and the collapse of domestic demand, imports fell by more than 33% and Thailand posted a 1998 trade surplus of US$12 billion. Foreign investment for new projects, the long-time catalyst of Thailand's economic growth, also slowed. The government closely adhered to the economic recovery program pre-scribed by the International Monetary Fund (IMF). This afforded the Thai currency stability and helped replenish foreign reserves. By 2000, recovery was underway. Tough measures, including passage of ade-quate bankruptcy and foreclosure legislation, as well as privatization of state-owned companies and recapitalization of the financial sector remain undone.

There are few non-Asian residents with whites (or "Farangs") mak-ing up less than 1% of the population. Until recently, Thailand was under-populated and willing to absorb all immigrants. Mass migra-tions, due to nearby Communist revolutions, caused the population of Thailand to triple during the past 40 years. Today, immigration is restricted. Residence permits and naturalized citizenship are limited.

Residency and Citizenship

The major reason for a foreign national to acquire Thai residence and/or citizenship is to make the nation your home and center of activity. This is especially true if your are non-Asian. A Thai passport is useful for Asian travel, but a westerner with a Thai passport will be asked more questions than an Asian. Most European countries will demand a visa and residents can't leave Thailand without an official tax clearance for each trip.

It's not easy for a foreign national to gain residence in Thailand (it restricts immigration to 100 new permanent residents for each country of origin.), but there are several categories under which one may qualify. Two of these are loosely described as "business" and "investor." No specific amount is demanded, but the government will want an organization chart showing all job positions including the total number of non-Thai aliens. Retirees also receive special treatment, but Thai laws give no description of the exact requirements. Other categories for admission are government officials, missionaries, evangelists, and "experts or advisors."

For investors, a B10 million (US$250,000) investment for at least three years ensures permanent residency. Applicants are charged B7,600 each for processing and B191,400 for issuance of a residency permit book, plus B95,700 for a spouse and each dependant under 20. The investment may be in a company, condominiums, bonds from the Ministry of Finance, or a fixed bank deposit. Applications should be submitted to the Immigration Bureau, Sathorn Road, Soi Suan Plu, Thailand. The process takes 45-60 days for approval.

For a foreign woman, marriage to a Thai man allows her to claim immediate citizenship. Any children born to the marriage are considered Thai citizens. The foreign husband does qualify for "favorable consideration" in obtaining permanent residence. After twelve years of residence, both husband and wife can apply for Thai naturalization.

Permanent Residence Permit

Requirements for permanent residence are as follows: The applicant must: 1) enter in a non-immigrant status and stay for a period not less than three years. Travel abroad is allowed, but the holder must return prior to the visa expiration date. Before leaving, an intention to return must be filed with the immigration office; 2) show proof of adequate assets and income, preferably with employment in a managerial or executive position. Proof of investment must be kept showing foreign amounts transferred into the Bank of Thailand; 3) invest in a Thai company or partnership shown by registration and trade certificates issued by the Commercial Ministry; 4) submit evidence of corporate tax and personal tax payments for three years must be submitted; and 5) accompany the application with a B2,000 fee. When approval is granted, another B5,000 fee must be paid.

Thailand grants only 100 permanent residence permits annually. This quota is waived for investors of more than B10 million and also waived in special cases.

Citizenship

Requirements for naturalization are as follows: 1) at least five years approved permanent residence; 2) 21 years of age or older; 3) no

Thai criminal record; 4) basic knowledge of the Thai language, enough to communicate; and 5) payment of a B5,000 application fee and another B5,000 for completion upon approval.

Contacts

Tourists staying for less than 30 days do not require a visa, but must possess a passport and onward/return ticket. Entry/visa information is subject to change without notice.

United States: U.S. citizen tourists staying for less than 30 days do not require a visa, but must possess a passport and may be asked to show an onward/return ticket. A Passenger Service Charge must be paid in Thai baht when departing the country from any of Thailand's international airports. When a traveler enters the country, Thai Immigration stamps the date on which the traveler's authorized stay in Thailand will expire in his or her passport. Any traveler remaining in Thailand beyond this date without having received an official extension will be assessed an immediate cash fine when departing Thailand. Any foreigner found by police to be out of legal status prior to departure (during a Thai Immigration "sweep" through a guesthouse, for example) will be jailed, fined, and then deported at his or her own expense, and may be barred from re-entering Thailand. In this regard, American citizens should be aware that private "visa extension services", even those advertising in major periodicals or located close to Immigration offices or police stations, are illegal. In 2003, more than ten Americans were arrested at border crossings when the visas and entry stamps they had obtained through these illegal services were discovered to be counterfeit. Thailand's Entry/Exit information is subject to change without notice. For further information on Thailand's entry and exit requirements, contact the Royal Thai Embassy, 1024 Wisconsin Avenue, NW, Washington, D.C., 20007, Tel: (202) 944-3600, Web site: http://www.thaiembdc.org, or the Thai consulates in Chicago, Los Angeles, or New York City.

Americans living in or visiting Thailand are encouraged to register, either online, or in person at the Consular Section of the U.S. Embassy in Bangkok or the U.S. Consulate General in Chiang Mai. At both locations updated information on travel and security in Thailand is available. The Consular Section of the U.S. Embassy is located at 95 Wireless Road in Bangkok the U.S. mailing address is APO AP 96546-0001. The central switchboard number is (66) (2) 205-4000 the American Citizen Services Unit number is (66) (2) 205-4049 and the fax number is (66) (2) 205-4103. The web site for the U.S. Embassy is http://bangkok.usembassy.gov/ American citizens can register online via the web site. Questions regarding American Citizens Services can be submitted by E-mail to acsbkk@state.gov. The U.S. Consulate General in Chiang Mai is located at 387 Wichayanond Road the U.S. mailing address is Box C, APO AP 96546. The telephone number is (66) (53) 252-629 and the fax number is (66) (53) 252-633.

United Kingdom: The British Embassy is located at British Embassy 1031 Wireless Road Lumpini, Pathumwan Bangkok 10330, Tel: (66) (0) 2 305 8333, Fax: (66) (2) 255 6051, E-mail: info.bangkok@fco.gov.uk, Web site: http://www.britishembassy. gov.uk/Thailand. There is also an Honorary Consulate located at 98 Bumrungraj Road, Muang, Chiang Mai 5000, Tel: (66) (53) 263-015. Fax: (66) (53) 263-016, E-mail: ukconsul@loxinfo.co.th.

Hong Kong

STATUS:	SPECIAL ADMINISTRATIVE REGION OF CHINA
POPULATION:	7,394,170
LANGUAGE:	CHINESE (CANTONESE), ENGLISH; BOTH OFFICIAL
CURRENCY:	HONG KONG DOLLAR (HK$)
AREA:	1,092 SQ KM
ETHNIC GROUPS:	CHINESE 95%, OTHER 5%
RELIGION:	ECLECTIC MIXTURE OF LOCAL RELIGIONS 90%, CHRISTIAN 10%

Situated at the south eastern tip of China, Hong Kong is ideally positioned at the center of rapidly developing East Asia. It includes Hong Kong Island, the Kowloon peninsula and the New Territories, which also includes 235 outlying islands.

Hong Kong was established as a British colony in 1841 and, under the terms of the 1984 Joint Declaration of the British and Chinese Governments, reverted to Chinese sovereignty on July 1, 1997. At that time, Hong Kong became a Special Administrative Region of the People's Republic of China retaining its current economic, social and legal system for a minimum period of 50 years. Since the handover, Hong Kong has continued to manage its own affairs, but with a diminished degree of local autonomy and under Beijing's constant watch and direction. Beijing has reneged on numerous guarantees of democratic procedures it made in 1997, including the scheduling of democratic elections.

Notwithstanding Beijing's controls, Hong Kong is rated as the world's freest economy by the conservative Heritage Foundation (2004) of Washington, D.C. and is a major trading center with total volume of trade in goods and re-exports (2002) of over US$400 billion. That makes the territory the 10th largest trading economy in the world.

Legal & Business Environment

The legal system in Hong Kong is based on English common law and an increasingly comprehensive body of statutory law passed by the local legislature. Hong Kong is has many lawyers including a number of overseas firms from the United Kingdom, Australia, Canada and the United States. The language of the law and of business is English. The local language is the Cantonese dialect and Mandarin Chinese is increasingly spoken. The Hong Kong Government generally has adopted a policy of 'Maximum Support and Minimum Intervention' and provides usually business-friendly conditions. Communications through Hong Kong are excellent and, in particular, telecommunications are efficient and cheap.

Since 1983, the Hong Kong dollar has been pegged to the US dollar at the rate of HK$7.80 to US$1.00 and there are no exchange controls. Hong Kong acts as a regional business center in Asia with well established commercial links with most Asian countries. In 2004 it began a significant revival from an economic slump that lasted several years.

Hong Kong is in a special position with regard to business in China. With China's entry into the World Trade Organization, Hong Kong is well positioned to increase its role as China's major commercial and financial link with the outside world. Hong Kong has signed a bilateral free trade agreement known as Closer Economic Partnership Agreement (CEPA) with Mainland China which will only increase trade.

Economy

Hong Kong is a major international financial center with a large number of banks offering services of all kinds, insurance companies, fund managers, venture capital companies and other financial professionals. It has the world's 10th largest trading economy, one of the world's four largest gold markets, the 7th largest foreign exchange market, the 12th largest banking center, and Asia's 3rd biggest stock market, the Hang Seng.

Hong Kong has always been a major trading center. There is little heavy industry and the economy is increasingly dependent on services. Hong Kong is the world's 10th largest exporter of services. Civil aviation, shipping, travel and tourism, trade-related services, and various financial and banking services are the main service components.

Hong Kong is also popular as regional head quarters for many multinational companies and has substantial local companies in fields such as hotel management, property development and telecommunications. The local economy is dominated by the real estate sector which is active both within the territory and increasingly overseas in China, Malaysia and Vietnam. Hong Kong has independent membership in several international bodies including the World Trade Organization. For international purposes it will continue to be treated as a an entity separate from China.

Privacy

Hong Kong has no Tax Information Exchange Agreement (TIEA) with the United States.

Until now, Hong Kong's banking laws did not permit bank regulators to give information about an individual customer's affairs to foreign government authorities, except in cases involving fraud. But Hong Kong has never had specific banking secrecy laws such as many asset and tax haven nations enjoy. As a matter of local custom, Hong Kong banks have always requested a

judicial warrant before disclosing records to any foreign government. Access is much easier for the local government, but there are no double-taxation agreements with countries other than the People's Republic of China. A mutual legal assistance treaty (MLAT) with the United States was signed in 1998 and came into force in 2000.

A strict anti-money laundering law is in place and is enforced. These laws and "know your customer" (KYC) rules have made the opening of bank accounts for international business corporations (IBC) much more difficult. Accounts applicants must declare to the bank the "true beneficiary" of an IBC or a trust with supporting documentation. Documentary proof must be shown for all corporate directors and shareholders of the registering entity and any other entities that share in that ownership.

Residency

In September 2003, the Immigration Department of Hong Kong introduced the "Capital Investment Entrant Scheme." Prior to its introduction, individuals seeking residency in return for investment in Hong Kong had to rely upon the visa known as the "Business Investment Visa." (See below). Experts who have examined these plans suggests the older BIA is of questionable value to the global investor seeking residency in Hong Kong unless that investor is very wealthy and merely intends to "park" himself in Hong Kong or otherwise "retire" to Hong Kong.

The new scheme has the following objective: "To facilitate the entry for residence by investment entrants..., i.e. persons who make capital investment in Hong Kong but would not be engaged in the running of any business here. The entrant is allowed to make his choice of investments amongst permissible assets without the need to establish or join a business."

The Scheme sets out criteria that must be met, conditions of stay, requires an application and nominal fee and is said to have generated marginal success since it began. It applies to foreign nationals, Macau residents, Chinese nationals who have obtained permanent resident status in a foreign country, stateless persons who have obtained permanent resident status in a foreign country with proven re-entry rights and Taiwan residents.

Further eligibility criteria include the following; 1) aged 18 or above; 2) net assets of not less than HK$6.5 million; 3) the making of an investment within six months; 4) a clean record; 5) proof of means of support. An intended investment of HK$6.5 million (US$834,000) in permissible investment asset classes includes real estate and financial assets exclusively in Hong Kong. The Scheme also imposes certain portfolio maintenance requirements and recognizes the volatility of financial assets allowing for changes in value.

Under the Scheme the successful applicant and his dependants (spouse and unmarried dependant children under 18) is granted a two year stay. Applicants must complete an application form ID(E)967 and pay the proscribed fee of HK$135 (US$17).

Business Investment Visa

Business Investment Visas routinely are granted to qualified applicants and are processed within 90 days. This visa often is granted if the applicant can demonstrate that a suitable business vehicle will be created, local jobs will be created, that local vendors will be used in planned commercial activities, that the industry within which investment activities are intended will be enhanced and that in the investment activities will have a sound business basis.

The Business Investment Visa for many years has been one of several visas available to people seeking Hong Kong residence. The visa objective has been to encourage global investors to engage in business activities within, and from, Hong Kong. The BIV is relatively inexpensive and easy to obtain.

Upon issuance of the visa, the applicant and his dependants (spouse and unmarried dependant children under 18) usually will be granted a one year stay. This is usually extended for two years on the basis that the commercial endeavors justify the extension. Others conditions which apply include not committing any criminal offence, continuous business activity and earning sufficient income so as not to become an economic burden to Hong Kong. The applicant must complete an application form ID(E) 936 and the proscribed fee is HK$135.

Of the two visas available, it is obvious that the less costly Business Investment Visa is not only the better bargain, it involves far less restrictions and conditions.

For further information see the web page of the Immigration Department of the Hong Kong Special Administrative Region of the People's Republic of China at http://www.immd.gov.hk/ehtml/hkvisas_13.htm

Entry & Exit:

A passport and evidence of onward/return transportation by sea/air are required. A visa is not required for tourist visits by U.S. citizens of up to 90 days. An extension of stay may be granted upon application to the Hong Kong SAR Immigration Department. Visas are required to work or study in Hong Kong. A departure tax and an airport security tax must be paid at the airport, unless these have been included in the traveler's airfare. Public transportation from Hong Kong 's International Airport at Chek Lap Kok to Central Hong Kong (about 25 miles) is readily available, as are taxis. Travelers should exchange sufficient money for transportation at the airport exchange facility located immediately outside the baggage claim area.

For the most current information concerning entry and exit requirements, travelers can consult the Hong Kong SAR Immigration Department, Immigration Tower, 7 Gloucester Road, Wanchai, Hong Kong (tel. (852) 2824-6111, fax (852) 2877-7711, Internet Home Page: http://www.info.gov.hk/immd/), or the Embassy of the People's Republic of China, 2300 Connecticut Avenue, NW, Washington D.C. 20008, tel. (202) 328-2500, Internet home page: http://www.china-embassy.org, or the Chinese consulates general in Chicago, Houston, Los Angeles, New York City, or San Francisco. Overseas, inquiries may be made at the nearest Chinese embassy or consulate.

Contacts

Henley & Partners Far East, 13/F Silver Fortune Plaza, 1 Wellington St., Central Hong Kong. Tel: (852) 2525 7818 Fax: (852) 2131 4253. E-mail: hongkong-office@henleyglobal.com Web site: http://www.

henleyglobal.com/hongkong.htm

United States: Americans living in or visiting Hong Kong are encouraged to register at the Consular Section of the U.S. Consulate General in Hong Kong and obtain updated information on travel and security within the Hong Kong SAR. Americans can register on-line at http://hongkong.usconsulate.gov, in person at the Consulate General or by fax or mail. The U.S. Consulate General is located at 26 Garden Road, Central, Hong Kong. The mailing address is PSC 461, Box 5, FPO AP 96521-0006, tel. (852) 2523-9011, fax (852) 2845-4845; Internet: http://hongkong.usconsulate.gov.

United Kingdom: British Consulate General, Hong Kong, No 1 Supreme Court Rd. Central Hong Kong. (P O Box 528) Tel: (852) 2901 3000. Fax: (852) 2901 3066. E-mails: visa@britishconsulate.org.hk or passport@britishconsulate.org.hk. Office Hours: GMT: Mon-Fri: 0030-0915. Local Time: Mon-Fri: 0830-1715. Web site: http://www.britishconsulate.org.hk/

It's No Secret Investing Offshore Can Help You Get The Most Out Of Your Money. And Now It's No Secret Who To Call For Help...

*T*he *Sovereign Society* has the one book that explains how to **protect and invest your money safely**. Discover how to obtain a second passport from almost any country to reduce your taxes and retire in luxury. Read about the secrets the super rich have used for years to lower their taxes and protect their assets. Learn how to organize your life to **pay ZERO taxes legally**. Find out how to disappear from government agencies, creditors and other snoops by using some simple privacy techniques.

Don't limit yourself to what your government thinks is safe banking; learn about the real asset havens around the world. Find out which country offers you big incentives to start a new business. Find out about the many ways to structure your money to **protect yourself from a lawsuit**.

To order call 1-888-358-8125 or if you're outside North America 353-51-304-557 for a copy of *Forbidden Knowledge*. These powerful secrets are available for only US$57 plus US$4.95 shipping and handling. When ordering please ask for code D190E801.

Don't waste another cent in excess tax. Order your copy today.

INTERNATIONAL FINANCIAL AND LEGAL NETWORK

Through a winning combination of experience, knowledge and understanding of international financial and legal services, IFLN can provide you with key advantages that few investors will ever have: truly independent advice and introductions to the right professional in the right place from the very start.

In particular, **IFLN** can assist you with:

❋ International Banking and Investment Management
❋ Tax and Estate Planning
❋ Asset Protection including Family Foundations, Foreign Trusts & Annuity Policies

❋ International Corporate Services
❋ Resident and Retirement Solutions
❋ Real Estate Acquisition and Structuring
❋ International Health and Life Insurance

For more information, our online assessment (at **www.ifln.com**) allows you to have your personal situation reviewed by IFLN specialists on the basis of a comprehensive questionnaire. An initial brief assessment and referral is free of charge. visit our web site, or contact us today:

IFLN International Financial and Legal Network
Florastrasse 44 8024 Zurich, Switzerland

Tel: +41(1) 265 1000 ❋ Fax: +44 (1) 265 1001
Email: info@ifln.com   ❋ Internet: wwwifln.com